D1220138

REVISION WORKBOOK

Jurisprudence:
THE PHILOSOPHY OF LAW

Second Edition

EDITOR: MICHAEL DOHERTY
BA Law, MA Criminology
Senior Lecturer in Law, University of Glamorgan

OLD BAILEY PRESS

OLD BAILEY PRESS
at Holborn College, Woolwich Road,
Charlton, London, SE7 8LN

First published 1997
Second edition 2002

© The HLT Group Ltd 2002

All Old Bailey Press publications enjoy copyright protection and the
copyright belongs to the HLT Group Ltd.

All rights reserved. No part of this publication may be reproduced or
transmitted in any form or by any means, electronic, mechanical,
photocopying, recording or otherwise, or stored in any retrieval
system of any nature without either the written permission of the
copyright holder, application for which should be made to the Old
Bailey Press, or a licence permitting restricted copying in the United
Kingdom issued by the Copyright Licensing Agency.

Any person who infringes the above in relation to this publication
may be liable to criminal prosecution and civil claims for damages.

ISBN 1 85836 427 2

British Library Cataloguing-in-Publication.

A CIP Catalogue record for this book is available from the British
Library.

Printed and bound in Great Britain.

Contents

Acknowledgement

Some questions used are taken or adapted from past University of London LLB (External) Degree examination papers and our thanks are extended to the University of London for their kind permission to use and publish the questions.

Caveat

The answers given are not approved or sanctioned by the University of London and are entirely our responsibility.

They are not intended as 'Model Answers', but rather as Suggested Solutions.

The answers have two fundamental purposes, namely:

a) to provide a detailed example of a suggested solution to an examination question; and

b) to assist students with their research into the subject and to further their understanding and appreciation of the subject.

Introduction

This Revision WorkBook has been designed specifically for those studying jurisprudence to undergraduate level. Its coverage is not confined to any one syllabus, but embraces all the major jurisprudence topics to be found in university examinations.

Each chapter contains a brief introduction explaining the scope and overall content of the topic covered in that chapter. There follows, in each case, a list of key points which will assist the student in studying and memorising essential material with which the student should be familiar in order to fully understand the topic.

Each chapter usually ends with several typical examination questions, together with general comments, skeleton solutions and suggested solutions. Wherever possible, the questions are drawn from the University of London external jurisdprudence and legal theory papers, with recent questions being included where possible. However, it is inevitable that, in compiling a list of questions by topic order rather than chronologically, not only do the same questions crop up over and over again in different guises, but there are gaps where questions have never been set at all.

Undoubtedly, the main feature of this Revision WorkBook is the inclusion of as many past examination questions as possible. While the use of past questions as a revision aid is certainly not new, it is hoped that the combination of actual past questions from the University of London LLB external course and specially written questions, where there are gaps in examination coverage, will be of assistance to students in achieving a thorough and systematic revision of the subject.

Careful use of the Revision WorkBook should enhance the student's understanding of jurisprudence and, hopefully, enable you to deal with as wide a range of subject matter as anyone might find in a jurisprudence examination, while at the same time allowing you to practise examination techniques while working through the book.

Studying Jurisprudence

The study of 'Jurisprudence and Legal Theory' and preparation for examination in the subject presents special problems for the student of law. Unlike other legal subjects there are no right answers to an issue; usually case law does not provide the solution. Instead, the student must approach the different theorists with an open mind, be prepared to criticise and evaluate and to consider law in wider social and political contexts.

The first difficulty for the student is where to begin. Jurisprudence is one of those subjects which becomes far more comprehensible when the student has completed the whole course. This will, however, be of cold comfort to the student still struggling to understand the subject at the beginning of the course. The best advice that can be given is that a student should not rely on writings about the theorists – they should as far as possible read the writings of the theorists. In other words, stick to primary sources wherever possible. Only then will critiques and analyses of those theorists become meaningful. This may sound daunting. However, the use of a good basic textbook and a sourcebook will ease the way. The student will benefit from the textbook commentary as a means of placing each theorist in an historical, social and political context and can then be guided by the extracts from original works as to the central elements of that theorist's thesis.

A mere understanding of the major theorists will not, however, be enough in itself to enable the student to obtain a good examination grade. Jurisprudence papers rarely call for straightforward analysis of theses; the student must be prepared to deal with familiar material in an unfamiliar way, to write answers comparing or contrasting more than one theorist, or even to answer a general question stretching across a whole spectrum of topics. In other words, the student should be prepared to think! A blind acceptance of what he or she has read or been told will not gain high marks. A recitation of a prepared answer on, for example, Kelsen, just because his name is mentioned in the question, will not impress any examiner. In jurisprudence, perhaps more than in any other subject, the three cardinal rules are: read the question; stop and think; plan.

So that the student may be in a position to do this, some hints on revising jurisprudence may be helpful. First of all, it is worth pointing out that no one could possibly read all the available literature. A pruning exercise is certainly required. Most tutors will have helped their students considerably here by producing concise digestible reading lists. The student may wish to be even more selective when the time comes to revise. But certain points should be remembered: jurisprudence is a subject where 'question-spotting' is impossible. Unusual topics are frequently juxtaposed and unusual slants on topics are common. To be too selective is therefore disastrous. The student should aim for a broad appreciation of the major schools and theorists as well as the major social, political and moral issues. Where a student can cut down his or her work lies in the fact that the need for rote learning is less great than in other legal subjects. Whilst the central elements of theses clearly need to be learned, the student can generally spend time more profitably in thinking about issues and constructing his or her own views than in learning masses of detail by heart.

The last sentence perhaps explains both the appeal of jurisprudence, and the reason why it frightens the more timid. The lack of clear answers, and the need to argue for one view or another inhibits those who like to have a 'right' answer to everything. But to those prepared to challenge and evaluate what they read or are told, and to come to their own conclusions, the study of jurisprudence is one of the most valuable and interesting opportunities in their entire course.

Revision and Examination Technique

Revision Technique

Planning a revision timetable

In planning your revision timetable make sure you do not finish the syllabus too early. You should avoid leaving revision so late that you have to 'cram' – but constant revision of the same topic leads to stagnation.

Plan ahead, however, and try to make your plans increasingly detailed as you approach the examination date.

Allocate enough time for each topic to be studied. But note that it is better to devise a realistic timetable, to which you have a reasonable chance of keeping, rather than a wildly optimistic schedule which you will probably abandon at the first opportunity!

The syllabus and its topics

One of your first tasks when you began your course was to ensure that you thoroughly understood your syllabus. Check now to see if you can write down the topics it comprises from memory. You will see that the chapters of this WorkBook are each devoted to a syllabus topic. This will help you decide which are the key chapters relative to your revision programme, though you should allow some time for glancing through the other chapters.

The topic and its key points

Again working from memory, analyse what you consider to be the key points of any topic that you have selected for particular revision. Seeing what you can recall, unaided, will help you to understand and firmly memorise the concepts involved.

Using the WorkBook

Relevant questions are provided for each topic in this book. Naturally, as typical examples of examination questions, they do not normally relate to one topic only. But the questions in each chapter will relate to the subject matter of the chapter to a degree. You can choose your method of consulting the questions and solutions, but here are some suggestions (strategies 1–3). Each of them pre-supposes that you have read through the author's notes on key points and any other preliminary matter, at the beginning of the chapter. Once again, you now need to practise working from memory, for that is the challenge you are preparing yourself for. As a rule of procedure constantly test yourself once revision starts, both orally and in writing.

Strategy I

Strategy 1 is planned for the purpose of quick revision. First read your chosen question carefully and then jot down in abbreviated notes what you consider to be the main points at issue. Allow yourself sufficient time to cover what you feel to be relevant. Then study the author's skeleton solution and skim-read the suggested solution to see how they compare with your notes. When comparing consider carefully what the author has included (and concluded) and see whether that agrees with what you have written. Consider the points of variation also. Have you recognised the key issues? How relevant have you been?

Strategy 2

Strategy 2 requires a nucleus of three hours in which to practise writing a set of examination answers in a limited time-span.

Select a number of questions (as many as are normally set in your subject in the examination you are studying for), each from a different chapter in the WorkBook, without consulting the solutions. Find a place to write where you will not be disturbed and try to arrange not to be interrupted for three hours. Write your solutions in the time allowed, noting any time needed to make up if you are interrupted.

After a rest, compare your answers with the suggested solutions in the WorkBook. There will be considerable variation in style, of course, but the bare facts should not be too dissimilar. Evaluate your answer critically. Be 'searching', but develop a positive approach to deciding how you would tackle each question on another occasion.

Strategy 3

You are unlikely to be able to do more than one three hour examination, but occasionally set yourself a single question. Vary the 'time allowed' by imagining it to be one of the questions that you must answer in three hours and allow yourself a limited preparation and writing time. Try one question that you feel to be difficult and an easier question on another occasion, for example.

Misuse of suggested solutions

Don't try to learn by rote. In particular, don't try to reproduce the suggested solutions by heart. Learn to express the basic concepts in your own words.

Keeping up-to-date

Keep up-to-date. While examiners do not require familiarity with changes in the subject during the three months prior to the examination, it obviously creates a good impression if you can show you are acquainted with any recent changes. Make a habit of looking through one of the leading journals – *Modern Law Review*, *Law Quarterly Review* or the *New Law Journal*, for example – and cumulative indices to law reports, such as the *All England Law Reports* or *Weekly Law Reports,* or indeed the daily law reports in *The Times.*

Examination Skills

Examiners are human too!

The process of answering an examination question involves a communication between you and the person who set it. If you were speaking face to face with the person, you would choose your verbal points and arguments carefully in your reply. When writing, it is all too easy to forget the human being who is awaiting the reply and simply write out what one knows in the area of the subject! Bear in mind it is a person whose question you are responding to, throughout your essay. This will help you to avoid being irrelevant or long-winded.

The essay question

Candidates are sometimes tempted to choose to answer essay questions because they 'seem' easier. But the examiner is looking for thoughtful work and will not give good marks for superficial answers.

The essay-type of question may be either purely factual, in asking you to explain the meaning of a certain doctrine or principle, or it may ask you to discuss a certain proposition, usually derived from a quotation. In either case, the approach to the answer is the same. A clear programme must be devised to give the examiner the meaning or significance of the doctrine, principle or proposition and its origin in common law, equity or statute, and, where appropriate, cases which illustrate its application to the branch of law concerned. Essay questions offer a good way to obtain marks if you have thought carefully about a topic, since it is up to you to impose the structure (unlike the problem questions where the problem imposes its own structure). You are then free to speculate and show imagination.

Examination checklist

a) Read the instructions at the head of the examination carefully. While last-minute changes are unlikely – such as the introduction of a compulsory question or an increase in the number of questions asked – it has been known to happen.

b) Read the questions carefully. Analyse problem questions – work out what the examiner wants.

c) Plan your answer before you start to write.

d) Check that you understand the rubric before you start to write. Do not 'discuss', for example, if you are specifically asked to 'compare and contrast'.

e) Answer the correct number of questions. If you fail to answer one out of four questions set you lose 25 per cent of your marks!

Style and structure

Try to be clear and concise. Fundamentally this amounts to using paragraphs to denote the sections of your essay, and writing simple, straightforward sentences as much as possible. The sentence you have just read has 22 words – when a sentence reaches 50 words it becomes difficult for a reader to follow.

Do not be inhibited by the word 'structure' (traditionally defined as giving an essay a beginning, a middle and an end). A good structure will be the natural consequence of setting out your arguments and the supporting evidence in a logical order. Set the scene briefly in your opening paragraph. Provide a clear conclusion in your final paragraph.

Table of Cases

Part A
Are Moral Judgments
Part of the Law?

Chapter 1

Introduction to Problems of Law and Morality

1.1   Introduction

1.2   Key points

1.3   Questions and suggested solutions

1.1 Introduction

This section, whilst important in its own right, can also be seen as an introduction to the chapters on positivism and natural law below. It is necessary for the student to keep clear the separate issues here: for example, whether unjust laws are law is not the same question as whether one has an obligation to obey the law, although the two points may well overlap. The student may also find it helpful to illustrate answers to questions on law and morality by practical examples such as apartheid or the Nazi regime.

1.2 Key points

In addition to the points raised below the student should keep in mind the whole nature of the positivist/natural law debate.

The connection between law and morals

a) Is it necessary? Fuller believes he has established an 'internal morality' consisting of eight principles.

b) Hart and Raz deny that this is a true morality. It could be argued that his principles are no more than a characterisation of the rule of law (which may not necessarily be an ideal anyway).

c) Fuller argues the existence of law to be a matter of degree.

Do we have a moral duty to obey the law?

a) This may depend on whether one considers unjust laws to be law or not (in Aquinas's words 'lex injusta non est lex').

b) If one believes that unjust laws are nonetheless law the question of a moral duty to obey becomes more acute. Such a duty might be absolute (though few support this theory) or prima facie (where the duty can be outweighed by other considerations such as the harm caused by an unjust law).

1.3 Questions and suggested solutions

QUESTION ONE

Is Fuller right to claim that there is a morality that is 'internal' to law?

Adapted from University of London LLB Examination
(for External Students) Jurisprudence and Legal Theory June 1995 Q12

General Comment

A good question to attempt by describing Fuller's eight principles of 'inner morality'. A detailed discussion of his main claim is required with a description of the principles. Hart's criticism can, on this occasion, be attacked and a general conclusion that Fuller's concept has merit, in part, can be made.

Skeleton Solution

Introduction to Fuller's claim – moralities of aspiration and duty – eight principles of the 'inner morality' – Hart's criticism – conclusion.

Suggested Solution

Fuller claims, in his criticism of legal positivism, that some things taken as legal facts are merely achievements of legal aspirations. He says that law can only be said to be binding if citizens believe or act as if it is, and that a genuine working legal system cannot be understood merely by looking at the rules consciously created by law makers. His justification is the American constitution which does not mention a requirement to legislate although all American legal authority flows from it.

Whilst Fuller does not seek to prove that substantive morality is bound up with law, he identifies perils when seeking to prove a relationship between a relativist, content-based concept of morality, and a content-neutral, universal conception of law. He argues that if morality must be seen as being relative rather than absolute, then if we seek to relate morality to law, such morality must be one specific to the nature of law. He concludes that legal morality must be a particular type of morality which is found in the nature of law itself rather than an abstraction from other moral norms.

Moralities of aspiration and duty

Fuller's concept of morality has a practical criterion with goals to which the legal system should aspire, thus his morality of aspiration is largely one of degree. A morality of duty can be distinguished in terms of the rules of a substantive morality such as 'thou shalt not kill'.

Whether there is an informal morality of law presents Fuller with a problem because he is concerned to relate a morality that is linked to his content-neutral concept of law. It seems not to follow the conventional approach of asserting that law respects certain substantive moral values. Therefore, the content of the internal morality of law looks remarkably like common-sense rules of good craftsmanship. His contention is that there is an inherent logic to the subjugation of human conduct to legal rules which, if ignored, lead to failure.

Eight principles of the 'inner morality'

Fuller asserts that the eight principles of the 'inner morality' of the law are as follows.

a) A legal system must be based on or reveal some kind of regular trends. As such law should be founded on generalisations of conduct such as rules, rather than simply allowing arbitrary adjudication.

b) Laws must be publicised so that subjects know how they are supposed to behave.

c) Rules will not have the desired effect if it is likely that your present actions will not be judged by them in future. As such, retrospective legislation should not be abused.

d) Laws should be comprehensible, even if it is only lawyers who understand them.

e) Laws should not be contradictory.

f) Law should not expect the subject to perform the impossible.

g) Law should not change so frequently that the subject cannot orient his action to it.

h) There should not be a significant difference between the actual administration of the law and what the written rule says.

These criteria are in the form of the moral rules of duty. Fuller expresses them as: principles or goals; generality of laws; promulgation of laws; minimising the use of retrospective laws; clarity; lack of contradiction; possibility of obedience; constancy through time; consistency between the word and the practice of law.

Fuller's evaluation speaks for itself:

> 'Though these natural laws touch one of the most vital of human activities they obviously do not exhaust the whole of man's moral life. They have nothing to say on such topics as polygamy, the study of Marx, the worship of God, the progressive income tax, or the subjugation of women. If the question be raised whether any of these subjects, or others like them, should be taken as objects of legislation, that question relates to what I have called the external morality of the law.'

Fuller states, by showing how the Nazi regime suffered a progressive decline in its adherence to such principles of legality, that the internal morality of law is neutral towards the law's substantive aims, with exceptions. The urge for legal clarity fights against laws that direct themselves against alleged evils which cannot be defined, such as racial discrimination. He cites *Perez v Sharp* (1948) 32 Cal 2d 711 where a statute which prevented the marriage of a white person to any Negro, Mulatto, Mongolian or member of the Malay race was held to be unconstitutional because the constitution required clarity.

Hart's criticism

One of Hart's more unfair criticisms concerns Fuller's assertion that beyond the satisfaction of a very minimal standard the legality of a system is a matter of degree: a legal system, some say, cannot 'half-exist'. Also, if a legal system exists only to a lesser degree, how can we decide when we do or do not have to take account of one point – how many people need to disobey a legal system for it to cease to be a legal system?

Fuller's eight principles, which loosely describe requirements of procedural justice, ensure that a legal system would satisfy the demands of morality to the extent that a legal system which adhered to all the principles would explain the all-important idea of 'fidelity to law' and command obedience with moral justification.

It is unfortunate that Hart's criticism has observed Fuller's main claim of a morality that is 'internal' to law. There is an important sense of legal justification where claims made in the name of 'law' are morally serious. A genuine claim for legal justification of an immoral, Nazi-style legal system must have some moral force about such a claim. Thus, when a claim is made about our 'law', it carries some moral force. It is submitted that a denial is insufficient and an explanation required – an explanation that can be found, in part, by Fuller's eight principles.

QUESTION TWO

Is Hart fair to Fuller when he criticises Fuller's eight principles of the 'inner morality' of law as being analogous to principles of the 'inner morality' of the poisoner's art?

University of London LLB Examination
(for External Students) Jurisprudence and Legal Theory June 1996 Q5

General Comment

This is a popular topic in the positivism/natural law separation of law and morality debate. What makes a good legal system? If the Mafia was to take over the United Kingdom, abolish Parliament and the judiciary and appoint its henchmen to make and enforce Mafia laws, would there be a legal system properly so-called?

Skeleton Solution

Background of Hart/Fuller debate – Hart's positivism as a response to Gustav Radbruch – Fuller's reply – the eight principles – Hart's counter-attack – evaluation and conclusion.

Suggested Solution

The background of the Hart/Fuller debate is rooted in the nature of the Nazi legal system. It was widely believed by natural lawyers that the evil nature of the Nazi legal system and the Nazi regime generally was partly supported by positivism. Gustav Radbruch, a positivist who lived through the Nazi atrocities, felt that the obnoxious acts of the Nazi regime would not have happened but for positivism. He renounced positivism and supported natural law principles. Radbruch's attack on legal positivism, and in particular his suggestion that positivism contributed to the Nazi atrocities, did not go unanswered.

Professor H L A Hart felt the attack on positivism was uncalled for and unjustified so he launched a defence of positivism. In an article, 'Positivism and the Separation of Law and Morals' ((1958) 71 Harvard Law Review, pp593–629), he defends his positivist thesis. The positivist slogan 'law is law' can be answered with a utitilitarian riposte that 'law may be law but too evil to be obeyed'. This is an evaluative statement which people can agree with as the statement separates law from morality. It is a completely different scenario to say that 'this law is invalid because it is too evil'. People who accept the validity of any law will find it difficult to accept this as they believe laws duly passed by lawfully-constituted authorities are valid laws.

Fuller disagrees with Hart and in his response 'Positivism and Fidelity to Law – a Reply to Professor Hart' ((1958) 71 Harvard Law Review, pp630–672), he criticises Hart for failing to take into account the nature of law. To Fuller, law aspires to morality. Referring to Hart's union of primary and secondary rules, he says such rules are fundamental rules of a legal system because they are rules not of law but of morality. They derive their efficacy from a general acceptance which in turn rests ultimately on a perception that they are right and necessary. It is fair to say that Hart will respond to Fuller's claim that there can be legal systems based on fear, but that does not mean people accept rules because of morality. To Fuller, law contains its own implicit morality and this morality must be respected if we are to create anything called law, even bad law. This is because, as he says, the authority to make laws must be supported by moral attitudes that accord it the competency it claims. This explains Fuller's position on the Nazi legal system.

It is against this background that Fuller propounds his eight principles which he calls the 'inner morality of law'. He says that for positivism to present the formal characterisation of human institutions like a legal system independent of their purposes is unjustified. To him the characteristic features of a legal system exist because they are related to the purpose of legal systems and this purpose is inherently a moral one. Thus an understanding of what law is cannot be separated from an understanding of what law ought to be in so far as an understanding of what law is involves an understanding of the moral aspirations that are implicit in the concept of law itself.

In his work *The Morality of Law* (1964), Fuller gives the eight principles which to him form the minimum features which together amount to a moral ideal which explains the purposive nature of law. The eight principles are:

a) rules must be general; meaning they must apply to all and not only a section of the population;

b) they must not be retrospective but prospective; this will eliminate unfairness in law;

c) rules must be published; this means making enacted rules public to avoid corruption;

d) rules must be intelligible; meaning people should be able to understand them;

e) rules must not be contradictory; meaning rules made should not make contradictory claims on people, for example: a law proclaims equality of sexes and yet bars women from holding public offices.

f) compliance with rules is possible; meaning people like the vulnerable in society should not be saddled with responsibility when they lack the necessary physical or mental capacity;

g) rules must not be constantly changed; meaning since people want certainty in the rules to enable them to pursue their goals and ambitions, constant changes of rules will badly affect them;

h) there must be congruence between the rules declared and the rules as applied; meaning rules must not say one thing while officials do the other.

Failure to comply with any one of the eight principles results in something that is not law at all.

Fuller calls the eight principles 'the inner morality of law'. Following the eight principles shows 'fidelity to law'. To Fuller the 'inner morality of law' is a morality of aspiration, so the eight principles should be thought of collectively as a moral aspiration for legal systems.

Hart's response to Fuller is that his eight principles are nothing more than principles for good and effective law making. To Hart, law is an instrument that can be used for good as well as bad purposes and its efficacy is not linked with morality. An example can be cited of the apartheid South African legal system. Laws made under the apartheid system were consistent with Fuller's principles yet many people regarded the apartheid legal system as amoral.

To Hart, Fuller has no justification for calling his eight principles the 'morality' of law. He says we can describe certain principles for effective poisoning which may read as follows:

a) administer a large dose but not large enough to kill;

b) choose a poison that can be masked so that it is undetected;

c) aim not to kill instantly;

d) choose a poison which is tasteless and odourless.

According to Hart, we could call the above steps 'principles' of a poisoner's art but it would be absurd to call these 'principles' the 'inner morality of poisoning'.

It is arguable that a government can rigidly follow Fuller's eight principles and yet pass obnoxious laws. This is what leads Hart to say an 'inner morality of law' is compatible with great iniquity. I do not think, however, that Hart is fair to Fuller at all. The fact that some regimes knowingly subvert the rule of law does not mean that law has no moral value. It can be said that consistency with the eight principles makes extreme forms of repression very difficult, though there still would remain unanswered questions about justice.

Fuller is concerned about the proper purpose of a legal system. He says that if a person describes a legal system, the person actually evaluates the degree to which that system is successful in achieving its purpose. To him, therefore, legal morality is a kind of morality intrinsic in law. Fuller's morality is based on goals that a legal system ought to aspire to in order to achieve procedural justice. Using Fuller's eight principles, we may ask if laws are to be effective should they not be published, made prospectively, not contradictory, intelligible, and must official actions and decisions not conform with the published law?

Fuller's response to Hart's poisoner's art attack is that evil aims lack the coherence moral aims have, and that paying attention to the coherence of law will ensure the morality of law. Is this not an overstated point Fuller is making? As Hart has forcibly pointed out, evil aims can equally be 'coherent', and having coherent principles toward a desired goal does not establish the morality of any practice. Indeed, there was coherence in the Nazi legal system and in the apartheid South African legal system.

Although Hart's poisoner's art response is very stimulating and instructive, I believe he misses the point of Fuller's argument. Fuller's 'inner morality of law' calls for procedural justice and fairness in any legal system. I believe this is a worthy idea. I do not think anybody would disagree with a demand that frankness and openness become virtues of a legal system. If Fuller's eight principles of 'inner morality of law' lead to transparency in a legal system I think that that itself has a utility value which gives it its moral status.

QUESTION THREE

Is there a prima facie moral obligation to obey the law?

Written by the Editor

General Comment

This is a fairly straightforward essay on the obligation to obey the law. The answer will be improved by reference to the difficult practical question of obedience to, for example, Nazi decrees or apartheid laws.

Skeleton Solution

Absolute obligation – prima facie obligation – are unjust laws law? – gratitude theory – promise – keeping theory – utilitarianism – duty to obey laws in a democracy – Peter Singer – fairness as compromise – participation – problem of unjust laws.

Suggested Solution

This question does not raise the issue of absolute obligation to obey the law (which few philosophers would accept) nor does it deal with non-moral reasons for obedience (such as sanctions, fear of social disapproval). It concentrates on the question of prima facie moral obligation: is there a moral obligation to obey the law which may in certain circumstances be outweighed by factors justifying disobedience? This is a rather different issue to that of whether, in Aquinas's words, 'lex injusta non est lex'. This answer will take the position that unjust laws are law, but that of course they raise special problems when considering the existence of a moral obligation to obey the law.

An argument used to support the view that there is a prima facie moral obligation is the 'gratitude' theory. This runs as follows: an individual has received benefits from the system of law and government, and thus has a moral obligation to obey the law arising out of gratitude. Smith has dealt with this argument succinctly: 'A government typically confers these benefits, not to advance the interests of particular citizens, but rather as a consequence of advancing some purpose of its own'. Viewed in this way the concept of 'gratitude' becomes meaningless, and it is clear that this theory thereby fails to establish an obligation for the individual.

A second common argument used to show a prima facie moral obligation to obey the law is that of 'promise-keeping'. This is closely linked with social contract theories; an individual owes obedience to the law in return for its protection. Clearly this argument must rest on individual consent to be valid – a 'contract' must be made by one exercising free will. Since being a member of society is non-voluntary, there can be no such free will or consent. The arguments from 'promise-keeping' are thereby unconvincing.

A third possible means of showing a prima facie obligation to obey the law lies in utilitarianism. The argument here is that breaches of the law will always diminish the amount of 'welfare' in society and there is thus a moral obligation to obey the law. One might well argue that such a general claim cannot be substantiated – can driving safely through a red light on a clear road really be said to diminish general 'welfare'? Surely the effect of each breach can only be judged individually, and as such one cannot claim a general moral obligation to obey the law. This argument could be answered by the submission that a breach of law **is** always detrimental to social 'welfare' because it sets a bad example and thus threatens social cohesion. Yet as Raz has pointed out, this argument is fallacious: some offences are never known to anyone but the offender (for instance, a minor undiscovered tax fiddle) and thus set no example at all.

It has been argued that none of the above arguments convincingly establishes a prima facie moral obligation to obey the law. Yet one is led to wonder whether part of the reason for their lack of persuasion is that all the arguments cited could apply to a dictatorship or an autocracy just as well as to a democracy. And one does have an intuitive feeling that there is more likely to be a moral obligation to obey law enacted in a democratic society than law enacted by a dictator. The crucial issue is whether this intuitive feeling can be supported by convincing theory. Peter Singer, in his book *Democracy and Disobedience*, suggests that a prima facie moral obligation to obey the law does exist, not in every society, but only where the law has been enacted by democratic means. His central argument is 'fairness as compromise'. By this he means that a decision-making process of equal say for each person provides a valid reason why individuals have a moral obligation to obey the law. Individuals should recognise the fairness of compromise in a society and thus obey the result of a majority decision rather than act on their own judgement. Singer also suggests that an individual who participates in the democratic process by voting is bound by a type of estoppel to abide by the outcome. Although this 'participation' theory does leave unclear the position of abstainers, it is submitted that Singer's argument for a moral duty to obey in a democracy is convincing. If one applied his theory to a country in South Africa where many are denied the vote, there would be no moral obligation to obey the law. But it then appears that Singer has left open a difficult question. Assume that a morally reprehensible group such as the Nazis are democratically elected to power, including the power to enact law. Is the democratic process itself enough to establish a prima facie moral obligation to obey those laws?

Singer does, however, have an answer to this puzzle. He suggests that disobedience to the law is justified where, despite a democratic process, there is:

a) a tendency for a minority group to be subjected to unfair laws; and

b) legal means of having those laws changed have proved unsuccessful.

He cites disobedience to law by the Catholic minority in Ulster as an example. But his theory would appear to work equally well for the example given above. Disobedience to Nazi laws where, for example, the Jewish minority are persecuted, would be morally justifiable even if those laws had been enacted according to a democratic process. It is thus submitted that Singer's theory gives a convincing answer to the question of prima facie moral obligation to obey the law which works well in relation to genuine practical dilemmas.

Chapter 2

The Separation of Law and Morals

A IMPERATIVE THEORIES

2.1   Introduction

2.2   Key points

2.3   Questions and suggested solutions

B THE PURE THEORY OF LAW

2.4   Introduction

2.5   Key points

2.6   Questions and suggested solutions

C MODERN THEORIES

2.7   Introduction

2.8   Key points

2.9   Questions and suggested solutions

A IMPERATIVE THEORIES

2.1 Introduction

Although Bentham is now generally considered to have postulated a more sophisticated imperative theory than that of Austin, the student should be prepared to deal with either, and to compare the two. It is also sensible to revise this section in conjunction with the modern theorists such as Hart and Raz who will provide useful standpoints of criticism of the traditional positivists. Since one of the most important issues in jurispurdence is the natural law/positivist debate, the imperative theories, like positivism generally, should be considered in the light of natural law theories.

2.2 Key points

The student should understand the similarities and differences between the theories of:

a) Bentham; and

b) Austin.

In particular the following aspects of both theories should be studied.

c) Law as 'commands'.

d) The concept of sanctions.

e) The concept of sovereignty.

Criticisms and comparisons with other positivists can be found in Parts B and C of this chapter.

2.3 Questions and suggested solutions

QUESTION ONE

'Austin's theory is not a theory of the rule of law – of government subject to law. It is a theory of the "rule of men" – of government using law as an instrument of power. Such a view may be considered realistic or merely cynical, but it is, in its broad outlines, essentially coherent.' (Cotterrell)

Discuss.

University of London LLB Examination
(for External Students) Jurisprudence and Legal Theory June 1995 Q4

General Comment

Beware that this question does not require a statement covering all you know about John Austin. It looks for a rational discussion of what Austin sees as the scope of jurisprudence, with the gloss that Cotterrell puts on it.

Skeleton Solution

Austin's definition of the scope of jurisprudence – Cotterrell's main criticism – the concept of sovereignty attacked – Hart's rejection of 'coercive order' – conclusion.

Suggested Solution

Within the context of Cotterrell's statement, John Austin's theory will include a concept of law as a species of command with an analysis of sovereignty. In *The Province of Jurisprudence Determined*, Austin defined what he saw as the precise scope of jurisprudence. To him, it involved drawing a clear distinction between morality and law.

Austin's theory has been much criticised, but in essence he regards the nature of law as based on the concept of power exercised by a superior and not on ideas which are perceived to be 'good or bad', or 'just or unjust'.

Jurisprudence, according to Austin, is concerned specifically with 'positive laws' or 'law properly so-called' as he puts it. Law is viewed as a species of command issued by a person or a body of people to whom habitual obedience was rendered. It was characterised by constituent elements:

a) command;

b) sanction;

c) duty;

d) sovereignty.

Law can be described as the command of a sovereign backed by sanctions.

Cotterrell's criticism

Austin's theory is criticised by Cotterrell who says it is not a theory of the 'rule of law', but more a theory of the 'rule of men'. The two separate concepts require distinction. De Smith sees the 'rule of law' as an abstract concept intended to imply that powers exercised by politicians and public servants require a legitimate foundation. Such powers are based upon an authority conferred by law, when the law conforms to certain minimum standards of justice, either procedural or substantive.

The 'rule of men' theory describes a position where deviation goes beyond what is acceptable, where executive discretionary power increases at the expense of individual freedom, and where the courts have the right to decide when legal preconditions for the loss of liberty are satisfied.

The validity of Cotterrell's view can be determined by the review of main criticisms levelled at Austin's theory. Initial criticism of Austin's theory revolved around his positivism which was denounced as 'a sterile verbalism which produced a travesty of reality' and also for an apparent 'narrowness of perspective'. Austin was accused of failing to understand the implications of his brand of positivism because his distinction between questions of 'law' and of 'morality' distanced him form an awareness of the real complexities of law within society.

Later criticism attacked Austin's 'simplistic view' of law saying he confused 'law' with the 'mere product of legislation'. Critics accused him of failing to understand that 'law' was much more than mere statutory measures because it included custom and international law which both received scant attention with his analysis. Further, Austin's analysis did not cover an adequate examination of 'judge-made' law arising from decisions of the courts.

Austin's command theory was also considered to have a linguistic looseness or ambiguity where the term 'command' has its own singular connotations. Command theory generally suggests the issue of order arbitrarily without using the word 'command' accurately when referring directly to the content of the large bulk of legislation. Austin also took criticism where the characteristics of a 'command' are absent from much contemporary legislation.

Sovereignty

Critics suggest that Austin's concept of sovereignty was 'over simplified' and incapable of an application to problems which arose from the legal structures of democratic society in particular. His view of 'the sovereign as possessing unlimited powers' was thought to have no validity within a parliamentary constitution. The indivisibility of a sovereign's power also created difficulties for those who sought to apply it to the analysis of a federal state.

Bryce says that Austin may have blurred the difference between a 'de facto' sovereign and a 'de jure' sovereign; a 'de facto' sovereign receives the habitual obedience of his subjects, whilst a 'de jure' sovereign is a law enacting institution. British constitutional law clearly distinguishes the Queen as sovereign from the Queen in Parliament. Austin had concentrated specifically on the form of 'law' and its outward manifestations relating to a sovereign and had given insufficient weight to the functional aspects of sovereign power in society.

Professor Hart has made serious criticism of Austin's theory when he rejected any model of law which was based merely on 'coercive orders'. Hart's justification was that 'coercive orders' were inapplicable to a large section of the modern legal system which confers public and private legal powers. Hart identified the mode or origin of law as being substantially misunderstood if it was seen as merely having emerged from 'orders plus threat'.

It can be concluded that Austin's analysis of 'law' in terms of a sovereign who is habitually obeyed as an omnipotent ruler exempt from all legal imitation does not account for the continuity of legislative authority which is the main characteristic of a modern legal system. In such circumstances, the sovereign cannot be identified either with a modern legislature or the electorate itself.

It is submitted that Cotterrell's contention that Austin's theory is more a theory of the rule of man rather that law flows logically from the substantial criticism levelled at Austin, most recently by Hart.

QUESTION TWO

'Analysing the content of Austin's theory of law can proceed without locating it within the historical and social conditions which gave rise to it, but appreciating the meaning of the theory cannot.'

Discuss.

University of London LLB Examination
(for External Students) Jurisprudence and Legal Theory June 1996 Q7

General Comment

Questions on Austin are popular among candidates. This particular question invites the candidate to consider whether it is possible to appreciate the meaning of Austin's theory without placing it within the context of the historical period that spawned it. You should not simply give an account of Austin's theory. Remember the question: does it matter to place it in its historical context?

Skeleton Solution

Austin's positivism – command theory – reasons for his stance located in historical and social conditions of his time – analysis of theory – appreciation of theory – conclusion.

Suggested Solution

John Austin establishes his positivist credentials with his opening line of *The Province of Jurisprudence Determined* (Austin, *The Province of Jurisprudence Determined* (1954), p9):

> 'The matter of jurisprudence is positive law: law, simply and strictly so-called; or law set by political superiors to political inferiors.'

To Austin, laws made by men for men are positive laws and natural law or law of nature is positive morality.

The historical and social conditions which gave rise to Austin's positivism could be said to be the prevalence of natural law doctrine that emphasised law as the law of nature, with which all laws made by men must conform in order to be valid. Austin was minded to propound a theory which stressed that all law was positive law in the sense that it was an expression of the will of a supreme authority. In other words, Austin recognised that what was needed was to advocate a view of law as a series of rational commands given by human beings with sanctions attached for non-conformity. Even though Austin did not explore fully the meaning of the word 'command', he believed his problem was solved by linking 'command' to the universally recognised doctrine of legal sovereignty.

Austin defines law as the command of a sovereign who is habitually obeyed. As noted above, Austin's problem was to link the word 'command' with legal sovereignty. In this suggested solution analysis of Austin's work will be limited to 'command', 'habitual obedience' and his sovereign.

Austin said in his first lecture that:

> 'Frankness is the highest compliment … I therefore entreat you, as the greatest favour you can do to me, to demand explanations and ply me with objections – turn me inside out.'

No doubt he has been very much obliged over the years with withering criticisms. Jolowicz (Jolowicz, *Lectures on Jurisprudence* (1963), p1) says that 'Austin's doctrine forms a very good target – we must set it up and see it clearly in order to throw bricks at it'.

Karl Olivecrona (Olivecrona, *Law as Fact* (1971), p32) makes the point that law is not identical with the declaration of will as Austin's theory says. Professor Hart says in *Essays in Jurisprudence and Philosophy* (1983) that the definition of law as a command is inadequate, saying a legal system, even a simple one, is distorted if presented as a command. Asking the question 'what is a command?', Hart says it is:

> '... simply an expression by one person of the desire that another person should do or abstain from some action, accompanied by a threat of punishment which is likely to follow disobedience.' (Hart, *The Concept of Law* (2nd ed 1994), p59.)

Accordingly to Hart, the command theory was simply a trilogy of command, sanction and sovereign, which he likened to a gunman threatening his victim for money: the gunman enforces conduct which differentiates 'obliging' from 'obligation'. To Hart, if one is under an obligation one has a legal duty to perform, whereas a gunman merely obliges conduct by threats; law, therefore, is 'surely not the gunman situation writ large and legal order is surely not to be thus simply identified with compulsion'. Even placing Austin's theory in its historical and social conditions it is difficult to appreciate why he thought law was a 'command'.

On the question of habitual obedience to a sovereign, Hart says it is wrong to think of a legislature with changing membership as a group of persons habitually obeyed. Hart would point to the legislatures in, say, the United Kingdom and America, and ask: 'since newly elected members had not known anything called habitual obedience how can they be called sovereign within Austin's definition'? He agrees that the idea is only suitable to a monarch sufficiently long-lived for a 'habit' to grow. Taking issue with the idea of the legally-untrammelled will of the sovereign who is above the law, Hart points out that legislators cannot make laws unless they comply with fundamentally accepted rules specifying the essential law-making powers. The point is that if legislators have to follow rules when making laws then their sovereignty is limited. Hart also brings home the point that procedural rules are not commands habitually obeyed, nor can they be expressed as habits of obedience to persons. Furthermore, he points out that other legal rules in society have quite different functions. They enable and empower people; they create rights such as rules enabling individuals to make contracts, wills and trusts. Hart quotes with approval Hagerstrom's analysis (Hagerstrom, *Inquiries into the Nature of Law and Morals* (1953), p217) that if laws were merely commands, the notion of an individual's right was inexplicable, for commands are something we either obey or disobey and are not right-conferring.

With reference to Hart's remarks on law being the command of a sovereign, I believe he has failed to direct his analysis to the fact that the body politic may not habitually obey a particular person or body of persons as the sovereign, but rather the institution they represent. In the United Kingdom, for example, people have habitual obedience to the Crown, an institution, and not the person of a King or Queen, so the institution is continually obeyed even when a new King or Queen is crowned on the death of the previous incumbent. As far as Parliament is concerned, it is composed of members of whom at least some vote against particular Bills during the process of law-making in

Parliament. Are such members said to have commanded anything as the sovereign? The fact that there is often a division in Parliament during the process of law creation reinforces the argument that sovereignty resides not in the Members of Parliament, but in the institution called the Crown-in-Parliament which is habitually obeyed. Again, however, when one reads Austin's theory against its historical and social conditions, it is difficult to appreciate the theory as clear-headed. Austin says that the House of Commons is merely trustee of the people's power so sovereignty resides in the Crown, the Lords and the electorate. Austin believes that in the United States sovereignty of each state and the federal union resides in the states' government forming one aggregate body; however he promptly contradicts himself by saying he means the body politic, in other words the electorate.

To Austin the sovereign is indivisible and illimitable. It is wondered if he was of the opinion that sovereignty in the United States resides in the aggregate body of the states, how is it that the electorate forms part of the sovereign? How can the bulk of the people be in a habit of obeying itself? Hart is right to say this is a picture of society divided into two halves, the sovereign giving orders for the subjects to habitually obey, but the blurring factor here is we have a society where the majority gives orders for the majority to obey.

Austin may reply that the majority has both private and public capacities. When it gives orders, it does so in its official capacity, and it obeys the orders in its private capacity. This leads to the absurd situation of the electorate undergoing metamorphosis, and Hart rightly asks: when does the metamorphosis happen?

There are inadequacies with Austin's command theory, and as the quotation in the question states, analysing the context of the theory can proceed without locating it within the historical and social conditions that produced it. The argument to be made here is that the institutions which he was writing about are still very much part of the constitutional firmament of both the United Kingdom and the United States of America, just as they were part of the constitutional set-up of these countries at the time he was writing. It is a valid argument that there is a clear lack of thoroughness with the theory and that has nothing to do with the historical and social conditions of the time he was writing.

It is appreciated that Austin wanted to propound a theory that required empirical explanation of law without metaphysics. He found it necessary to separate what was a legal rule from what was a moral rule, and he needed to think of a prior command, a sort of order given by human beings to be obeyed by human beings, and he linked all this to the legal concept of sovereignty. However, this does not mean that he could not have done better than presenting law as the command of a sovereign.

As Hart says, it is better to offer a theory that does not trace law to any particular author. Thus describing law as a system of rules should be enough. Hart accuses Austin of propounding a theory on the back of definition. I believe this is a valid criticism of Austin's work. Austin himself said that frankness is the highest compliment he could be paid and invited readers to turn him inside out. I join in obliging him. The historical and social conditions prevailing at the time he was writing cannot be used as an excuse for the flaws in his theory. Appreciating the theory does not require it to be located in any historical or social conditions. The institutions which Austin wrote about are still with us – very much part of the constitutional make-up of both the UK and USA. That is why his theory can still be criticised today by referring to these same institutions he used as paradigms.

QUESTION THREE

'The purpose of command theories is not to justify the existence of law but to justify its application by states.'

Discuss.

University of London LLB Examination
(for External Students) Jurisprudence and Legal Theory June 1999 Q6

General Comment

The essence of this question is to consider the purpose of the command theories of law. You must consider whether the command theories sought to justify the existence of law – that is to say, why do we have law?

Skeleton Solution

Definition of law by Bentham and Austin – analytical discourse of Austin's position – summary and conclusion.

Suggested Solution

The object of the command theorists (Bentham and Austin) was to attempt to clearly distinguish law from other social phenomena, like moral rules, social custom and traditional norms, with which it can easily be confused.

Jeremy Bentham (Jeremy Bentham, *Of Laws in General* (1970)) was surprised at how Blackstone had mixed-up moral notions and legal principles. To Bentham, Blackstone had merely espoused an adulterated cocktail of moral rules and prejudices under the guise of law. He famously poured scorn on Blackstone's efforts, and called natural law 'nonsense on stilts'. This is because he believed that the science of law must clearly show the demarcation between law and morality. This demarcation would make it clear that legal and moral issues are separate, and that each has a special validity and importance.

Bentham defined law as the mandate of the sovereign, whilst Austin's definition (John Austin, *The Provincial Jurisprudence Determined* (1832)) states that law is the command of the sovereign who is habitually obeyed. To Austin, the subject matter of jurisprudence is positive law – law strictly so-called and set by political superiors to be obeyed by political inferiors. This gives the impression that law is merely an expression of power (Roger Cotterrell, *The Politics of Jurisprudence* (1996)). If we consider Austin's theory, law is a rule laid down for the guidance of an intelligent being by an intelligent being who has power over him.

Austin defines law as a species of command. Two classes of such command, which he calls laws properly so-called, are divine law and human law. Human laws form the province of jurisprudence and are positive law. These laws are set by political superiors acting in such a capacity, or by others delegated to do so.

Bentham sees law as an assemblage of signs declarative of volition. It is arguable that Bentham also sees law as a species of command; it is an expression of power. To Austin, moral rules set by public opinion differ from laws strictly so-called. What they have in common is generality. A command, such as a directive from one government department to another to consider a particular case, is not law in Austin's sense. He argues that generality can be understood in two senses. It can apply to acts required or prohibited, and to persons addressed by the command. Generality as to acts, therefore, means that the command applies to a class of acts and not a specific one. When applied to persons, it indicates a class of people or the general polity subject to the command, not a particular individual or a number of specified individuals.

To Austin, law therefore consists of rules addressed to individuals, business organisations and agencies, or addressed to the general public or a section of it. Austin gives us an impression of law as a technical instrument of government and administration, which should be efficient and aimed at the common good (as determined by utility). In this sense, law, for Austin, is effective government.

Like Bentham, Austin is impatient with the idea of natural rights. To him, there are no rights or laws which are inherent to the human condition. All laws, rights and duties are created by positive law and are laid down by government. This means that there is nothing sacred about civil or political liberties. To the extent that they are valuable, they are the by-product of collective government in the common interest. Austin states that liberty has been erected onto a plinth like an idol, extolled with extravagant praises by its doting and fanatical worshippers. He says that the purpose of government is to serve the common good, and so the protection of civil and political liberties is valid only in so far as it serves this common good. Thus the limitation of liberty is sometimes more conducive to the common good than the maximisation of it.

This is a governmental view of law which states that (a) duties are more important than rights; and (b) the law's command allows the individual to make a specific claim on others through the legal system. Since sanction is an essential element of this command, duty then becomes the automatic consequence of being addressed by a potentially enforceable command.

The above essay has attempted to look at the command theories of Bentham and Austin analytically, and the conclusion that we can draw is that these theories do not seek to justify the existence of law, but to explain and justify its application by states. States apply the law for the common good, which is a sound utilitarian goal.

QUESTION FOUR

Explain and evaluate the reasons Hart gives for rejecting the view that the law of any society consists in the general orders of a 'sovereign'.

University of London LLB Examination
(for External Students) Jurisprudence and Legal Theory June 2000 Q1

General Comment

This question requires an analysis of Hart's criticisms of a model of a legal system akin to that of Austin. You have to do more than state the reasons that were put forward by Hart; you have to go to evaluate them. In this enterprise an examination of the strengths of Hart's approach in terms of linguistic analysis is valuable. The devices used by Austin, orders, sanctions and the sovereign, are insufficient and in particular the device of a rule is missing. The better answers will include reference to the Postscript which was added to the second edition of *The Concept of Law*.

Skeleton Solution

Austin – positive law – commands – sovereign – Bentham – Hart – methodology – critique of Austin – need for rules – officials – internal attitude – discretion – Raz – Dworkin – Postscript.

Suggested Solution

The idea of law being the general orders of a sovereign was central to the work of both Austin and Bentham, the latter providing a more sophisticated version of it. Hart in *The Concept Of Law* developed his own version of legal positivism by criticising a model of the legal system similar to that of Austin. Hart's ideas were in turn to be criticised and developed by other jurisprudential writers. This series of developments in ideas have been the most important movement in jurisprudence in the last 50 years.

Austin thought that the matter of jurisprudence is positive law, this being law strictly so-called and being set by political superiors to political inferiors. He saw law as a rule laid down by an intelligent being by an intelligent being having power over him. He excluded natural or divine law. He put international law into a category based on opinion or sentiment which also included fashion. Every law properly so-called was a command. The theory is one of imperatives or commands. He said that if you express a wish that another should do something or stop doing something and if this is backed by a sanction, then that wish is a command. That person is bound or obliged by the command and is under a duty to obey. The device of the sovereign was also used. If a determinate human superior, not in the habit of obedience to a like superior, receives habitual obedience from the bulk of the population, that determinate human superior is the sovereign and there is a political society. Bentham also presented an orders or imperative theory in which concepts such as sovereignty and command are put to work but in a more subtle manner than in the case of Austin. Bentham, for example, does not resort to an indivisible or illimitable sovereign. He accepts divided and partial sovereignty. He also takes a broader view of human motivation, including, for example, alluring motives. His approach is designed with a wider range of law than the criminal law in mind. He puts to work the concept of permissive laws. He also saw the will of the sovereign as being more complex than Austin's notion of a command. Bentham does not have to utilise the idea of nullity as a sanction or set up fictions such as tacit command.

Hart's work is the most thorough attack on a model of law similar to Austin's. He was aware of Bentham's ideas and he utilises some of his strengths in order to provide a theory which stresses the need for both primary and secondary rules. Hart attempts to produce both a descriptive sociology and a linguistic analysis in which he is keen to find the meaning of words. Hart criticised Austin's work in a variety of ways. For example, a command will explain a criminal law but not why a statute applies generally and also applies to its framers. Equally, many laws do not contain threats. Secondly, there are other varieties of laws, notably powers. Thirdly, Austin's habit of obedience fails to explain succession to sovereignty. Succession to sovereignty occurs by virtue of the acceptance of a rule entitling the successor to succeed, not because of a habit of obedience. The idea of a determinate person or body as the issuer of commands does not fit in well with the complexities of the present time. As Duguit suggests, with social legislation the State would be commanding itself. Austin also exaggerated the role of sanctions within legal systems as our motivation towards the law is influenced by more than fear. We may agree with many of the laws and realise that they provide advantages of various sorts to us all. Many laws may in fact be permissive providing a means by which we can achieve our aims. Hart incorporated this reality into his theory by the device of power confering rules.

Hart thought that law should be understood as a system of rules. Societies need a system of rules and he makes use of two types of rule – primary and secondary rules. Primary rules of obligation state what must or must not be done. These are duty imposing rules. Examples are to be found in the criminal law. Hart tells us that primary rules are needed concerning the free use of violence, theft and deception to which human beings are tempted but which they must, in general, repress, if they are to coexist in close proximity to each other. There are secondary rules of change, recognition and adjudication. They are power confering rules which are designed to supplement the primary rules. They affect the operation of the primary rules. It is the union of primary and secondary rules which produce a legal system. For a legal system people would have to, on the whole, obey the primary rules and the officials who administer the system would also have to accept (have to have an internal attitude towards) the rules of change, adjudication, and recognition. For Hart rules will have an internal aspect – that is people will have a critical, reflective attitude towards them.

The patterns of behaviour they contain set a common standard. This attitude will be seen in criticism and self-criticism, demands for conformity with the standards and general acknowledgement that such criticism and demands are justified. In short the rules are accepted when you have this attitude. Thus adherence to the rule can be more than a habit or a result of a command that includes the threat of a sanction, as in Austin's system. The external aspects of a rule refer to the idea that an observer of a legal system would be aware of the existence of particular rules through his observation of them. Habits possess only an external aspect whilst rules have both external and internal aspects. Most societies could not get by with just primary rules. Problems would arise and the secondary rules provide the means to solve these problems. Hart states that there are two fundamental conditions for the existence of a legal system. Rules (in particular the rule of recognition) must be obeyed and the secondary rules must be accepted by the community's officials as common public standards in relation to official behaviour.

As was noted earlier, these ideas produced by Hart have been criticised. Finnis, for example, tells us that Hart tells us little about the state of mind of the officials. Raz thought that Hart's ideas were too limited and attempted to develop Hart's work, for example, expanding the categories of rules beyond primary and secondary rules. Dworkin suggested that in hard cases, ie difficult ones, the judges apply principles – these being requirements of justice or fairness – such as no man may profit from his own wrong. Principles have a dimension of weight or importance that rules lack. Principles are a push in a particular direction, whilst rules are applied in an all or nothing fashion. Dworkin suggests that schemes such as Hart's cannot accommodate principles and as a result are driven to rely on the notion of discretion. MacCormick has in fact formulated a positivist theory that includes principles. He shows that it is possible to incorporate non-rule standards into positivism. Dworkin suggested that judges do not make law, that they will always be able to find a right answer. Hart of course thought that the judges had discretion and that they sometimes engaged in law making. It seems easier to agree with Hart on this. The following cases seem to involve judicial law making: *Donoghue* v *Stevenson* [1932] AC 562, *Rylands* v *Fletcher* (1868) LR 3 HL 330, *British Railways Board* v *Herrington* [1972] AC 877, *Pepper* v *Hart* [1993] 1 All ER 42 and *Burmah Oil* v *Lord Advocate* [1965] AC 75.

Hart's second edition of *The Concept of Law* was published in 1997, two years after his death. In a Postscript, which was included in that edition, Hart deals with some issues raised by critics – particularly Dworkin, and in general he sticks to his guns. Hart does not accept that rules are as different to principles as Dworkin had suggested. Hart suggests, for example, that the case of *Riggs* v *Palmer* 115 NY 506 (1889) involved a rule as regards inheritance and a principle of unjust enrichment rather than two principles as claimed by Dworkin. He does accept that he did fail to pay attention to principles. Hart rejected the proposition that ideas of morality have a role to play in identifying rules of law. Hart sticks to his view that the Nazi system was a legal system. Hart is of the view that the judges sometimes make law. But he does not see this as being problematic, which is hard to swallow, as it amounts to retrospective law making. He now tells us that by descriptive sociology he meant morally neutral. He does not accept Dworkin's criticism that he has committed the sin of the semantic sting – ie concentrated on how people speak. It depends really which bits of Hart's work you read: the early parts seem very linguistic, but not so much at the end. Hart denies Dworkin's claim that the purpose of law is to justify coercion.

As Lloyd tells us, Hart's description of a legal system in terms of a union of primary and secondary rules provides a tool of analysis for much that has puzzled both jurist and political theorist. At the same time it may be wondered whether too much is not claimed for this new view of old problems. There are times when Hart would appear to have moved little from Austin's command theory. Thus he writes: 'So long as the laws which are valid by the system's tests of validity are obeyed by the bulk of the population this surely is all the evidence we need in order to establish that a given legal system exists'. Further he concedes that there is more to a legal system than a union of rules. In particular, he stresses the open texture of rules, as well as the distinctive relationship of law to morality and justice. We have to conclude that whilst Hart was able to produce a powerful critique of the idea of law as the commands of a sovereign, his own reasoning was itself criticised and developed in a variety of ways. Hart remains the leading contributor to jurisprudential thought in the last 50 years.

B THE PURE THEORY OF LAW

2.4 Introduction

The pure theory of law was developed by Kelsen, and has been said by Lloyd and Freeman in *An Introduction to Jurisprudence* to be the most 'illuminating analysis of the legal process' this century. Kelsen shared many characteristics with other positivists – for example, his insistence on sanctions as being central. But the most crucial and outstanding element of Kelsen's analysis is his norm theory: that an 'ought' statement is derived from another 'ought' statement or norm, until one ultimately arrives back at the Grundnorm. In revising Kelsen students should consider his theory in the light of positivism generally. It might also be useful to consider comparisons with other types of theories such as Realism.

2.5 Key points

Why is Kelsen's theory 'pure'?

a) It aims to explain law free from the taint of other social sciences, sociology, and particularly, morality.

b) Kelsen makes a distinction between the prescriptive and the descriptive – one of his criticisms of Austin and Bentham was that they mixed prescriptive and descriptive propositions.

The hierarchy of legal norms

a) A norm is prescriptive of conduct, and is an 'ought' statement.

b) Each norm or 'ought' statement is validated by a higher norm, and the higher norm by a still higher one.

c) The chains of norms stretch back to the basic norm or Grundnorm which is the presupposed ultimate rule. It provides the criteria by which one may assess whether any particular norm belongs to the legal system.

As with the imperative theories, the pure theory of law stresses the importance of sanctions. For Kelsen, law consists of norms backed by coercive sanctions. There are many criticisms of a sanction – based view of law.

The important relationship between validity and efficacy

a) Norms are valid where they have ben made by the correct procedure. Validity can be traced back to the Grundnorm. A valid norm is binding in legal terms in that it guide behaviour.

b) Efficacy means that people do actually behave in the way that the legal norms prescribe.

c) Validity and efficacy are thus separate: but if the system as a whole ceases to be efficacious then the validity of individual norms is lost.

Kelsen addressed the issue of revolution. For him, if a new order takes over and becomes generally efficacious, then that new order will be valid and a new Grundnorm presupposed. It has been argued that his theory gives a judge no assistance in revolutionary situations.

2.6 Questions and suggested solutions

QUESTION ONE

What is the function of Kelsen's basic norm? Is it an unnecessary complication in his theory?

University of London LLB Examination
(for External Students) Jurisprudence and Legal Theory June 1999 Q7

General Comment

This question is very straightforward. You must try to find out whether the basic norm is of any value to us at all – in other words, examine the practical usefulness of the basic norm.

Skeleton Solution

Kelsen's pure theory – methodology – the Grundnorm/the rule of recognition – usefulness of the Grundnorm – conclusion.

Suggested Solution

The aim of Kelsen's pure theory (Hans Kelsen, *The General Theory of Law and State* (1946)) is to show that the essence of law is positive law. Law is not discoverable from the realities which exist in the human condition.

Whereas other legal theorists take a sociological view of normative legal theory (Roger Cotterrell, *The Politics of Jurisprudence* (1996)), Kelsen rejects such an approach. To him, there can be no link between legal theory and the theory of a purely legal science and sociology. He believes that they are completely different conceptual discourses, appropriate to their specific subject matter. Legal theory, as he understands it, must be purged of any connection to foreign concepts and methods.

His theory, called the Pure Theory of Law, is not concerned with the law as it ought to be, because this belongs to the realms of politics or moral philosophy. The subject matter of the pure theory is simply positive law.

Kelsen calls the law a 'norm', which means that something ought to be or ought to happen, with particular regard to the fact that a human being ought to behave in a specific way. To this extent, legal science is normative. The law, which is made up of ought propositions, is addressed to the officials of the legal system: if X circumstance occurs, officials ought to apply sanctions. Thus, law is always addressed to the officials of the legal system.

We may balk at this idea, since we generally believe that law addresses the general public. Kelsen's theory argues that it does not. It addresses the officials, and the citizen or the individual may only trigger the circumstances necessitating the application of sanctions. The individual is said to cause the act which will trigger the official reaction.

The norms in a legal system are in a hierarchical structure. At the top of the hierarchy is the basic norm (the Grundnorm). The function of the Grundnorm is two-fold: (a) to validate all other norms in the legal system; and (b) to give unity to the legal system. This means that we have a sequence of the authorisation of norms, which can be traced back from the decision of a court through to that of Parliament or a statute enabling a specific act, through to the constitution, which enacts the statute to the pure theory of law, deliberately postulating a further single norm – the basic norm, standing behind and giving validity to the constitution. The basic norm is a theoretical necessity, which Kelsen insists we must presuppose in our juristic thinking.

Professor Hart takes issue with Kelsen with regard to the basic norm. Hart believes that this basic norm is an 'unnecessary luxury'. His own theory believes that at the apex of a legal system of rules is the rule of recognition, validating all rules within the system. The actions of officials are taken into account in identifying the rule of recognition as being in existence. Hart is an empiricist which forces him to say that the rule of recognition is identifiable by the actual practice of officials. It is an actual legal rule found in real legal systems. Viewed externally, the rule of recognition is an observable social fact: officials act uniformly on presuppositions as to what counts as law. Internally officials have presuppositions in order to administer the legal system.

Kelsen is a conceptualist, and thus finds his theory in no need of an empirical rule of recognition. However, we could say that his Grundnorm, which we must presuppose, informs us that law is an intellectual discipline, so legal practice must relate to a logical form about all norms within a single legal system. To say that the basic norm is effective means that the unity of the legal system is actually being presupposed in legal thought and practice.

Hart's theory distinguishes between situations where one is 'obliged' to do something by another, and the situation where one is under an 'obligation'. To Hart, where one is under an 'obligation', it means that an existing law places a duty on the individual: obeying the law is seen by the individual from the 'internal point of view' – the critical reflective attitude we all have. Similarly, Kelsen's theory argues that in situations (as Hart points out) there is no rule of thumb as to how we should react, and so we must make a presupposition in order to understand the physical world.

As a positivist, Kelsen's idea is controversial, but if we consider the influence from Kantian epistemology, where he asks how we can explain the subjective notions of, for example, a sovereign's command into objective rules of law without the help of God or nature, then we can see where he is coming from. If we must identify the 'law which is' from the 'law which ought to be', as positivism demands of us, then we must presuppose the existence of the basic norm to give objectivity to the law.

Seen in the light of the above interpretation, Kelsen's theory argues that in situations where a successful revolution has replaced a democratically elected government, we need not fret about what constitutes law and the legal system, but merely create a theoretical construct (called the basic norm) which sits behind the original constitution, albeit one introduced by the usurper, which says we must act in accordance with the original constitution. Despite the controversial nature of this theory, it is arguable that it gives us a real life purpose, and imposes a practical order on our lives by asking us to be engaged in real life situations.

QUESTION TWO

Discuss critically what Kelsen means by saying that the validity of the basic norm is to be presupposed.

University of London LLB Examination
(for External Students) Jurisprudence and Legal Theory June 2000 Q9

General Comment

You must provide a critique and not just descriptive material that focuses on the Grundnorm. Whilst the role of the Grundnorm can be explored as indeed can the issue of validity, you must make as much as you can of the notion of a presupposed basic norm. You do this because the question asks you to do it. Consider, for example, who does the presupposing – jurists, judges, citizens or some or all of them?

Skeleton Solution

Science of law – normative relations – directions to officials – hierarchy of norms – Grundnorm or basic norm – concretisation of norms – the principal of effectiveness – presupposition – fictional character.

Suggested Solution

Kelsen wanted to explain law of all types and to this end attempted to produce a pure theory of law, a science of law free of metaphysical elements. To do this it was necessary to isolate the key elements necessary for such an endeavour. He was concerned with what the law was and not what it perhaps ought to be. He presented law as a series of normative relations. This was a normative approach: he is concerned with what ought to happen – but in an entirely different way to metaphysical propositions. Kelsen sees laws as normative propositions detailing what should happen within a legal system.

If, for example, s22 Theft Act 1968 creates an offence of handling stolen goods, which has penalties attached to it, and Arthur handles stolen goods, then the magistrate or judge ought to apply the appropriate penalty. For Kelsen as opposed to Austin this is not just saying that the official is under a duty but it would also cover situations where the official had power or discretion. Kelsen sees laws as being directions to officials instructing them as to the application of sanctions in particular circumstances. In the example he would suggest that it is far more appropriate to concentrate on the direction to the official as to sanction rather than the offence or the offender.

The validity of a law is to be tested in terms of other higher laws from which it is derived. There is a hierarchy of laws or norms at the top of which is a Grundnorm or basic norm. Moral, social and political considerations are thus irrelevant to the validity of legal norms. Such a hierarchical system would explain a system of delegated legislation. The norms themselves become more concrete as you descend the hierarchy – this is the concretisation of norms. The basic norm is the norm that performs the task of validating all other norms within a legal system. It is not validated itself and each legal system will have a basic norm. Within England and Wales in the pre-EC era it may have been appropriate to think of the authority of the Queen in Parliament as supplying the basic norm. Now of course the situation is more complex. Where there is a written constitution then the hierarchy of norms may be based upon its propositions. This is in the sense that it will provide directions as to how officials should act. The constitution itself, since it is a fact rather than a normative proposition, could not be the basic norm. You must not talk about giving validity to the basic norm. In any constitution it is rather like an elephant; the suggestion is that you will know it when you see it. This norm is thus presupposed or assumed.

Kelsen tells us (Kelsen *Introduction to the Problems of Legal Theory* (1996)) that the Pure Theory works with the basic norm or Grundnorm as a hypothetical foundation. There is a presupposition that the basic norm is valid and thus the legal system resting on it is also valid. He states this in the following terms:

> 'The basic norm confers on the act of the first legislator – and thus on all other acts of the legal system resting on this first act – the sense of "ought", that specific sense in which legal condition is linked with legal consequence in the reconstructed legal norm, the paradigmatic form in which it must be possible to represent all the data of the positive law. Rooted in the basic norm, ultimately, is the normative import of all the material facts constituting the legal system. The basic norm is valid not as a positive legal norm – since it is not created in a legal process, not issued or set – but as a presupposed condition of all lawmaking, indeed, of every process of the positive law. The Pure Theory aims simply to raise to the level of consciousness what all jurists are doing (for the most part unwittingly) when, in conceptualizing their object of enquiry, they reject natural law as the basis of the validity of positive law, but nevertheless understand the positive law as a valid system, that is, as norm, and not merely as factual contingencies of motivation.'

As Cotterrell explains, norms are traced back from court decisions, through the statutory norms providing jurisdiction, through the constitutional norms authorising enactment of the statute, to the original constitution. Then the Pure Theory of law postulates a further norm that gives validity to the original constitution. The basic norm is a presupposition or hypothesis, a theoretical necessity. In later writings Kelsen terms it a fiction. Jackson explains (Jackson *Making Sense in Jurisprudence* (1996)) how the system operates in the following terms:

> 'Kelsen argues, we experience the legal system as one within which objective, and not merely subjective, legal meanings are produced – if, that is, we experience the legal system as having the sense of objective validity, and not merely as being a reflection of the subjective wills of those who deploy power (as it would be, for example, according to the Command Theory) – then logically we must presuppose the existence of a norm superior to the constitution, which gives validity to that constitution.'

In practice Kelsen's work has proved to be disappointing when applied to the real world. I've already noted that a basic norm for the constitution in England and Wales is elusive at the present time. Attempts to apply his work to revolutionary situations have been of limited success. However, the following are some examples of real cases in which his ideas have been applied. *Madzimbamuto* v *Lardner Burke* [1969] 1 AC 645, *Dosso PLD* 1958 SC 533, *Sallah* v *Attorney-General* (1970) CC 54, *Jilani* (1972) SC 139 *Matovu* (1966) EA 154. It might be that such situations are so unsettled that it is difficult to know if you have a legal system at all. For Kelsen a legal system was characterised by a settled system. The norms of the legal order have to be by and large effective – this is the principle of effectiveness. What is certain is that there is a legal system in England and Wales with an elusive basic norm. Part of Kelsen's approach is that he is an advocate of monism this being the idea that there is one legal system with international law being higher in the system than domestic law. This is a notion that is difficult to accept and leaves Kelsen open to strong criticism. As Freeman tells us, it disregards the realities of the situation.

It is apparent that some of what Kelsen said is unclear – for example, in relation to the nature of the basic norm. Most fundamentally, consider who does the presupposing of this basic norm – jurists, judges, citizens, jurists or some or all of them? Also, he changed his ideas over the years; for example his ideas on the basic norm. In some of his writings he even entertained the idea that there could be more than one basic norm.

QUESTION THREE

'The pure theory of law … establishes the law as a specific system independent even of the moral law. It does this not … by defining the legal norm as an imperative, but as an hypothetical judgment expressing a specific relationship between a conditioning circumstance and a conditioned consequence.' (Kelsen)

Explain and discuss critically with particular reference to the practical implications of his theory.

University of London LLB Examination
(for External Students) Jurisprudence and Legal Theory June 1996 Q4(a)

General Comment

Questions on Kelsen always appear in the examination paper in one form or another. This question invites you to think about the nature of Kelsen's ought propositions. What must be kept in mind is that Kelsen intends his ought statements not to be an imperative like the command theory but as a hypothetical judgment. Ask yourself whether there are occasions when judges do not apply the law for any reason.

Skeleton Solution

The nature of Kelsen's pure theory of law – law as an independent entity – methodology – difference between science of law and other sciences – difficulties of drawing a strict line of demarcation between science of law and other sciences – question of probability.

Suggested Solution

Kelsen's pure theory of law establishes the law as an independent entity devoid of any impurities. His aim is to free law from the value judgments common to other sciences; his pure theory seeks to free the science of law with a methodology that eschews any reliance on politics, ethics, theology, psychology or biology.

By establishing the independence of law, Kelsen seeks to liberate law from its traditional association with morals. Natural law makes morals part of law, and this makes the legal norm an imperative. For example, the traditional association of law and morals makes 'thou shall not kill' a legal norm as well as a moral imperative. Law and morals are interlinked. To Kelsen, law's liberation from morals means the pure theory is to be seen as a theory of positive law. The pure theory does not question the requirement that law must be moral. It questions the view of natural law that law is part of morals and every law must therefore have some moral input. The quotation in the question shows that if the moral law is imperative Kelsen's legal norm is not, so there is a difference between the moral norm and legal norm. The difference is shown by separating law from other sciences which explain causal, natural processes.

The law of nature links a particular circumstance – the cause – to a particular effect. Law links the legal condition (a conditioning circumstance) to the legal consequence (a conditioned consequence). There is a relationship here. With the law of nature the link is explained by the principle of causality: if A, then B. The pure theory, on the other hand, says that law has a 'specific relationship' which is a special and peculiar principle of law. Law, then, is a hypothetical judgment, an imputation, because when a conditioning circumstance (delict) happens it says nothing with regard to value, the moral or political value of the ensuing relationship.

According to the pure theory, the legal rule says: 'if A is then B ought to be'. The ought is a pure a priori category which expresses no moral or political value between A and B. Kelsen says there is no cause and effect between A and B. The example Kelsen gives is that punishment does not always follow a delict as cause upon effect. The legal rule, therefore, only expresses a hypothetical judgment, eg: 'if someone steals he ought to be punished'. The ought statement is the hypothetical judgment because A may steal and not be punished. Here the law is not followed so there is no cause and effect. There is no imperative analogous with a moral norm. To Kelsen the ought category of law indicates the 'specific sense' in which the legal condition and the legal circumstance are understood in the legal rule.

What Kelsen is saying is that by being a hypothetical judgment the rule of law is different from the rule of nature because while natural science describes its objects by the principle of causality, law describes its objects by the principle of normativity or imputation. Therefore, a normative rule is valid even if it is unenforced. For example, a normative rule which says 'if someone kills he ought to be punished' is still valid even if in a given case someone who murders is not punished. This is because an 'ought' statement which is a hypothetical judgment (explains why the killer in this case is not punished) is different from an 'is' statement which says if someone kills he is actually punished.

The difference between a legal norm and the law of nature is not seen by examining the elements that connect them but by the manner of their connection. Whereas the rule of law connects the conditioning circumstances and the conditioning consequence with an 'ought', the law of nature connects two elements by an 'is'.

There is a difficulty in drawing a strict line of demarcation between a rule of law and a law of nature as presented by Kelsen. He agrees that both a legal norm and a law of nature follow hypothetical judgments attaching certain consequences to certain conditions. If both have this logical form how can he make any watertight compartment between the two? He says the difference between the rule of law and the law of nature as far as connection between the two elements is concerned is that whereas the rule of law uses 'ought' to connect two elements, the law of nature uses an 'is'. However, if punishment ought to follow upon the commitment of a delict by someone is this not the same as causality? If both a legal norm and a law of nature employ hypothetical judgments, is it then not correct to say that if a law of nature is characterised by probability (in that there is nothing absolute about a law of nature which cannot be contradicted by another law of nature), is it also not the case that a legal norm can be contradicted by another legal norm?

Kelsen is not convincing about the specific relationship between a conditioning circumstance and a conditioned consequence as far as law is concerned. Punishment may not follow upon a person committing a delict but that may be because another legal rule rescues the person from punishment. For example, the law exempts children under ten years of age from punishment. If a child in this age group escapes punishment it is because the law exempts the child, and it is misleading to say the law was not enforced because it is only expressed as an imputation. If the logic of this argument is followed then the pure theory cannot establish any binding force in law.

The problem with the pure theory is that Kelsen sees law as a hypothetical judgment. If a law says 'if someone steals he ought to be punished', and a thief escapes punishment, it is not the case that the judge deciding the case sees the law as a hypothetical judgment but that in all probability the thief was able to rely on another law as a defence or that the thief was let off on a technicality. It is not that because the thief escapes punishment because the judge chooses not to enforce the law without reason. In practice the pure theory, by relying on hypothetical judgment will admit value judgment, moral or political. The pure theory may properly be called a theory of positive law in that it seeks to separate what is a legal rule from what is a moral rule, yet describing a legal rule as a hypothetical judgment has its own problems in practice if not in theory. The practical implication of this theory is that a legal rule has no force until enforced by a judge or an official.

QUESTION FOUR

Explain critically Kelsen's idea that legal validity depends upon a 'transcendental epistemological postulate'.

University of London LLB Examination
(for External Students) Jurisprudence and Legal Theory June 1996 Q4(b)

General Comment

Your knowledge of Kelsen's theory must be comprehensive enough to give you the confidence to tackle this question. If Kelsen's Grundnorm or basic norm is not validated by any other norm but must, as he says, be presupposed in our juristic thinking, is one not right in arguing that Kelsen's Grundnorm, like a phantom, can be based on anything?

Skeleton Solution

The idea of the norm and legal validity – the idea that a higher norm validates another norm – hierarchical structure of norms – the basic norm or Grundnorm – Kantian epistemology – criticism by Julius Stone – Kelsen's response – Hart's criticism of the basic norm – MacCormick.

Suggested Solution

The law is a legal norm in Kelsen's pure theory of law. A legal norm is valid and the reason for its validity is that it is validated by a higher norm. This means that norms are in a hierarchical structure, and we trace the reason for a particular norm's validity up the hierarchy.

However, the search for validity cannot go on indefinitely. For example, if we want to trace the validity of a local authority bye-law we trace it up the hierarchy to a statutory instrument whose validity can be traced to an enabling Act of Parliament; the validity of the Act of Parliament can be traced to a constitution which empowered legislators to make law. The first constitution sits at the apex of the hierarchy. How does the first constitution achieve its validity? Here Kelsen says the final norm is presupposed because it is not created by an authority whose competence will have to be anchored on a still higher norm. Though the legal validity of this final norm cannot come from another higher norm, its validity cannot be questioned. This presupposed final norm is called the basic norm or Grundnorm. All norms whose validity can be traced to the same basic norm form a system of norms – this becomes a normative order.

Kelsen's idea is that in tracing the validity of a norm we eventually arrive at a historically first constitution whose validity could not be traced to a positive law created by a legal authority. For example, the historically first constitution may have been promulgated after a successful revolution. This revolution may have breached a legal order based on a constitution. Therefore, in considering a particular national legal order, validity is traced to a presupposed basic norm. That is how a constitution imposed by a revolutionary regime can be said to be binding. The presupposed basic norm is important in that the validity of the constitution makes it possible to interpret acts made or done under it or its application of valid rules, as well as acts performed according to valid rules.

To help us understand what the basic norm is, Kelsen says it must be kept in mind that it refers directly to a specific constitution which is established by custom or is of statutory creation and is by and large effective. It is only by presupposing the basic norm that we are able to interpret the subjective meaning of an act made under the constitution as an objectively valid norm. To interpret the subjective meaning or constitution-created acts as objectively valid norms, Kelsen employs Kantian epistemology which asks:

> 'How is it possible to interpret without a metaphysical hypothesis, the facts perceived by our senses, the laws of nature formulated by natural science?' (Kelsen, *Pure Theory of Law* (1967), p202.)

Drawing on this, Kelsen asks:

> 'How is it possible to interpret without recourse to meta-legal authorities like God or nature, the subjective meaning of certain facts as a system of objectively-valid legal norms describable in rules of law?'

The pure theory's epistemological answer is that it is by presupposing the basic norm that one ought to behave in accordance with the constitution. The function of the basic norm is to underwrite the objective validity of a positive legal order, and it does this by interpreting the subjective meaning of acts of human beings by which the laws of an effective legal system are created as their objective meaning.

Problems raised by commentators about the pure theory of law have centred on the idea that the validity of a norm depends on a 'transcendental epistemological postulate'. According to Professor Julius Stone, the basic norm conceals:

> '... an ambiguity, swinging between, on one hand, a norm that is at the top of the pyramid of norms of each legal order, and on the other, some other norm which remains outside this pyramid, and is wholly meta-legal, and amounts to a general presupposition requiring that in each and every legal order "the constitution" shall be obeyed.'

Kelsen's response is to emphasise that the basic norm is only presupposed in juristic thinking as the constitution in a legal-logical sense. This distinguishes a constitution presupposed in juristic thinking in a legal-logical sense and a constitution in a positive legal sense. This means that the basic norm presupposed in a legal logical sense in juristic thinking is not created by the real act of will of a legal organ. Kelsen says the basic norm is meta-legal if we say that it is not created by a positive law, and it is 'legal' if we are to understand things with legal significance; so the basic norm presupposed in juristic thinking has the function of interpreting the objective validity of the requirement of a community's constitution.

At first sight it would seem that Kelsen's Kantian epistemology is false in the sense that, as Professor Stone points out, the juristic thinking employs a meta-legal concept or value judgment not created by any positive law. This way Kelsen's epistemology relies on some meta-legal authority, possibly nature.

Professor Hart's criticism of the pure theory is that to say that a rule is valid is different from Kelsen's idea of validity. According to Hart a rule is valid if it passes the test of validity provided by the rule of recognition. Kelsen's response is to ask when one looks back to the ultimate constitution or to Hart's rule of recognition what is it that makes this rule of recognition valid? Hart dismisses such a question. To him questioning the validity of the rule of recognition is just like asking whether the metre-bar in Paris used for measuring metre lengths is itself a metre in length.

To Hart the validity of the rule of recognition is a fact. This can be demonstrated by pointing to how officials identify the law. When officials identify rules of their systems it means they accept and use the rule of recognition. Kelsen's reply will be that since the rule of recognition is not created by any positive law it is also 'meta-legal' or at best presupposed. Kelsen can say that, like the rule of recognition, when officials of a system identify rules and apply them, it is because they have presupposed a basic norm and can trace individual norms to a basic norm. To Kelsen the basic norm is a theoretical construct, performing a theoretical function. It becomes the norm that stands behind the historically first constitution.

MacCormick in *H L A Hart* (1981) supports Kelsen and says the pure theory of law aims to establish what makes possible knowledge of the law as an objective normative order. To MacCormick, there is a presupposition of a non-positive basic norm according to which the human act of creating the historically first constitution of a legal order is valid.

The idea of the presupposed basic norm giving validity to all other norms in the legal order makes sense if we think that after a revolution a new regime makes a new constitution and the legal order of that particular territory is in general effective due to validity given to the constitution. Since the basic norm is a fiction, a theoretical construct, it remains free of any value – this is why the validity of norms in the legal order depends upon a transcendental epistemological postulate.

QUESTION FIVE

Are the critics right to label Kelsen's 'pure theory' an 'exercise in sterile formalism'?

University of London LLB Examination
(for External Students) Jurisprudence and Legal Theory June 1998 Q6

General Comment

Candidates frequently say that Kelsen is difficult to understand. What they really mean is that they are frightened of engaging in clear and careful thinking. It is important for law students to sharpen their intellect and Kelsen offers a sound basis for putting on the thinking cap.

Skeleton Solution

The idea of a norm and legal validity – the idea of a hierarchical structure of norms – the basic norm (or Grundnorm) – the relevance of the basic norm – summary and conclusion.

Suggested Solution

Kelsen (Hans Kelsen, *General Theory of Law and State* (1946)) calls law a legal norm in his pure theory of law. He argues that a legal norm is valid because it is validated by a higher norm. Norms in the legal order form a hierarchical structure.

The trace for the validity of any norm is found by going up the hierarchy. The search does not go on forever; eventually, a cut-off point will be found. When we reach that point we discover the first historical constitution, which confers legal validity on all other norms. For example, if we want to trace the validity of a local authority's bye-law, we have to trace it up the hierarchy until we come to an enabling Act of Parliament. The Act of Parliament confers authority on the local authority to make the bye-law.

Legal validity is given to the historically first constitution by the final norm (which is a higher norm). This final norm is called the basic norm (or Grundnorm). The functions of the basic norm are two-fold: to give validity to all norms within the legal system and to give unity to the system. The legal validity of this basic norm (or Grundnorm) does not come from another legal norm. Kelsen says we must presuppose the existence of this basic norm in our juristic thinking.

This basic norm, which is presupposed, stands behind the constitution, which may have been created in a positive way or may have been promulgated after a successful revolution. This revolution may have breached a legal order based on a constitution. Once we have discovered the historical first constitution, then the basic norm we have presupposed tells us that 'one ought to act in accordance with the constitution'. This means that it is not necessary for anyone to accept the validity of any particular social order. In Kelsen's theory, as long as we have presupposed the basic norm, we understand that we are to act in accordance with the constitution, however it came into existence.

Kelsen's theory is a challenging way of looking at the law. We have long been conditioned into thinking that the law applies a particular technique: it addresses a particular group of people – members of society. However, Kelsen's theory introduces us to a new way of looking at the law. It does not speak to us as citizens, but rather to officials of the system, who must apply sanctions if certain circumstances occur. We may say that this is a refreshing new approach to the law. If you direct your mind sufficiently to what Kelsen is saying, you may come to agree with him. For example, s1 Law of Property Act 1925 may be said to be addressed to officials to consider what constitutes an estate in land.

Furthermore, the idea that the basic norm is this higher norm, giving validity to all norms in the legal system and also supplying unity to the system, opens up a new horizon for us. We presuppose this basic norm in our juristic thinking; in other words, we use our intuition to determine this basic norm which tells to us that we have to act in accordance with the historically first constitution. I believe this theory has a wholesome way of impacting on our lives. Just think about it. Here is a theory which invites you to use your intuition in order to articulate that specific acts are required by a constitution which may have been introduced by a usurper.

To further explain, consider how the revolution cases have real meaning and purpose in life. In the case of *Madzimbamuto* v *Lardner Burke* [1968] 1 AC 645, Kelsen's theory must be applied to understand why the Rhodesian court failed to order the release of Madzimbamuto from detention without trial if, as some people think, Mr Ian Smith had acted illegally by declaring Unilateral Independence from Britain. If the Smith regime was illegal, the court should have declared the detention without trial of Madzimbamuto illegal and ordered his immediate release. That this did not happen illustrates the point that, in any real life situation where a revolution has occurred, Kelsen's theory is helpful in clarifying the fact that a proclamation of a usurping regime is valid as the new constitution: the basic norm we presuppose simply directs us to act in accordance with the new constitution. This is real life.

Similarly, in *Uganda* v *Commissioner of Prisons, ex parte Matovu* [1966] EALR 514 the High Court of Uganda declared (through Sir Udo Udoma CJ) that the 1966 constitution was the legally valid constitution and the supreme law of Uganda, in the sense that the previous constitution of 1962 had been abolished by a victorious revolution in law and therefore no longer formed part of the laws of Uganda. This victorious constitution was merely a statement by the Prime Minister on 22 February 1966 that, in the interest of national stability, public safety and tranquillity, he was taking over the powers of the Government of Uganda.

If we also consider Kelsen's positivism, which states that law and morals must be kept separate, we see the point made by jurists such as Hart, that the individual must distinguish his conscience from the demands of the state. By so doing, the individual is not susceptible to any confusion regarding the totally different issues of law and morality. This certainly has relevance in our lives. Our ability to distinguish between the two is crucial to the decisions we make about our actions in life.

It goes without saying, after this careful study of Kelsen's theory, that the critics are wrong to label Kelsen's theory as 'an exercise in sterile formalism'.

C MODERN THEORIES

2.7 Introduction

This section focuses on Hart (who is particularly important for examination purposes) and Raz, and the extent to which they have advanced the positivist debate. It should be noted that Hart actually eschews the term 'positivist' yet he sees no necessary connection between law and morals. His *The Concept of Law* is undoubtedly one of the leading contemporary jurisprudential works. It is clearly and elegantly written, and the student must read it. Apart from putting forward his own theories, Hart provides an excellent standpoint of criticism of other positivists. No student should ignore Hart.

Raz's theory attempts to take the debate a stage further, by meeting the criticisms levelled at Hart.

2.8 Key points

'The Concept of Law' – *Hart's great contribution to jurisprudential debate*

a) The union of primary and secondary rules form the centre of a legal system.

b) There is an internal and an external aspect to rules (and this distinguishes a rule from a mere habit)

c) Law is different from 'orders backed by threats' – there is a contrast between being obliged and being under an obligation.

d) No evaluation of Hart is complete without consideration of Dworkin's *Law as Integrity* which is dealt with in Chapter 14.

Raz has sought to advance upon Hart's theory in *The Concept of a Legal System*. The student should consider Raz's theory in the light of criticisms levelled at Hart.

In studying Hart and Raz, one should be aware of their criticisms of Austin, Bentham and Kelsen (see Chapter 2, sections A and B).

2.9 Questions and suggested solutions

QUESTION ONE

'My aim in this book has been to further the understanding of law, coercion, and morality as different but related social phenomena.' (Hart, *The Concept of Law*.)

How successful has Hart been in achieving his aim?

University of London LLB Examination
(for External Students) Jurisprudence and Legal Theory June 1993 Q1(a)

General Comment

This question is a very wide one and for that reason candidates are advised not to produce an 'all they know about Hart' type answer because the examiners will pay more than usual attention to an attempt to answer the question. The question asks for an account of Hart's purpose in writing his work on legal positivism and calls for a detailed assessment of whether Hart has met up with his own standards.

There is an infinite number of ways it could be done. Here is a suggestion: first, a brief description of his theory, second, a consideration of why he produces it which entails a discussion of the points outlined in Hart's famous *Preface*, and the 'three recurring issues' outlined in Chapter 1, with others relating to his general methodology, and third, a consideration of how well he attains his purpose.

However, there are other possibilities. For example, one could examine whether the command theory, in the end, is all that different from Hart's theory. Hart, after all, tries to distance himself from it by referring to the difference between coercion and law; but he is still a positivist and his explanation of law refers to an authority that is as barren of moral authority as Bentham's and Austin's sovereign.

Skeleton Solution

Consideration of question – three recurring issues – Hart's methodology – the legal as opposed to pre-legal world – the rule of recognition – his theory of law briefly described – the wider conception of law and its advantages – consideration of the virtues of positivism.

Suggested Solution

The discerning of Hart's purpose is not easy as his book suggests at least two. These are the describing of an entity which he obviously regards as law 'out there' in much the same way as an historian would describe some event that 'had occurred' or a scientist might describe some properties of something that exists in the real world. Hart does, after all, describe his work as 'an essay in descriptive sociology', by which he meant, presumably, that his work was to be just descriptive of the world, in Dworkin's 'plain fact' sense (see Guest, *Ronald Dworkin*, Chapter 5, for example).

But a second purpose in his work expresses a desire that seeing law as separate from morality is good from a moral point of view, because then people would not confuse what the State demanded with what it was morally right to do, as perhaps was inherent in the allegedly moral excuse of the Nuremburg tribunals – 'I was just obeying (legally valid) orders'.

How do we find these two strands in Hart's work? He refers early on to 'three recurrent issues' in Jurisprudence: the distinction between coercion and law; the distinction between moral and legal obligation; and the question of what constituted a social rule. In what sense are these 'important' issues? I suggest that they are important for him because he is not just interested in description but justification as well; he wants a theory that draws a distinction between the bank robber ('obliging' a victim) and a legislature who can create 'obligations'. Further, he obviously thinks that it is of practical importance to distinguish moral obligations from legal obligations since, as a positivist, he thinks that there can be laws so immoral that we have no duty to obey them. Thirdly, he regards an explanation of the nature of a social rule as important, given his extended discussion in Chapter 7, to explain the law-making discretion judges have in making decisions within the penumbra of law.

It seems, then, that Hart's methodology may combine elements of description and justification: the purpose of his theory is to draw a map of law as well as to commend it to us as a way of solving practical problems: keep law and morality distinct and the three recurring issues will be answered.

There is further, and stronger, evidence of his two purposes in the distinction between his pre-legal and legal worlds. He commends, by dignifying with the label 'legal', a view of law in which courts, legislatures and rules of certainty, created by the three secondary rules, exist to 'cure' the 'defects' of the 'pre'-legal world. Here there is clear evidence of Hart's justifying purpose to produce a theory of law that helps society. And the rule of recognition is the most important. It cures uncertainty and makes the chief virtue of a legal system the certainty with which it identifies what is and is not law.

The theory of legal positivism he finally produces then distinguishes law from morality so that, as he says in Chapter 9, the fact of legal validity 'is not conclusive of the question of obedience'. This is very important for Hart because this theory endorses a 'wider conception of law' which includes 'morally iniquitous laws' unlike the 'narrower' conception, the natural law conception, which excludes them. (In fact, the use here of two possible 'conceptions' of law sits a little unhappily with the title of Hart's work, which is, after all, the *Concept of Law*. This title is much more consistent with the 'plain fact' strand isolated earlier in his work; there is a concept of law 'out there' and there is no room for alternative accounts.)

How successful is Hart in these two purposes? Positivism does describe law, in the UK anyway, in a significant way. The sort of clear law that solicitors and law students love is the clear law that speaks with certainty in a 'black and white' way. On the other hand, Hart doesn't seem to account very well for the way in which barristers argue and judges decide in what Dworkin calls the 'hard cases', where there is uncertainty. But Hart could reasonably reply that this law is not important law. Rather, it is penumbral to what centrally should be thought to be law. This attitude is central to his method of definition, after all.

What about the second, justificatory strand to Hart's work? This places the principle of 'justice as certainty' at the very heart of the theory; remember the criterion of legal validity, the rule of recognition was to 'cure' uncertainty. But I suggest that legal certainty is only one of a number of desirable virtues for a legal system; flexibility is another, especially in constitutional cases, or cases of tort, where the justice of the instant is far more important than the justice of 'having one's reasonable expectations' fulfilled. In fact, the virtue of certainty really only reaches its height in Chancery, land law-type cases.

To sum up; Hart's purposes are two-fold and in each he succeeds to the extent of describing and justifying a legal system from the point of view of either an historian uninterested in the minutiae of hard cases or a Chancery solicitor interested in giving precise predictions to her clients. Overall, however, he fails to give a satisfactory account, both descriptively and normatively, of cases of which we are all experienced where the question of what the law is remains uncertain.

QUESTION TWO

'*The Concept of Law* is primarily aimed at historians or sociologists who want clear criteria of what it means to say a legal system exists and has no direct use to lawyers who want to know what "the law" is on some point.'

Discuss.

University of London LLB Examination
(for External Students) Jurisprudence and Legal Theory June 1996 Q2

General Comment

It is easy to misinterpret this question. It is not simply asking you to reflect on Hart's famous statement that his work, *The Concept of Law*, is 'an essay in descriptive sociology'. It is also easy to make the mistake of thinking that 'an essay in descriptive sociology' is of more relevance to sociologists and historians than lawyers. Using Hart's methodology you can establish the relevance of his work to the legal practitioner.

Skeleton Solution

Consideration of Hart's stated aim in the preface of *The Concept of Law* that his work is an essay in descriptive sociology – Hart's methodology – his elements of law – the existence of a legal system – virtues of legal positivism – wider concept of law – hard cases – Dworkin.

Suggested Solution

Hart's claim in the preface to *The Concept of Law* (2nd edn 1997) that his work is an 'essay in descriptive sociology' suggests that he wants to describe an entity which he regards as existing 'out there', just as a sociologist or a historian would report or describe an event that happened somewhere. It can be said, therefore, that Hart probably wants his 'essay in descriptive sociology' to be a description of a legal system.

To achieve this end he employs a methodology which uses strands of description and prescription to help our consciousness, and provide a view of the law which he highly recommends to us in our search for practical solutions to problems: keep law and morality separate and distinct. Hart's methodology, which is variously called the 'existence thesis' or 'development thesis', shows Hart's purpose in producing a theory of law that helps society. He imagines a pre-legal society with only primary rules of obligation. The rules contain restrictions on the free use of force or violence, theft and deception to which human beings are tempted, but which must be suppressed if they are to live in close proximity with one another. Such a society may show tension between those who voluntarily accept rules and those who do not. The rules of the group do not form a system but are simply a set of separate standards without any common identifying mark. Such a society, according to Hart, has three defects which are:

a) uncertainty about which rules are members of the system – which rule is a moral rule and which is legal;

b) static nature of rules: the society is rigid through lack of any means of quickly changing rules and introducing new ones;

c) inefficiency: when disputes arise through myriad social pressures it is impossible to find what rules are applicable.

To cure these defects in the pre-legal society, Hart recommends remedies which will cure them: (a) the rule of recognition; (b) the rule of change; and (c) the rule of adjudication.

The rule of recognition will specify features which a rule has to possess to be taken as conclusive affirmation that it belongs to the group. The rule of recognition may be no more than an authoritative list or text of the rules to be found in a written document. What is important is that there is now a reduction into writing of hitherto unwritten rules, which becomes a reference point and is authoritative.

The second defect, the static nature of rules, is cured by the introduction of the rule of change to deal with the slow process of growth within society. This empowers an individual or a body of persons to introduce new primary rules for the conduct of the group. To Hart, it is in the 'rules of change' that the process of legislative enactment and repeal is to be understood. The rules, besides specifying the person or persons to legislate, also define the procedure to be followed in legislating.

The third defect is that of inefficiency of the diffuse social pressures by which rules are maintained in a simple society. There is a waste of time in such a society through lack of organisation in catching and punishing wrongdoers. The remedy for this regime is to introduce 'rules of adjudication'. These are secondary rules empowering individuals to make authoritative determination of questions about breaches of rules. The secondary rules of adjudication define the procedures to be followed and also define the concepts of judge, court, jurisdiction and judgment.

The remedy for each of the three defects, as has been noted, consists in supplementing the primary rules of obligation in the simple society with secondary rules. The introduction of each remedy for a defect might be considered a step from the pre-legal into the legal world. Each remedy has its own elements which permeate law. Together the three remedies are enough to convert the regime of primary rules into what is indisputably a legal system.

This is the existence thesis of a legal system which at first sight is enough to support the suggestion that Hart's primary aim in *The Concept of Law* is to proffer the criteria or test that will enable the sociologist or the historian to recognise legal systems in any political system.

It would, however, not be correct to say that is the primary aim of *The Concept of Law*. To say that is to ignore Hart's other purpose, which is to distinguish between the state and the individual. To Hart, law is the demand of the state 'out there' which is separate from the individual as a moral being. In Chapter 9 of *The Concept of Law*, he introduces the narrow concept of law which says the certification of something as valid is not conclusive of the question of obedience. In saying that law is the demand of the state 'out there', Hart seeks to emphasise legal positivism's claim that law is separate from morals. The 'wider concept of law' includes morally repugnant laws and is distinguished from the narrow concept – the natural law concept – which forbids morally unjust laws.

It can, therefore, be said that Hart emphasises positive law, the kind of law which is sought by lawyers who want to know what 'the law' is on some point. The law is the black letter rule. The lawyer who wants to know what the law is on some point must simply work out the black letter rule – check the sources of law to find out what the law says on the issue. As Hart says, the existing law is the demand of the state 'out there', so morality must be separated from questions of law.

Hart has a dual purpose which I believe he fully succeeds in establishing. He succeeds in his first purpose of offering sociologists and historians a test for recognising the existence of a legal system, and he succeeds in the second purpose of offering a practical help to the lawyer who wants to know what 'the law' is on some point. The practical advice to the lawyers from Hart's legal positivism is clear – the law is the demand of the state 'out there' which must be separated from our individual consciences. The rule of recognition was introduced to clear the air, to positively distinguish legal rules from what are not legal rules, to introduce certainty into the law. The rule of recognition possesses the criteria of validity of rules of the system so that the practitioner will be able to know positively what the law says on some point. Hart's legal positivism is therefore of practical help to the lawyer.

The only unfortunate thing about Hart's positivism is his analysis of hard cases. His analysis does not match the way barristers speak or argue in court. Hart says in hard cases there is a gap in the law since the law here is indeterminate, inconclusive or there is a gap in the law. Hart believes that the judge has to legislate to fill in the gap in the law when deciding cases. This means that in hard cases, there are no laws until the judge makes a decision. Dworkin disputes this view of law presented by Hart. To Dworkin the law is always complete without gaps. The law is explained, justified and underlain by principles so in hard cases there is always law to be consulted.

Dworkin's argument supports the way barristers speak and argue cases. The barrister always cites an existing law and never says there is no law to be consulted because of gaps in the law. Following Hart's account of hard cases it seems the barrister will not be able to know what 'the law' is in a hard case until the judge makes a decision. The barrister, from experience, might disagree as he or she, following Dworkin's approach, can always argue what 'the law' is on an issue.

Hart succeeds in *The Concept of Law* in doing two things: firstly, providing us with a methodology for recognising the existence of a legal system, which helps everybody including the sociologist and the historian; and secondly, providing the legal practitioner with the tool for recognising and distinguishing between law and morality. The rule of recognition helps the practitioner in identifying statutes and precedents – what 'the law' is on any issue.

QUESTION THREE

How does Hart approach the question of defining 'law'? What are the difficulties he identifies in doing so?

University of London LLB Examination
(for External Students) Jurisprudence and Legal Theory June 1999 Q1

General Comment

This question should excite the candidate since it deals with Hart's attitude to the definition of 'law' by others. Hart claims defining 'law' is difficult because there are some crucial features of law which any definition must encompass. A careful reading of chapter one of his book *The Concept of Law* is a good start.

Skeleton Solution

The 'what is law' question – definitions of law by others – standard cases and doubtful cases – three recurrent issues – evaluation and conclusion.

Suggested Solution

Hart (H L A Hart, *The Concept of Law* (2nd edn, 1997)) states that the question 'what is law?' has been persistently asked and answered in different (and sometimes strange) ways by serious thinkers throughout history. For example, the American Realist, Karl Llewellyn, says 'what officials do about disputes is the law itself'. Justice Oliver Wendell Holmes claims that the law is the prophecies of what the courts will do. Hans Kelsen argues that law is the primary norm which stipulates the sanction. Whereas John Austin considers law to be the command of the sovereign who is habitually obeyed but who does not habitually obey anyone.

To Hart, these definitions are 'illuminating' in the sense that they throw some light on the law. However, the light is so dazzling that we are in danger of not having a clear picture of the law.

He considers that the problem of finding a definition for law has persisted because of the difficulty posed by the existence of clear standard cases, as embodied in a modern municipal legal system, and the doubtful cases whose 'legal quality' is disputable. To him, primitive law and international law fall within the doubtful cases. International law presents a problem because there is no single legislature responsible for passing any law, and (because states cannot be bound by international law without their consent) there is no sense that the law is made by any identifiable municipal organised legal system.

Similarly, we find difficulty with primitive laws because they lack the crucial feature of a modern municipal legal system. Sometimes, the difference between a standard case and a doubtful case is merely one of degree. For example, a man with a shining head is clearly bald; another with a full head of hair is not; but whether or not the man with a strand of hair here and there is bald is a debatable point.

Hart claims that defining law has been difficult because there are recurrent issues which must come together in order to capture the nature and essence of law. The three issues remove the difficulties with the definition of law. The first of the three issues is the difference between law and coercion.

According to Hart, the existence of law means that certain human conduct is no longer optional but obligatory. We can illustrate the difference between the existence of law and coercion by looking at a situation where one man forces another to do something purely because he threatens the other with unpleasant consequences if he refuses to comply. An example is where a gunman orders his victim to hand over money or be killed. Where the intended victim complies, we say that the gunman has obliged his victim to carry out a particular conduct. This is a naked coercion: the use of brute force. There is no existing social rule that says that people must hand over money to gunmen.

The difference between the above situation and the existence of a legal system is that there is a permanence about law which is normative, in that it guides human conduct. The difference between a statute and a gunman's orders is that statutes are generally addressed to a group of people who normally obey such orders. People obey law because they see it as a duty required by law. The gunman situation is totally different.

The second recurrent issue is the relationship between legal and moral obligation. A legal system obviously contains elements closely connected with certain aspects of morality. There is a temptation to see in this close relationship a common identity. Not only do laws and morals share a common vocabulary, but all municipal legal systems reproduce the substance of certain fundamental moral requirements. For example, murder, violence and fraud are instances where law and morality coincide. Furthermore, the expressions 'justice of the law' and 'justice according to the law' are used to show the link between law and morality. Hart maintains that making this close assimilation between law and morality confuses one kind of obligatory conduct with another, and this leaves little room to explore the difference between legal and moral rules. To Hart, it is an exaggeration to claim a relationship exists between legal and moral obligation, because legal rules and moral rules impose different obligations.

The third recurrent issue relates to what a rule is. For example, a group of people may decide to meet every Sunday for lunch. This is a mere convergence of behaviour. If someone fails to turn up, there is no sanction applied to that person. Yet where a rule exists specific conduct is prescribed, and breaches of that conduct are met with sanctions by officials. The existing rule employs words such as 'must', 'should' and 'ought to' to show that the conduct in question is required by a rule.

We have seen that Hart claims that there are difficulties in defining law, because any good definition must address the three issues that he has isolated. However, Professor Lon Fuller points out that if the only issue facing us is to find a meaning for the word law in pursuit of intellectual clarity, then there is justification for treating Austin (John

Austin, *Province of Jurisprudence Determined* (1832)), Gray, Llewellyn and Holmes as working in the same direction. I agree with Fuller's observation, because if our object is to obtain clarity (which comes from explicit definitions) then we can plausibly argue that the conception of the meaning of law offered by the jurists mentioned in this essay will suffice. The justification for this conclusion is this: if Hart is concerned about the separation of law and morals, the definitions of law that these jurists have provided avoid any confusion between law and morals, and certainly leave us in no doubt as to what meaning they propose to attribute to the word law.

While we may say that Hart has offered us powerful points upon which to ponder, we can equally argue that Austin, Holmes, Kelsen and Llewellyn may also have problems with Hart's approach. This is a matter of one's subjective judgment.

QUESTION FOUR

Does Hart take sufficient account of sociological facts in *The Concept of Law*?

University of London LLB Examination
(for External Students) Jurisprudence and Legal Theory June 1998 Q2

General Comment

This may appear to be a difficult question. However, a careful thought about Hart's book *The Concept of Law* is all that is necessary to provoke an understanding of what the question requires. Ask yourself whether you can think of any 'sociological facts' about Hart's theory. Hart provides these in his book.

Skeleton Solution

Hart's methodology – criticisms of Hart's methodology – answers to criticisms – conclusion.

Suggested Solution

Hart writes in the Preface to his book (H L A Hart, *The Concept of Law* (2nd edn, 1997)) that his work is 'an essay in descriptive sociology' of the law. He claims that he will focus attention on the language of law in order to discover what the phenomenon entails. This concentration on the language of law has made other philosophers of law critical of Hart's work. It is said that Hart is engaging in linguistic philosophy and not attempting to discover the phenomenon of law: Hart is merely playing with words.

One such critic is Professor Lon Fuller (Lon Fuller, 'Positivism and Fidelity to Law' (1958) 71 Harvard Law Review), who argues that it is not true that we are concerned with the definitions of single words in a statute, for instance. He says we are concerned with interpreting the whole passages or paragraphs of a statute, and not the single words in them as Hart suggests.

Another critic of Hart's method is Professor Ronald Dworkin (Ronald Dworkin, *Law's Empire* (2nd edn, 1991)), who claims that Hart has succumbed to the semantic sting in that he is too obsessed with language. To Professor Dworkin, Hart has it wrong because law is an argumentative attitude. Law concerns the argument parties can construct relative to their rights and duties, and thus the language of the law is couched and is only instrumental.

The general sense behind the criticisms of Hart's method is illustrated by the way that Hart claims that a society with only obligation or duty-imposing rules is a pre-legal society. We can see from these criticisms that Hart talks about this pre-legal society with only duty-imposing rules, but fails himself to investigate why there is the need for law at all in society. In other words, the critics claim Hart should have made it his business to find out about the impact that law has in any society.

The criticisms have their basis in Hart's declaration that his book is an essay in descriptive sociology. To these critics, anybody with a remote interest in sociology would look at how law affects the people he studies. The critics say that Hart fails to do this with the pre-legal society, and his work is, therefore, devoid of any sociological facts.

These criticisms are easily countered. A careful study of Hart's book will show that Hart pays attention to 'sociological facts' in his work. We must first of all look at the three recurrent issues that Hart isolates as crucial to law. The first point Hart makes is that it is a sociological fact that where law exists conduct is no longer optional but obligatory. He illustrates this with the analogy of a gunman's coercive orders to a victim backed by threats. When the victim obeys the gunman, there is a sense that the gunman has 'obliged' his victim to comply with his orders because of the possible threat of evil consequences.

This situation is different from the nature of a penal statute which imposes an obligation on citizens. What must be understood is that it is a sociological fact that law imposes duties on citizens. Whereas there is no law requiring citizens and others to hand over monies to gunmen as a matter of course, law is different: for example, tax law requires citizens and others to pay their taxes as a matter of course.

Another sociological fact investigated by Hart is the relationship between legal and moral obligation. Both law and morality make conduct obligatory rather than optional. The investigation centres on those elements closely connected to both legal rules and moral rules. To Hart, there is a difficulty in identifying the precise nature of this relationship, and this leads to the tempting assumption that both are the same. The reasons for this assumption are that, not only do law and morals share the same vocabulary (there are both legal and moral obligations, duties and rights), but all legal systems reproduce 'the substance of certain fundamental moral requirements'. For example, both legal rules and moral rules prohibit killing and theft. If we cared to look deeply we would also note that the concept of justice unites them both, and we seem to know what we mean when we talk of the 'justice of the law' and 'justice according to law'. These are sociological facts which suggest that law is a 'branch' of morality or justice. Hart points out that it is the height of confusion to suggest that moral rules and legal rules are the same, because there are differences and divergences in the requirements of both.

Hart also investigates the question of what a rule is. Although there are many social rules that govern what we do, some of them are not made in order to make conduct mandatory. Sociologically, when we say that a rule exists, we mean that a group of people (or most of them generally) behave in a certain way in certain circumstances. However, we can distinguish mere convergence in behaviour from the instances where a rule exists. For example, if a group of friends decide to meet at a particular restaurant every evening at 7pm for dinner, that is only the conduct of such persons converging. There is no rule in existence that they meet at 7pm every evening. However, where a rule exists requiring specific conduct, we can tell it is a rule by the sociological fact that words like 'must', 'should' and 'ought to' are employed to emphasise this fact.

Hart's theory of law does not seek to analyse law to find out what causes rules and how the law affects people in society. This task can be left for others. Hart is only concerned about giving us an account of what law is. This is a legitimate sociological enquiry and others can be entrusted with the responsibility of investigating the other sociological matter relating to how this thing called law comes about or affects people.

QUESTION FIVE

Explain the distinction which Hart draws between 'primary' and 'secondary' rules. On what grounds does he make this distinction? What purpose does it serve? In what sense, if at all, is it correct to say that law is a 'union' of 'primary' and 'secondary' rules?

University of London LLB Examination
(for External Students) Jurisprudence and Legal Theory June 1992 Q1

General Comment

This question involves an analysis of the use made by Hart of the notion of a rule.

Skeleton Solution

Introduction: Hart's *The Concept of Law* – law and legal system – meaning of primary rules – meaning of secondary rules – distinction between primary and secondary rules – purpose of distinction – evaluation – clubs – international law – Dworkin.

Suggested Solution

Hart's *The Concept of Law* proposes a theory of law which, to a certain extent, equates 'law' with 'legal system' in that it focuses on the difference between primitive or pre-legal societies and societies which may be described as having a legal system. It is in relation to this aspect of the theory that the distinction between 'primary' and 'secondary' rules and the notion of the union between the two arises.

Hart attempts to explain how a legal obligation can be recognised and distinguished from, for example, human conduct which is the result of mere habit. In Hart's view a habit will be the result of common behaviour but a rule, unlike a habit, will have some 'internal aspect' which renders a particular type of conduct in some sense obligatory. This internal aspect of obligation is the identifying feature of Hart's 'primary' rules. Rules which are necessitated by the nature of man as a partly selfish, partly cooperative creature with a will to survive in a world of limited resources may fall into this category. Such rules might, for example, forbid killing, stealing or deception and are described by Hart as 'the minimum content of natural law'.

Hart suggested that primary rules may exist in pre-legal societies. However, in such societies the process of changing the content of the rules will be slow, adjudication upon the rules will be unregulated, and it may be difficult to distinguish legal rules from other social rules. In order to facilitate the three functions of change, adjudication and recognition of primary rules of obligation, Hart proposed the existence of secondary rules. Secondary rules of change would allow society to adjust the content of primary rules in a relatively efficient manner. Rules of recognition would allow the identification of the form and content of legal rules more quickly than in pre-legal societies where one would have to 'wait and see' if a particular rule were to be accepted as such. Rules of adjudication would provide for officials who could enforce the rules and punish wrongdoers. For example, Hart suggested that in England the supreme rule of recognition might be 'Whatever the Queen in Parliament enacts is law'.

Primary rules can be distinguished from secondary rules on the grounds that the latter are in a sense parasitic upon the former. Primary rules regulate conduct of individuals in society, whereas secondary rules regulate the primary rules themselves and are the concern of officials of the state rather than individuals generally. The purpose of the distinction in the context of Hart's theory is to provide a means of identifying advanced social systems. Hart was concerned to move away from the view, expressed by Austin and others, that law was the result of the command of the sovereign. For Hart such a theory could not explain why individuals would obey the commands of the successor to the sovereign, nor could it explain why old laws could remain laws today. Mere rules of obligation, which were characteristic of the 'command theory', could not, in Hart's opinion, explain these phenomena. It was for this reason that Hart proposed the existence of secondary rules and, in particular, the rule of recognition.

In Hart's view, it is the 'union' of primary and secondary rules which provides the basis for a legal system. If rules of behaviour, primary rules, are generally obeyed, and rules of change and adjudication are generally accepted as common public standards of behaviour by officials, then Hart thought a legal system could be described as being effectively in force.

Although the logic of Hart's theory is compelling it leaves certain questions unanswered. For example, Hart's theory does not adequately deal with the difference between social institutions such as clubs, which have both rules of obligation and 'secondary' rules of change, recognition and adjudication, and the state. Furthermore, international 'law' fails to meet Hart's test for an advanced legal system in that it does not have a central organ of adjudication with compulsory powers, has no method for changing rules other than by agreement (tacit or express) of states, and has no clear rule of recognition. Although the question of international law as law is an oft-debated subject, few would argue that it is not some form of legal system, albeit different from systems of municipal law. Perhaps the essential difference derives from the fact that the 'subjects' of international law are states, which are not in a position of 'approximate equality' as Hart considered man to be. This is a distinction which Hart recognised. One must question whether the union of primary and secondary rules is the essential characteristic of all advanced legal systems or whether, on the contrary, there may be different criteria applicable in certain situations.

Finally, it is worth bearing in mind that the very basis of Hart's theory, in company with the theories of legal positivists generally, is that law is solely comprised of rules. This premise has been criticised by Dworkin for failing to recognise that there may be other principles which may legitimately be described as forming part of the law. Dworkin identifies as standards which are not rules the policies and principles which may be referred to by a judge in a 'hard case' in order to reach a decision. Policies are defined as community goals, such as a goal that car accidents should be decreased. Principles are defined as standards to be observed generally, such as 'a man may not profit from his own wrong'. Any conclusion as to the validity of the description of law as the union of primary and secondary rules must question in the first place whether, as Dworkin argues, rules alone are simply not enough.

QUESTION SIX

How effective is Hart's Postscript in meeting the objections of his various critics?

University of London LLB Examination
(for External Students) Jurisprudence and Legal Theory June 1999 Q3

General Comment

This is a question anyone who is familiar with the content of Hart's book *The Concept of Law* should be able to answer. This is because the Postscript is nothing but a diatribe against Ronald Dworkin, who has been the greatest critic of Hart's positivism. Hart originally intended to use the Postscript to answer several critics, but he did not go beyond Dworkin: the Postscript is used by him to robustly defend his theories in *The Concept of Law*.

Skeleton Solution

The pictures of law painted by both Dworkin and Hart – rule and principle distinction

– the rule of recognition, principle and pedigree criteria – the way lawyers talk – judicial law-making.

Suggested Solution

Originally, Professor H L A Hart (H L A Hart, *The Concept of Law* (2nd edn, 1997)) presented a picture of law as being incomplete and indeterminate, with gaps waiting for the judge to fill during adjudication by exercising his discretion. Dworkin rejects this picture of law painted by Hart. To Dworkin, the law's empire is coherent with no gaps, which follows from principles which fit both the legal system and its institutional history, and provides the best moral justification for it. In any difficult case, therefore, the principles underlying and justifying the law will lead the way, even though they will not conclusively determine a case. We have here two rival theories – Hart's positivism claiming law is exhaustive of convention, and Dworkin's which claims that principles decide cases.

Hart uses the Postscript to go over all the areas of his positivism that Dworkin's theory conflicts with. While giving credit to Dworkin (Ronald Dworkin, *Taking Rights Seriously* (1977)) for pointing out the role that principles play in adjudication, he attempts to explain the difference between rules and principles. He explains that, relative to rules, principles are broad, general or unspecific: in other words, what would be regarded as a number of distinct rules can be exhibited in the form of a single principle. He believes that principles refer to some explicit purpose, goal, entitlement or value, and so are regarded as desirable to maintain (or to adhere to), since they not only provide an explanation or rationale for the rules they exemplify, they at least contribute to their justification.

Dworkin disagrees with Hart's characterisation of legal principles. To him, a principle is a standard to be observed because it is a requirement of justice or fairness or some dimension of morality. The difference between legal principles and legal rules is that principles direct or point to a particular decision regarding a legal obligation in certain circumstances; legal rules, on the other hand, are either applicable or not. The crucial difference between rules and principles means that principles have a dimension of weight or importance, whereas rules function in an all-or-nothing way – they are either important or unimportant, applicable or inapplicable.

Hart also says in his Postscript that to agree with Dworkin that his rule of recognition cannot capture legal principles, and so it must be abandoned, is a matter for some consideration. He says that the rule of recognition can 'capture' and identify some principles by their 'pedigree' criteria, meaning the manner of their creation or adoption by a recognised authoritative source. Hart claims that principles such as the one applied in *Riggs* v *Palmer* 115 NY 506 (1889) – no man may profit from his own wrong – passes the 'pedigree' test because they have been consistently invoked by courts in cases as providing reasons for a decision which must be considered. We can lock horns with Hart and ask why if his rule of recognition can capture principles did it fail to identify or recognise the previously unformulated 'neighbour principle' in *Donoghue* v *Stevenson* [1932] AC 562, which extended the duty of the manufacturer to the ultimate consumer?

Hart's argument is unsatisfactory. It is only a rehearsal of Dr Raz's institutional support concept, which suggests that judges take account of particular principles cited by many judges over a period of time. Raz points out that some principles can be brought together under a social rule of recognition. His theory states that these principles will form a cluster of social rules, which will stand alongside Hart's conventional rule of recognition and together provide a test for law. I believe that Hart found this idea attractive and tried to use Raz's idea to support his pedigree criteria in the Postscript.

The doctrine of strong discretion in adjudication can be rejected, because persuasive arguments can always be used during adjudication. As Dworkin points out, these arguments must include arguments on issues of normative political theory (like the nature of society's duty to equality) that go beyond the positivist's conception of the limits of the considerations relevant to deciding what the law is.

Hart describes as false a typical picture of the judicial process and the methods by which the courts decide difficult cases. He rejects Dworkin's view, which argues that judges do not talk about making or creating the law, even in difficult cases. However, he concedes that, very often when deciding difficult cases, judges cite some general principle or some general aim or purpose, which an area of the existing law can be understood as exemplifying or advancing, and which therefore points towards an answer for any particular case.

It is difficult to understand how Hart can make this point and yet still claim that this process is false. He accepts that judges do not talk about gaps in the law with a view to creating new law to fill in those gaps, and yet he argues that, since judges play a big role in the affairs of society, they must be given law-making powers. This is very disappointing coming from Hart. It is unfortunate that he is indifferent to the principle of the separation of powers.

Hart does not defend a better thesis in the Postscript. We may turn to other jurists, who have attempted to improve his theory, for answers to objections that Hart's critics have raised regarding *The Concept of Law*.

QUESTION SEVEN

'[The judge's] statement that a rule is valid is an internal statement recognising that the rule satisfies the test for identifying what is to count as law in his court, and constitutes not a prophecy of but part of the reason for his decision'. (Hart)

Discuss.

University of London LLB Examination
(for External Students) Jurisprudence and Legal Theory June 1996 Q1

General Comment

This question examines Hart's attitude to the predictive theory of obligation. It is necessary to consider what the rule of recognition is, together with analysing what are internal and external statements of law. The essay requires careful thought as it is easy to lose sight of the crux of the matter – one judge's decision says nothing about the behaviour of other judges.

Skeleton Solution

Test provided by the rule of recognition – meaning of an internal statement – question of validity and external statements – comparison of rule of recognition and the basic norm or Grundnorm.

Suggested Solution

Professor Hart offers an illuminating discussion about the day-to-day life of a legal system in his book *The Concept of Law*; at the heart of a legal system is the rule of recognition which contains the criteria of validity of all rules of the system. The rule of recognition is seldom formulated expressly as a rule, though occasionally courts declare the importance of one criteria of law relative to another. For example, in the United Kingdom courts declare Acts of Parliament supreme over other sources of law. Mostly the rule of recognition is unstated, but its existence is shown in the way in which rules are identified and applied by courts and other officials.

There is a difference between the use made of the rule of recognition by courts and the use made of the rule by others. The crucial difference is that when courts reach a decision on the basis that the criteria provided by the rule have identified as a member of the legal system that decision has special authoritative status.

Hart likens the rule of recognition to the scoring of a game like cricket or football. The general rule defining the activities which constitute scoring (runs, goals, etc) is not formulated in the course of the game, yet it is used by the umpire, referee and players in identifying the particular phases of the game which count towards winning. It is important to note that the declarations of the umpire or referee have special authoritative meaning attributed to them by other rules. The difficulty with this analogy is that rules of cricket or football, although not formulated in the course of the game, are set by the governing bodies of the respective sports – so presumably Hart is saying that because the rules of the game have already been set by a governing body the referee, umpire or players can positively identify them by using what could be called a rule of recognition.

When unstated rules of recognition are used by courts and others in the identification of rules of a legal system, it is said that such usage is characterised by the internal point of view. This means that those who use the rules of recognition show their acceptance of them as guiding rules. This acceptance of the rules of recognition as guiding rules is accompanied by a particular kind of expression used not only by judges but also by ordinary citizens living under a legal system when they have identified any rule of the system. Thus an expression like 'it is the law that parking on a red line is punishable by a fine' or 'out' or 'goal' is the language used by someone who assesses a situation by reference to rules which are commonly acknowledged as appropriate for this purpose.

The language such a person uses is called an internal statement in that it manifests the internal point of view and is naturally used by people who accept the rule of recognition and apply it in identifying some specific rule of the system as valid. The internal statement is to be contrasted with the external statement which is made by the outsider or observer who says, for example: 'In the United Kingdom it is accepted as law whatever the Crown in Parliament enacts'. This is the language of an observer who does not accept the rule of recognition, but states that it is a fact that others in the United Kingdom accept it.

The internal statement governs the question of the validity of a rule of the legal system. The internal statement says that a particular rule of a legal system is valid. This means that it is recognised that a given rule passes all the tests provided by the rule of recognition, and is thus a rule of the legal system.

When one makes an internal statement about the validity of a particular rule of a system, one may be said to presuppose the truth of the external statement of fact which says the legal system is generally efficacious. The catch here, however, is that it would not be wholly correct to say that any time anyone makes an internal statement it means the legal system is generally efficacious. There may be rules of the legal system which are obsolete or dormant but still remain rules of the system. The efficacy of a system cannot be measured by such obsolete or dormant rules.

There is a common theory known as the predictive analysis of obligation which says that the internal statement that a given rule is a valid rule of the system and the external statement that the system is generally efficacious assert the validity of a rule, and so predict its enforcement by judges or other officials. The predictive theory is advanced to avoid metaphysical interpretations: either (a) that the statement which says a rule is valid suggests some mysterious content that cannot be detected; or (b) it predicts the future behaviour of officials of the system.

What the predictive theory does is to mistake the specific character of an internal statement, and treat it as an external statement about official behaviour. Therefore, when a judge makes an internal statement about the validity of a rule of the legal system in a judicial decision, the judge presupposes but does not state the general efficacy of the system. Neither does the judge predict his or her own and others' official behaviour. Accordingly Hart says the judge's 'statement that a rule is valid is an internal statement recognising that the rule satisfies the test for identifying what is to count as law in his court, and constitutes not a prophecy of but part of the reason for his decision'.

As far as the judge's internal statement and validity are concerned, the judge only remarks that a particular rule identified by the system's rule of recognition is valid because it satisfies the criteria provided by the rule of recognition. This is why that rule forms part of the reason for the judge's decision. It is not a prophecy or a prediction of the judge's own or others' future actions.

The rule of recognition can be compared with Kelsen's basic norm. Kelsen's basic norm supplies the criteria of validity of all norms in a legal order. Similarly the rule of recognition supplies the criteria of validity of all rules in a legal system. However, whereas Kelsen's basic norm is a theoretical construct, a fiction, Hart's rule of recognition is a fact as well as law. The basic norm is presupposed in our juristic thinking, and stands behind the historically first constitution with which people ought to behave in accordance. There is nothing in both Kelsen and Hart which says that because a judge pronounces a rule valid because it satisfies the criteria supplied by the rule of recognition, or that it is validated by a higher norm, the judge's decision is a prophecy or a prediction of the behaviour of others in future.

The predictive theory's mistake is to treat a judge's internal statement about legal validity as a prediction of the general efficacy of the legal system, and to a larger extent a prediction of what others may do. Hart refuses this and says the judge's internal statement is about what he or she through the criteria supplied by the rule of recognition identifies as law to count towards a decision in a case.

QUESTION EIGHT.

'It is because a rule is regarded as obligatory that a measure of coercion may be attached to it; it is not obligatory because there is coercion.' (Goodhart)

Consider the theories of Austin and Kelsen in the light of this statement.

University of London LLB Examination
(for External Students) Jurisprudence and Legal Theory June 1994 Q10

General Comment

This question requires the cross-referencing of theories between effectiveness and validity when discussing political philosophy in general and legal philosophy in particular. Austin equated might with legal right whilst Kelsen (and Hart) took the view that there was an additional element of authority arising from a commitment to an 'internal attitude'. Austin's command theory, including the idea of a sanction inside the command itself and not merely commands backed by sanctions, needs to be compared with a critical discussion of Kelsen's Grundnorm.

Skeleton Solution

Coercion – Austin and Kelsen compared – the Grundnorm – conclusion.

Suggested Solution

Norms, to Kelsen, were not commands but depsychologised commands. Austin, who relied on the idea of a command as an expression of will, ignored the normative character of legalising rules because he believed in reliance on each other and not on an active will. On the Kelsen model, for example, where the norm is that the judge orders the payment of damages by a defendant, then damages ought to be levied under coercion, if necessary, on the principle of enforcement of a judgment. It is neatly contrasted between the authorised demands of a tax collector and the unauthorised demands of the gunman, exemplified by Hart.

With sanctions, Austin saw the primary norm as the 'do not murder' part, while Kelsen saw the primary norm as a directive to apply the sanction. Kelsen agrees with Austin that coercion is one of the essential features of law but he rejects Austin's reliance on motivation by fear.

Austin is seen to have failed to capture what has been described as the 'dynamic quality of law'. He ignored the dynamic process of law whereby there is the creation of law occurring throughout the hierarchy of norms and which derive validity from the constitution.

Austin saw the law and state as separate entities, called dualism. To Kelsen, they were the same thing with the state merely the personification of the legal order and the sovereign merely the order's highest organ. Austin, however, made the error of basing the validity of his legal order (or sovereignty) on a factual situation such as habitual obedience. He ignored the logical objection to basing the validity of a norm on anything but another norm.

The Grundnorm

Kelsen's model of a legal system comprises an hierarchy of norms where each norm is 'validated' by a prior norm until the point of origin of legal authority is reached with the basic norm: the basic norm becomes, or is, the Grundnorm. The structure of 'norms' excludes moral, political and social values and is concerned with the actual working of active functional legal norms. Kelsen describes it thus:

> '... the basic norm ... must be formulated as follows: Coercive acts sought to be performed under the conditions and in the manner which the historically first constitution, and the norms created according to it, prescribe.'

Initially, Kelsen treated the Grundnorm as the basic element of national or municipal life and this remains essentially so. In later work, Kelsen considered a broader view, examining the relationship between public international and national or municipal law, postulating an international Grundnorm ranking higher than the municipal Grundnorms of particular states, though such a view does not affect the Grundnorm when viewed at national level.

Austin, writing at a time when international law was institutionally much less developed, relegated the system to the sphere of 'positive morality'. Hart, however, identified that international law approaches the closeness of a 'legal' status without actually achieving it, with Kelsen reassessing the Grundnorm internationally.

Austin's view that public international law is not 'law', but instead 'positive international morality', when he wrote that Grotius, Pufendorf and others had fallen into 'a confusion of ideas', where 'they have confounded positive international morality, or the rules which actually obtain among civilised nations, ... with their own vague conceptions of international morality as it ought to be' is a misunderstanding by Austin as to the claims of Grotius and others.

In the early nineteenth century, as today, there is no international sovereign commanding public international law. The United Nations operates sanctions for the international community covering economic sanctions and military action, as seen in Iraq and Bosnia. Morrison has criticised Austin, writing that if Austin had investigated whether a particular sovereign with whom he was concerned recognised the system of international law, 'he might have been led to a much more standard view of the basis of authority on international law than the snap conclusion he made'.

A subtle contrast can be illustrated here by concluding 'does public international law serve the same ends in the community of nations which positive law (or Austin's laws 'properly so-called') plays nationally?' It has been argued that Austin's exclusion of public international law as 'law properly so called' appears to have an unduly narrow definitional focus.

QUESTION NINE

'[W]e shall take legal positivism to mean the simple contention that it is in no sense a necessary truth that laws reproduce or satisfy certain demands of morality, though in fact they have often done so.' (Hart)

Discuss Hart's attitude towards legal systems whose laws do not 'satisfy the demands of morality'.

University of London LLB Examination
(for External Students) Jurisprudence and Legal Theory June 2000 Q3

General Comment

Hart's position is that the fact that a rule may be the product of a legal system and thus a law does not provide an answer to the question of whether or not at the moral level we should in fact obey that rule. A range of theorists such as Fuller and Dworkin could be utilised on this issue to supplement your material on Hart. Whilst examples on evil legal systems such as that of the Nazis or the experience of Apartheid are instructive and should be used, there is much more to this question than an account of case law of the Nazi informer type.

Skeleton Solution

Separation of issues of legal validity and moral content – core of good sense in natural law – clarity, certainty and objectivity – the need for a moral test or benchmark – Radbruch and Fuller – inner morality of law – the Nazi regime – hard choices.

Suggested Solution

Hart wanted as features of his theory of law: clarity, certainty and objectivity. To that end, he advocated a strict divorce from the question of the identification of what is valid law from the question of obedience of the law. Hart utilised the device of a rule of recognition as a means of supplying the ultimate criterion of legal validity. Law in such a system is that which is identified by whoever has official power or authority to perform this role. Hart thought that the point of distinguishing questions of legal validity from the question of what is morally right is to drive a wedge between personal conscience and what the State demands in the name of law. That is, a citizen of a state should always be able to say, 'Yes, this is the law, but it is too evil to be obeyed'. What the State demands must always be subject to scrutiny. Hart's theory of law is a theory of individualistic liberalism, consistent with the strong democratic underpinnings of Western legal systems. It justifies a particular relationship between the citizen and the State. Despite this approach, elsewhere in his writings Hart argues that there is a core of good sense in natural law thinking, that certain rules would emerge as a result both of aspects of the human condition and that we are not a suicide club. Rather we want to co-exist within society.

There are of course other views. Fuller as a natural lawyer suggests that legal systems necessarily have a moral content, brought about by the attention paid to the eight principles of the inner morality of law. Despite Hart's strong attack that these eight principles are analogous to such things as 'the poisoner's art' of the carpenter's trade that is 'neutral' on the question of producing 'hospital beds or torturers' racks', there is perhaps a moral element that runs through them. This is that the eight principles assert implicitly the principle of procedural fairness that rulers should proceed carefully with those they rule; they should be general, prospective, open, fair, stable, not require the impossible and so on. The rulers command obedience in Fuller's legal system but they must do it in a fair way, one which recognises individual moral divergences in its citizens. Fuller would reject the Nazi regime as amounting to a legal system and would also be opposed to the argument that I was only following orders, authorised by the purported legal system, when this is offered by way of a defence or justification by the perpetrator of some atrocity. Fuller's view then of the Nazi legal system was that it did not measure up to the requirements of this moral core and thus should be denied the title legal system. Further, there would be no moral obligation in relation to it. The Nazi system and the regime in South Africa may well have satisfied at least some if not many of Fuller's criteria. The point then is that the criteria suggested by Fuller are overly concerned with notions of procedural fairness.

Much discussion arose as a result of events during the Nazi regime in Germany. It caused some to become natural lawyers, as in the case of Radbruch. He argued that to be a law, a provision would have to be in accord with basic principles of morality. In West Germany after the Second World War, trials took place in relation to informers. Such behaviour would have been lawful when carried out in the context of Nazi Germany. In one such case a wife, who had a grudge against her husband, reported him to the authorities, on the basis that he had criticised Hitler. The provision that authorised her behaviour was repealed and she was brought to trial, under a legal provision that prevented people from unlawfully depriving others of their freedom. The court was prepared to condemn the Nazi law as one that offended justice and decency. This is the sort of approach promoted by Radbruch. The problem is that you have to choose between the evil of the Nazi law and the evil of retrospective legislation. Hart still favours the idea of separating issues of validity and their moral content but thinks that in extreme cases such as the one above you may have to make a choice between the two evils. Rather than obscure the issues, as Radbruch's approach would be likely to do, Hart suggests that if you go for the retrospective law then you avoid confusion by making it clear that that is what you have done.

On these issues, you may find the example given by Guest (Guest S (2000), Why the Law is Just, '*Current Legal Problems*', Oxford: Oxford University Press, pp31–32) instuctive:

> 'In the film Crocodile Dundee, the hero, Mick, is confronted in New York by a Lower East Side hooligan who pulls a flick-knife on him in a dark alley. "Call that a knife?" mocks Mick, as he pulls out a huge Bowie knife, almost a foot long. Although it is unlikely that the hooligan had studied philosophy, if he had, he might have said:
>
>> "The necessary and sufficient conditions of the truth of the proposition that this thing I hold in my hand here is a knife are fulfilled. It has a handle and a cutting edge, arid the fact that it happens to be smaller than yours, is neither here nor there as to its being a knife."
>
> We can imagine Mick's reply. We understood perfectly well what Mick said. He charged or loaded the word "knife" with a meaning that reflected its purpose in that context. The hooligan perfectly well understood that, because he fled.
>
> To generalize from this, a charged meaning is one that achieves the most from the circumstances. Mick is in potential danger, and "knife" takes on the meaning, in this Lower East Side context, of "'that sort of knife, the pulling of which, wins fights. Other sorts of knives aren't properly called knives." '

You can see where I am heading. Law is a 'charged' concept. Like Mick Dundee, we can say of unjust laws 'call that a "law"?!' or, as we might have said, perhaps following Fuller, of the Nazi legal system, 'call that a "legal system"?!'

Hart, in his Postscript to the second edition of *The Concept of Law*, rejects any kind of view which says that moral judgments about what people's rights are, are part of the identification of their legal rights. He says that the reason simply is that legal rights and duties are the point at which the law protects or restricts individual freedom by allowing individuals the power to avail themselves of the law's coercive machinery. He also maintains his belief that the Nazi-type legal system, while undeniably one of moral wickedness, is nevertheless law since the various features it shares with other modern municipal legal systems are too great for a universal-descriptive legal theory, such as he claims his theory to be, to ignore. He points to Dworkin's suggestion that such a legal system might be described in a pre-interpretive sense but then says that Dworkin's concession there about the flexibility of legal language strengthens rather than weakens the positivist's case, because it allows the positivist's assertion here to make use of the flexibility of language as well.

It is difficult to offer a strong conclusion. There may well be behaviour that we wish to condemn. But if that is the case we face the difficulties of being able to justify our moral position. This is the strength of Hart's approach: he thinks matters are clearer if you separate questions of legal validity from questions of morality or an obligation to obey the law. Calling something a law and encouraging societies to be watchful of the content of law has much to recommend it.

Chapter 3

Modern Natural Law and its Historical Background

3.1   Introduction

3.2   Key points

3.3   Questions and suggested solutions

3.1 Introduction

The central tenet of natural law theories is that there is a set of principles or moral values which are discoverable by man's reason, and according to which all things ought to behave. There is a necessary connection between law and morals. Those moral values or principles are universal, unchanging and absolute. The student will realise at once the dichotomy between these natural law theories and those of positivists; natural law and positivism must be studied in conjunction. Natural law in general is also important for the law/morals debate, especially that between Hart and Fuller.

3.2 Key points

The historical development of natural law

a) The Greeks – Aristotle, Cicero.

b) The Scholastics – Aquinas.

c) The secularisation of natural law.

The central propositions prior to Finnis

a) There are objective moral values that can be discovered by the use of reason on the realities of the human condition.

b) These are universal, unchanging and absolute.

c) Any law violating these moral values is not a law.

Finnis' restatement

a) His seven basic goods are 'self-evident'. He thus avoids the illegitimate 'is-ought' derivation of traditional natural lawyers.

b) A validly made, unjust law is still law. The natural law/positivist dichotomy is thereby narrowed so that the issue of obligation to obey the law becomes all the more important.

3.3 Questions and suggested solutions

QUESTION ONE

'All theories of natural law have relied upon some thesis that value is inherent in nature. Since that thesis is plainly wrong, all theories of natural law are incoherent and illogical.'

Discuss.

University of London LLB Examination
(for External Students) Jurisprudence and Legal Theory June 1996 Q12

General Comment

The difficulty positivism has with natural law will continue to dog jurisprudence for a very long time to come. This is a straightforward question that invites you to consider the positivist position that natural law is illogical and whether you agree with that position.

Skeleton Solution

Positivism/natural law dichotomy – David Hume's is/ought argument – Kelsen's attack on natural law – difference between 'is' and 'ought' propositions – Finnis – conclusion.

Suggested Solution

Positivism denies any connection between law and morality, thus whilst natural law theories have relied on some intrinsic value of nature in discovering what the law ought to be, positivism refutes the illogicality of such a thought process, and claims all natural law theories are, therefore, incoherent and illogical.

The first positivist attack on natural law as made by David Hume in *A Treatise of Human Nature* (1874), who criticised the deductive fallacy of natural law philosophy. According to Hume, the starting point of natural law theories is human reality, particularly human nature, and then the theories derive value judgments from such starting point. To Hume this is illogical reasoning by which an 'ought' statement is derived from an 'is' statement. According to Hume, a deductive argument is invalid if it derives a conclusion based on a value judgment from premises which are facts. Instead of the valid connection between propositions being 'is' and 'is not', natural law propositions are connected with an 'ought' or 'ought not'. An example of such deductive fallacy is seen in the following syllogism: Bettie is a cat; Bettie is black; therefore, all cats called Bettie ought to be black.

The fallacy of this deduction is that an 'ought' conclusion is derived from 'is' premises.

This is better explained by Thomas Aquinas' use of natural inclination. In any system of morality, statements about human nature describe what people are and do. Men ought to behave in certain ways because that is the nature of things. It can be seen that statements which are prescriptive, evaluative and normative are derived from the empirical statements that say something 'is'. Hume considers this kind of reasoning invalid because the conclusion does not follow from the premises, and there are no 'oughts' in the premises either.

Hume's attack on natural law gains support from Kelsen. In his book *What is Justice?* (1957) Kelsen attacks natural law from the scientific viewpoint. He says that natural law extinguishes the difference between the rules whereby natural science describes its objects and the rules whereby ethics and jurisprudence describe objects, namely, morality and law. In natural science two phenomena are connected to each other by the principle of causality – cause and effect. To use Kelsen's example, if a metallic body is heated it expands. The relation between cause and effect is not attributable to any human or paranormal powers. However, when we speak of morality or law we refer to rules prescribing human behaviour, rules which are the specific meaning of acts of human or superhuman beings. An example is the moral rule of Christ which says that a person has to be his/her brother's/sister's keeper, or a legal rule which prescribes punishment for stealing. Ethics describe the situation which exists under a moral rule: be your brother's keeper; jurisprudence describes the situation under the legal rule: if a man steals, he ought to be punished. It can be seen from this that the rule of morality, like the rule of law, connects the condition with its consequence. This follows the principle of imputation. Natural law, for example, is expressed as: if A is, then B is. On the other hand, the rule of morality, like the rule of law, is expressed in this form: if A is, then there ought to be B. The difference between natural science and morality or law is the difference between the 'is' of causality and the 'ought' of imputation.

To Kelsen, it would be better if a general norm was presupposed which prescribed a certain type of human behaviour so that any particular behaviour not in accordance with the presupposed general norm can be characterised as good, bad, or correct behaviour. These are recognised as value judgments and the term is used in an objective sense because the value is in accordance with a presupposed norm. Kelsen distinguishes a positive value from a negative one. A positive value is derived from a presupposed norm. A value which does not conform to a presupposed norm is a negative value. If an individual's behaviour is described as good or bad, this means that the person's behaviour is in accordance or not in accordance with a presupposed norm, therefore, the value judgment is expressed as: 'a person ought to or ought not behave in a certain way'.

Kelsen says that without presupposing a general norm we cannot make a value judgment in the objective sense that something is permitted or forbidden. According to Kelsen, value is not inherent in the object adjudged valuable but it is in the relation of the object to the presupposed norm. He asserts that value is not inherent in natural reality; therefore, value cannot be deduced from reality. This means that it does not follow from the fact that something is, then it ought to be done, to be, or not to be done. His interesting example is that it does not follow that if in reality a big fish swallows a small fish it implies that the behaviour of the fish is good or that it is bad. The conclusion is that there is no logical inference from the 'is' to the 'ought' of natural reality to moral or legal value.

Furthermore, what under one system of morality is good may under another system of morality be bad; similarly what under one legal system is a crime may not be a crime under another legal system. Value, then, is relative. Natural law doctrine dwells on the point that value is inherent in nature and that this value is absolute; in other words a divine will is inherent in nature. Kelsen makes the point that only by presupposing that value is inherent in nature can natural law claim that law is deducible from nature and that this law is absolute justice. Kelsen's damning conclusion is that the assumption that value is inherent in nature is metaphysical and unacceptable from the scientific point of view. This being the case, natural law doctrine is based on an illogical fallacy, deriving 'is' from an 'ought'.

Kelsen says that the norms allegedly deduced from nature are tacitly presupposed and are based on subjective values presented as the intention of God – a supreme legislator. Kelsen's verdict on natural law is well worth quoting:

> 'Before the tribunal of science, the natural law doctrine has no chance. But it may deny the jurisdiction of this tribunal by referring to its religious character.'

This is a serious indictment of natural law. Does the theory falsely claim value is inherent in nature? Finnis, in *Natural Law and Natural Rights* (1980), says that it is not true that natural law theories entail the belief that obligations and duties of human beings are deducible from propositions about their nature. Thomas Aquinas has said that the first principles of natural law specifying the basic forms of good and evil can be understood by everyone of the age of reason and are not demonstrable. They are self-evidence, and are informed neither form facts, speculative principles, metaphysical propositions about nature nor what is good or evil. In short, they are not derived or inferred from anything. Principles of right and wrong are derived from pre-moral principles of practical reasonableness, and not from any facts, metaphysical or otherwise.

According to Finnis, when one distinguishes what is good to be pursued, intelligence operates in a different way yielding a different sort of logic form when distinguishing in a historical, scientific or metaphysical way, what is the case. Finnis does not see any reason for saying that there is a rational operation of intelligence in the historical or scientific case of intelligence. The basic form of good that practical understanding offers is what is good for human beings considering the nature they have. To Aquinas, practical reasoning takes place by experiencing one's reason from inside – by following one's inclination. These are not psychological or metaphysical judgments about human nature, and there is no process of deduction. People just do not judge that they have an urge to make some inquiries and conclude that knowledge per se is a good or a value to be pursued. On the contrary, people understand that the object of the urge they experience is an example of a general form of good for themselves.

Criticisms can be levelled at Aquinas' theory of natural law. D J O'Connor in *Aquinas and Natural Law* questions just how the specific moral rules which need to guide our conduct can be shown to be connected with allegedly self-evident principles. Finnis rejects any suggestion that Aquinas derived an 'ought' from an 'is'. He believes that the argument that natural law is based on value judgments is because the phrase 'natural law' brings an image that refers to the norms of natural law as being based on judgments about nature. In his ethics and theology Aquinas points out the analogies running through the whole order of nature. Human virtue is similar to the virtue that can be based on anything of nature which is good. To Aquinas, therefore, human virtue is in accordance with the nature of human beings. The opposite of human vice and criteria for conformity or contradiction to human nature is reasonableness. Reasonableness is an underived first principle which makes no reference to human nature but only to human good.

Finnis bridges the dichotomy between positivism and natural law with his seven basic goods which he says are self-evident. He does not start from any facts about nature or man so there is no derivation of an 'is' in Finnis' theory. What he says is that everybody can recognise that his seven basic goods – life, knowledge, friendship, procreation, practical reasonableness, play, aesthetic experience and religion – are aspects of human existence which as such are good, ie worth having.

Positivists mount a strong indictment of natural law but the important question is whether it is true that natural law derives an 'ought' from an 'is'. I agree with Aquinas that natural law is not derived from any fact about human nature. It is underived and therefore, there cannot be any fact of nature which imbues natural law doctrines with value. Saying that the criterion for conformity or nonconformity with nature is reasonableness is not the same as saying nature has an inherent value. It cannot be correct to say, therefore, that all theories of natural law are incoherent and illogical because they do not make the claim attributed to them. Since natural law is based on the principle of reasonableness which is underived from any fact, it follows that Kelsen's argument that natural law presupposes a moral norm from which it derives its subjective conclusions cannot be right either.

QUESTION TWO

'A belief in natural law is humane, if not rational.'

Discuss.

University of London LLB Examination
(for External Students) Jurisprudence and Legal Theory June 1998 Q8

General Comment

Natural law questions are always popular with candidates. This question is straightforward enough. Although you must demonstrate why you think natural law is irrational, you must be careful to answer the question fully. State whether you think 'a belief in natural law is humane, if not rational'.

Skeleton Solution

Classical natural law theory – criticisms of the theory – revival of natural law – attractions of natural law – conclusion.

Suggested Solution

For over 2,000 years natural law theories have dominated legal philosophy. There must be good reason for the enduring appeal of the natural law doctrine.

We may trace the origin of the classical natural law doctrine to the ancient Greeks. Aristotle, for example, believed that men naturally lived by reason, which is common to all men, and through reason universal laws by which men could live were discovered. Among the early philosophers to discuss natural law is the Roman philosopher Cicero, who was of the opinion that natural law was everlasting, universal and unchanging. The point about man and his reason is captured by the classical natural law theory, which states that there is a higher law which is discoverable by reason, and that all man-made law ought to conform with this higher law in order to be valid.

In the thirteenth century, Thomas Aquinas divided law into four parts:

a) divine law – God's revelation through the scriptures;

b) eternal law – divine reason, known only to God, and it is God's plan for the universe and man;

c) natural law – participation of the eternal law in rational creatures. Natural law is the same for all men because it is proper for all men to be inclined to act according to reason;

d) human law – the law of the human authority which derives its validity from natural law.

According to Thomas Aquinas the purpose of the human law was to promote the good of society. The law-giver must not exceed his powers, and the burdens of the law must not be imposed unequally on people. Where the human law infringes these principles it becomes an unjust law in the sense that it does not conform to natural law, and that unjust law is no law – *lex injusta not est lex*. However, Aquinas believed it was better to obey an unjust law, because disobedience of the law would lead to consequences which would be far worse than the unjust law itself.

In the Reformation era, natural law became secular and its influence began to dwindle. Philosophers, like the Dutch protestant Hugo Grotius, advocated that natural law was possible without basing it on a belief in God. Natural law was simply discovered by applying one's reason.

The arrival of legal positivism further dealt a severe blow to the reputation of natural law. The Reformation era was particularly harsh on natural law because it was the age of reason. It was said that there was no application of reason in natural law thinking. Positivism insists on the separation of law and morals. The inability of natural law to separate law from morals was frowned upon by positivism, which believes that law and morals are two separate realities.

David Hume in his book (David Hume, *A Treatise of Nature* (1874)) criticised the illogicality and sophistry of natural law. To Hume, natural law made a value judgment which was an 'ought', derived from human reality which is an 'is'. This is non-cognivitism which means that there is no rational procedure by which we can objectively know what is morally right and wrong. Hume's point is that the conclusions of natural law do not follow logically from stated premises. For example: first premise: all men marry and produce children; second premise: David is a man; conclusion: therefore, David ought to marry and produce children.

The instructive logic in this is false because it contains an ought not found in the premises. David may marry and not produce children. The charge against natural law that it is illogical has been established so robustly.

Hans Kelsen (Hans Kelsen, *What is Justice?* (1957)) says that natural law extinguishes the difference between the rules, whereas natural science describes its objects and the rules, whereas ethics and jurisprudence describe objects, meaning, morality and law. To Kelsen, the value judgment of natural law makes it subjective. The withering criticism of natural law is that its claim (that there is a higher law discoverable by the application of reason) is illogical, unscientific and metaphysical.

The doctrine of natural law has, however, experienced a revival of late. Finnis (John Finnis, *Natural Law and Natural Rights* (1980)) has produced the most significant restatement of natural law in recent times. He rejects much in the classical natural law tradition and aims to rescue it from its preconceptions associated with philosophers like Aquinas and Aristotle.

Finnis claims that natural law does not mean a belief that morality is reflected in rational principles of behaviour. He also denies that it demands that laws which do not conform to natural law principles are invalid. To him, natural law is a set of principles of practical reasonableness in ordering human life and the human community. His version of natural law is based on the assumption that there are seven basic goods for human beings which we find worth having in life. These basic goods are, therefore, aspirational and objective values. The seven basic goods are: life, knowledge, play, aesthetic experience, sociability or friendship, practical reasonableness and religion.

The basic goods must be seen from the point of view of the human community. Practical reasonableness dictates that the basic goods are desirable to pursue. Finnis' theory of the central or focal meaning of law and the peripheral meaning of law helps to bridge the dichotomy between positivism and natural law. In this sense natural law does not deny the legal validity of an unjust law: it merely takes the peripheral meaning of law, which uses natural law as a moral barometer to judge the content of the positive law.

According to Professor H L A Hart (H L A Hart, *Essays in Jurisprudence and Philosophy* (1983)), Finnis' account of natural law has great merits. Hart himself has restated natural law with his minimum content of law, because to Hart natural law contains a core of good sense to which human beings must pay attention as long as we are what we are and continue to want to establish a viable society.

Professor Neil MacCormick (Neil MacCormick, 'Natural Law Reconsidered' (1981) 10 JLS 99) has also said that Finnis' restatement of natural law requires us to abandon our caricature version of what a natural law theory is. MacCormick concludes that the age-old rivalry between positivism and natural law is no longer useful. According to MacCormick, it is important to appreciate that law, like all social phenomena, makes sense relative to its aspirations. The aspirational nature of law which MacCormick calls the 'essential moral aspiration of law-giving', evidences why law cannot be understood without recourse to the values of justice and public welfare. He argues that John Finnis' work illuminates the sense in which law and morality are related but are also separate forms of practical reasoning. The conclusion is that every system of positive law also contains non-positive standards.

In a world where positivism holds such a sway over many people, we must try to find out why the natural law doctrine is still attractive. Curzon (Curzon, *Jurisprudence* (1979)) says that natural law theory is often condemned as basically reactionary, untrue, inadequate and derived from questionable logical foundations. But Friedman's reminder is important. The history of natural law is a tale of the search of mankind for absolute justice and its failure. It has mirrored man's belief that there is, in the scheme of things, something higher than the positive law to which appeal can be made and from which valid criteria of justice on earth might be deduced. Herein lies the human face of the natural law doctrine. It is the only doctrine which we can use to question man's inhumanity to man in this world torn by myriad catastrophes.

In a world where tyrants and dictators will stop at nothing to demonstrate their might and power in callous disdain to established and received civilised norms, only an appeal to natural law can lead to heart-searching and a re-examination of the principles of human law and government. At least we can all join the philosopher Immanuel Kant and proclaim that to be moral is to be rational.

QUESTION THREE

'Given survival as an aim, law and morals should include a specific content.' (Hart)

Discuss, with particular reference to Hart's minimum content of natural law.

University of London LLB Examination
(for External Students) Jurisprudence and Legal Theory June 1991 Q1

General Comment

The question requires an account and critique of Hart's position on natural law aided by the use of material from Finnis and Fuller.

Skeleton Solution

Hart's theory – positivist view of natural law – form/is versus substance/ought distinction – empiricalism versus normativity – lack of empirical basis – uncertainty of consequences – other human aims; Fuller – wider interpretation of 'survival'; Finnis' theory.

Suggested Solution

Hart's 'minimum content of natural law' was posited by him as being the product of a sociological and empirical enquiry as to what basic function a legal system must perform in order to ensure human survival. In turn, human survival was seen as the ultimate 'telos' (purpose) of human existence. Following on from this, Hart concluded that by virtue of six invariable characteristics of the human condition (human vulnerability, limited resources, limited altruism, limited understanding, limited will power and approximate equality) all legal systems must have a specific content. In other words, the law must ensure a minimum level of protection, otherwise human survival would be impossible. Although Hart does not provide us with any specific substantive rules, he does state that this minimum content of natural law would have to protect persons, property and promises.

Hart was at pains to reduce the concession he had made to natural law, hence the term 'minimum'. This is hardly surprising given his declared aim of presenting law from a positivist viewpoint. Hart, like other legal positivists, felt that the law could be looked at as a mere structure, or form, without the need to describe it as including certain universal principles, such as justice. Legal positivists criticised natural lawyers for failing to keep separate the universal form of law from its varying content, or substance. Positivism sees the law as having a specific and universal form, whereas its substansive content was variable.

The implications of this view were that, for example, laws promulgated under the Nazi German regime, although iniquitous and immoral in content, nevertheless still bore the structure of laws and were therefore legally valid. Another way of seeing this distinction between form and substance is to see legal positivists as claiming to analyse law as it 'is', as opposed to making normative claims as to how it 'ought' to be.

By conceding that law had a specific content it would prima facie seem that Hart has contradicted his positivist claims. However, he stresses that this specific content does not entail certain higher or fundamental principles with which all laws must comply. The specific content of law is merely dictated empirically by the universal nature of the human condition. Theoretically, therefore, should the six fundamental conditions Hart mentions alter in the future, the declared minimum requirements of the law needed to ensure human survival would also be subject to change.

A number of criticisms have been made of this minimal inclusion of natural law within Hart's anti-natural law theory. Firstly, Hart claims that the concept of what law is is provided by an 'exercise in descriptive sociology'. Likewise, he claims that his minimum content of natural law is empirically necessitated. D'Entreves has argued that there is a lack of any empirical basis for Hart's view of the human condition. It may therefore be said that Hart has merely made an intuitive assumption; if this is true he can be justly accused of making the very normative (instead of factual) assumptions so criticised by legal positivists. On the other hand it is true to say that his minimum conditions are, on common sense grounds, largely true.

Secondly, there is some vagueness in Hart's theory. It is uncertain what protective laws would flow from his premises concerning the human condition. For example, limited resources may justify a claim that the law should protect those resources in limited supply but there are many societies in which the exploitation of resources is encouraged. Even when such protective laws exist, Hart's theory is of no help in the debate as to how much protection to allow, as in the environmental questions that concern us today.

Finally, in allowing for a minimum level of natural law, Hart may be forced to concede to more radical natural law claims. Fuller has stated that the ultimate aim of human beings is communication, rather than survival. He asserts that it is through our ability to communicate that we acquired the knowledge that has in turn ensured our success in competition with other, often stronger, animals. Proceeding from this premise, Fuller claimed that a universal 'anatomy' or 'inner morality' of law existed. This was in the form of certain essential procedural requirements within the structure of any efficiently functioning legal system. It could be stated that such requirements, such as the non-retrospectivity of laws, are Fuller's own minimum content of natural law. The difference between Hart and Fuller lies in their description of human existence and its aims. Both use the same methodology of making normative assumptions concerning the ultimate aim of life.

If we concede, however, that survival is the central aim of human existence, it might then be claimed that Hart's account of natural law is too minimal. A natural lawyer such as Finnis, might give a wider interpretation of survival as being synonymous with human flourishing. This notion forms the basis of his assertion that all legal systems must provide the conditions under which citizens can attain so-called 'basic goods' with which they can flourish.

Whether we stick with Hart's claim as to the central position of survival as a human aim, or challenge it as not being empirically proven, his minimum content of natural law can be attacked as being too minimal. Furthermore, his theory is open to allegations of uncertainty and, most fundamentally, internal incoherence; in that it seems to undermine the central tenets of legal positivism to which Hart purports to adhere.

QUESTION FOUR

Is Hart's discussion of the five considerations, which amount to the 'core of good sense' in traditional natural law thinking, satisfactory?

University of London LLB Examination
(for External Students) Jurisprudence and Legal Theory June 1999 Q2

General Comment

You may well wonder what a positivist like Hart is doing dabbling with natural law in the light of the fundamental disagreement between the two schools of legal philosophy regarding the relationship between law and morals. Should a positivist be bothered about natural law teaching at all? Will a positivist be able to challenge a natural lawyer on a natural law teaching? An understanding of these points should help you to answer this question well.

Skeleton Solution

Hart's positivism: the separation of law and morals – the connection between law and morals – law and morals must have specific content – criticism of Hart's approach – conclusion.

Suggested Solution

Professor Hart exhibits his credentials as a positivist by defining legal positivism in the following terms in chapter nine of his book (H L A Hart, *The Concept of Law* (2nd edn, 1997)): 'it is in no sense a necessary truth that laws reproduce or satisfy certain demands of morality, though in fact they have often done so'. This definition illustrates the difference between legal positivism as a legal philosophy and natural law thinking.

Classical natural law theory suggests that human beings and other objects aspire to an ultimate end or goal. This, in natural law teaching, is the teleological conception of nature. Natural law governs the natural progression of every creature in the universe. To Hart this theory is too grand. He argues that the proper goal of man is survival. Most men want to continue to survive most of the time and make social arrangements to this end.

According to Hart, there are five human conditions which properly call for the coincidence of law and morals. Given the five facts of human condition, the natural law we must have to achieve the goal of survival is minimum only. To Hart, the minimum content of natural law found in the five conditions of man he discusses form the core of good sense in natural law, to which we must pay attention if we seek to establish a viable society.

The five considerations which give rise to the minimum content of law we need are as follows.

a) Human vulnerability: all men are vulnerable – even the weakest is able to kill the strongest when he is asleep and therefore even the strongest is vulnerable. We need law to restrict the use of violence.

b) Approximate equality: human beings differ from each other in characteristics but no one is invincible, so in order to make life less nasty, brutish and short lived, aggression must be restrained. People must co-operate for the benefit of all.

c) Limited altruism: since human beings are neither angels nor devils, selfishness must be controlled. Co-operation is needed.

d) Limited resources: since resources are scarce in any community there must be rules to regulate property and prevent people from stealing what belongs to others.

e) Limited understanding and strength of will: because of the excesses of some people we are prepared to establish a legal system with rules and other agents of law to deal with any anti-social behaviour.

Hart says that because of these five facts, he considers it a 'natural necessity' for the minimum of natural law (represented by these five facts) to exist in order to protect life, property and promise.

It is interesting to find Hart take on natural law in this way. Why should the natural lawyer fear anything about Hart's 'survival thesis'? If the teleological conception states that we need law for every pursuit in life, why should Hart believe moral rules only deal with murder, theft and fraud? Human beings do not just want to survive at the cost of hideous misery. We want to flourish, so why do we not simply create more law?

Moreover, Hart fails to tell us what would happen if people flout the rules within has minimum natural law. Hart's minimum content is too restrictive, because law coincides with morals outside his core of good sense. Surely moral rules may even come into play in rules governing buying and selling, establishing a company, and the relations between two or more countries? I believe that flourishing is compatible with natural law's teleological conception of nature. We need laws to govern trading, competitions and other cultural activities: should we not need a further necessary content of law as natural law teaches?

Professor Lon Fuller (Lon Fuller, *Law and Morality* (1969)) points out that Hart's minimum content says nothing about who should be included in the community that seeks the realisation of the community-shared objective of survival. As I have already pointed out, most people would not want to survive at the cost of hideous misery. Fuller argues that Hart's is a dubious claim, and undermines any assertion that survival is a necessary condition for the attainment of other ends.

A challenge against Hart's thesis comes from Fuller who argues that if we were to select the principle which best supports human endeavour it would be communication. No-one would enjoy a vegetative existence where we could not articulate our thoughts with each other.

The classical natural law theory about a further necessary content of law to aid the teleological conception of nature makes sense. It is difficult to understand why Hart felt this theory outlandish and in need of reform into his arbitrary 'core of good sense'. His efforts are largely unsatisfactory.

QUESTION FIVE

What are Fuller's principles of the 'morality of law'? Why does he posit them? Are there any practical problems which might be resolved by recourse to these principles?

University of London LLB Examination
(for External Students) Jurisprudence and Legal Theory June 1993 Q11

General Comment

This is a giveaway question to someone who has studied Fuller properly, which means reading his book *The Morality of Law*. (This book is readily available and enjoyable to read; it is not difficult and rewards the student with many insights.)

First, state what the eight principles of the 'inner morality of law' are. Do this fully; merely stating them is parroting and each one has its own ramifications and interest. Then consider why it is that he posits them. These reasons may be gleaned from his remarks in response to Hart in the famous Hart-Fuller debate, although you might consider the general question why people devise theories of law in the first place, in order to pep up your answer (and reference to Finnis would be useful here). Then consider what practical problems could be solved, given the light of Fuller's overall purpose (which is to explain, remember, the human 'purposive' element in law). You should come to some sort of conclusion that rules of procedural fairness have very good point and go back to illustrating four or five of the principles of the 'internal morality of law' applying.

Skeleton Solution

The eight principles – why Fuller posits them – Finnis's attitude to this kind of theorising – Hart's response in talking of the virtues of positivism (from the Hart/Fuller debate and his review of Fuller's *The Morality of Law*; see also Fuller's reply to Hart's criticisms in the revised edition of *The Morality of Law*) – how the rules of the inner morality of law have virtue as 'procedural rules of fairness' – conclusion that Fuller's views have a number of virtues.

Suggested Solution

Fuller was a natural lawyer, strongly opposed to the positivistic insistence that law and morality were distinctly separate; he therefore thought that there was a logically necessary relationship between any statement about what the law was and some correct moral statement. For example, to say that such and such a law was part of a legal system, was to say that a legal system concurred with a certain degree of morality. The test case is that of the Nazi legal system. Since it did not have a moral core, it could not correctly be called a 'legal' system, and thus any rules that emanated from it could not properly be called 'laws' and could have no moral obligatory effect. This view strikes an intuitive chord in us; there was clearly great evil in the Nazi legal system. 'Laws' that purportedly authorised sadistic murders and torture in inhumane 'camps' don't seem properly to be called 'law', which idea we appear to associate with justice, fairness, or at the very least, some basic level of human decency. Here Fuller is at his strongest in his attack on Hart, because it is quite clear that Hart regards his own theory as able to provide criteria according to which Nazi law, however 'iniquitous' is nevertheless law (and Hart's reason was that seeing the law in this way would provide useful and essential clarity, certainty and objectivity). According to Fuller, Hart's positivism presents law as an 'amoral datum'; as a piece of scientific matter, not to be endowed with any sense, as Fuller puts it, of 'human striving and purpose' in which the great ideal of 'fidelity to the law' can be explained. This idea is attractive but how does Fuller get to it?

He says that a large part of the necessary conditions to be in place in order to say that a legal system exists consists of the eight principles of what he calls the 'inner morality of law'. The greater degree of conformity that a set of rules purporting to govern society has to these 'principles', the closer to a fully working legal system – which to him means one that commands moral fidelity from citizens – the set of rules becomes. These principles of 'inner' morality are contrasted with the 'external' morality, which is the morality 'that makes law possible', and is a simply understood idea through the relatively straightforward idea of the community, or its officials, accepting the basic constitutional arrangements from the moral point of view.

What are these 'inner' principles? Laws must be general, that is, they must apply to classes of people, and to classes of acts, and not to individuals only (see Austin's extension of the meaning of command, in *The Province of Jurisprudence Determined*). This makes sense; a legal system in which laws applied to some individuals and not to others would be open to the charge of arbitrariness. Laws must also not be *secret*; if they were, this would lay the way open for corruption since there would be no public check on what the officials were doing. Laws must not, generally, be retrospective, for otherwise there would again be unfairness, since people would not know what was expected (although Fuller thought that the occasional retrospective law could be useful to right a former injustice). Laws must be clear; otherwise, people would again not be able find out what was expected of them. Law must not require the impossible; so, for example, it would be wrong for laws to lay heavy responsibility on those who lack the capacity to bear such responsibility, such as infants or the mentally disordered. So, too, would it be wrong to institute too many laws that impose strict liability. For similar reasons, Fuller thinks that laws ought not to require people to have to do contradictory things; for example, it would be silly to have a law that required people to have their number plates changed on a national holiday, when garages were not free to trade. Law also must not be subject to frequent change; this would result again in people being in a secure position about how to plan their lives (which is a fairness issue). This admonition against frequent change is particularly apt in the case of property law; if the Law of Property Act 1925 was altered dramatically, year in and year out, people would not be secure in their property rights. Finally, Fuller's eighth principle was that there should be a congruence between official pronouncement and official action. The sort of thing Fuller was getting at is the situation where what the law says in the books is quite different from what actually happens in practice; an example is the Statute of Frauds which for centuries was 'applied' by the courts in a way that was quite unrelated to the wording of the statute.

Fuller thinks that the Nazi 'legal system' abused most of these eight principles and therefore could not be properly called law and, consequently, the 'obligations' that these laws purported to create were unreal. The practical upshot is that claims such as 'I was only obeying orders' made no coherent claim for moral excuse from blame for atrocities done in the name of law. But it is useful to consider Hart's response. Hart thought that the eight principles were good principles of legal craftsmanship, but in no way guaranteed that the legal system would be moral. He says that it is possible for us to envisage a society in which all eight principles are adhered to, but where there is a fairly evil legal system in place (eg possibly in South Africa). He says that any activity could have 'principles of craftsmanship' extrapolated from it which would not necessarily guarantee that the use to which the thing crafted was put was a moral one; for example, he imagined principles of the 'inner morality' of poisoning (eg use odourless poisons, poisons that don't induce vomiting, etc) which could aid murder, or principles of 'good' carpentry that would be neutral between the production of hospital beds and torturers' racks!

This fairly devastating attack by Hart can be shown to be misguided by Finnis's account of moral reasoning securing, in legal theory, the moral basis behind the reasons that legal theorists such as Fuller and Hart have for producing their theories. Fuller is motivated by the moral concerns of 'moral consistency and fair play between governors and governed'; these principles of craftsmanship can therefore be seen to be part of the ideal of a legal system which, for Fuller, lies in adherence to principles of procedural fairness. Possibly he doesn't succeed in spelling out the principles in full enough detail, and perhaps his list is not sufficiently long; nevertheless, this view is that if lawyers pay attention to the nitty gritty of procedural fairness, in the end the law will 'work itself pure' and substantive fairness will finally be achieved. This view is a distinctly American view and finds echoes in the work of Dworkin and some others.

If we accept this view, we find that Hart's concerns for clarity, certainty and objectivity, to be achieved by his insistence on a rule of recognition, empirically determinable, are not dissimilar. Hart wants a clear wedge between the citizen and the state; in other words, he wants an 'above the board' public distance between them. One way to achieve this is, of course, in conjunction with the requirement for use of rules of procedural fairness. For these reasons, it can be seen that Fuller's eight principles of the inner morality of law do, contrary to what Hart claims, have a strong connection with the moral requirements of law and legal systems.

Part B
Legal and Social Theory

Chapter 4

Sociological Jurisprudence and the Sociology of Law

4.1   **Introduction**

4.2   **Key points**

4.3   **Questions and suggested solutions**

4.1 Introduction

Although a distinction is often claimed to exist between 'sociological jurisprudence' and 'the sociology of law', the student should revise the two subjects in conjunction. There are obviously significant overlaps – both see law as essentially a social phenomenon and both employ the techniques of social sciences – so that it is convenient to deal with them together.

4.2 Key points

Sociological jurisprudence

a) Roscoe Pound was predominantly concerned with law reform, and with law as a social fact. He developed a concept of 'social engineering' whereby the law operates to ensure social cohesion by balancing conflicting interests. Where such interests cannot be accommodated Pound develops the concept of jural postulates. For him these are the means of testing new interests; they are the presuppositions of legal reasoning.

b) It will be helpful for the student to have a brief knowledge of the salient points of other sociological jurisprudential writers, eg Ehrlich, Ihering.

The sociology of law

a) Max Weber sought to explain the relationship of law and capitalism. He can perhaps best be understood as offering a response to the Marxist attack on capitalism. In particular he criticised Marx for his (as Weber saw it) sole reliance on economic factors as the determinant of the nature of society. Weber also offered a typology of law: legal systems are characterised by either rationality or irrationality. He believed that formal rational legal systems were unique to developed Western society.

b) Emile Durkheim also attributed much importance to law in developing an understanding of society in general. For Durkheim there were two types of social cohesion: 'mechanical solidarity' (where there is no division of labour) and 'organic solidarity' (where there is much specialisation of labour). The latter form of cohesion will exist in more advanced societies. The type of law prevalent in society indicates the type of 'solidarity' existing. Law is largely penal where there is mechanical solidarity but more restitutive where there is organic solidarity.

4.3 Questions and suggested solutions

QUESTION ONE

Evaluate critically the following statement concerning Roscoe Pound. 'For him, jurisprudence is not so much a social science but a technology.' (Charles Conway)

University of London LLB Examination
(for External Students) Jurisprudence and Legal Theory June 1984 Q8

General Comment

Analysis of the methodology employed by Pound is required here. A comparison with other practitioners of the sociological approach will aid the production of a critique rather than a descriptive account of what Pound said.

Skeleton Solution

Sociological jurisprudence – lacked complete theory of law in sociological context – social science techniques – American Realists – socio-legal surveys – technology – social engineering – balancing of interests – jural postulates.

Suggested Solution

I think the quotation makes a valid point in an overstated way. It is not true to say that Pound did not see jurisprudence as a social science, but it is true to say that his was a 'sociological jurisprudence' viewpoint which lacked a completed theory of law in its sociological context. Rather, he poses the role of law in society and sees how it plays the role thus ascribed to it: and to do this he uses an engineering analogy. This practically explains why it is accurate to say that he considered jurisprudence to be a 'technology'. It cannot be denied that Pound was intending to apply social science techniques and thought to jurisprudence. His influence as a leader in this field was great. He sets out a 'programme' for the sociological study of law, including the study of the actual social effects of legal institutions, precepts and doctrines; the study of the means of making legal precepts effective in action and the study of juridical method. This emphasis on studying what actually happens was similar to that found with the American Realist writers who wrote after Pound; this new emphasis created the impetus for the many – and useful – findings of socio-legal research in relatively recent years.

It is true to say that Pound did not have a complete sociological theory into which law fitted. He was not, therefore, a sociologist. He saw and explained law's position in society, its 'role' or job; his explanation might not find favour with sociologists because it is too simplistic and (more particularly) based on a now unfavourable consensus view of society, with law as one factor in holding that consensus together. Nevertheless, Pound clearly saw law as a 'social science'. The lack of theoretical underpinning does not diminish this fact. I would go further and say that the emphasis on sociological techniques in studying day-to-day law encouraged by Pound and resulting in many recent socio-legal surveys has been of more real and direct value than the considerable theorising that has gone on under the label of 'legal sociology'.

We can say that though Pound does not see jurisprudence through the eyes of a sociologist, he does see it as a social science: he does see that law should be considered with the tools and from the viewpoint of a social scientist. The first part of the quotation must be rejected as inaccurate. Is it correct to say that he sees jurisprudence as a 'technology'?

Certainly the language and analogies that he uses suggest that this is indeed the case. Law is 'social engineering' designed to minimise the 'friction and waste' from the process of balancing the interests which compete in a society. Law then is seen as a 'technology', a means by which society can achieve the balancing of interests required. This is functional jurisprudence; it rests, as I have pointed out, on a consensus model of society which sees law as a cohesive (rather than divisive) force.

Pound devotes much space to this theory of competing interests on their different levels, to the balancing process and to the jural postulates which are to be used in cases of conflict. Much has been written and said about the meaning and force of what he says. Pound has provoked much controversy. What is, however, clear is that Pound's view of law is that it is a tool whereby this balancing process is carried out. The study of law is therefore a 'technology', in the sense of a study of a complex tool and its efficiency in performing a given task.

Contrary to the quotation, Pound saw jurisprudence not as a social science rather than a technology, but as both a social science and a technology.

QUESTION TWO

Evaluate Weber's analysis of the relationship between law and capitalism.

Written by the Editor

General Comment

Quite a general question on the work of Weber. The evaluation should cover both the strengths and weaknesses of his work.

Skeleton Solution

Capitalism – rational legal order – formally rational legal systems – Marxism – economic factors – class instrumentalism – legitimate authority – limitations of theory – England – relevance today.

Suggested Solution

Max Weber sought to understand and explain the distinctive characteristics of modern Western society. In doing so he was the first theorist to develop a comprehensive sociology of law. For him the most important feature of Western society was capitalism. He believed that a rational legal order was crucial to the development of capitalism in Western society. In assessing Weber's exposition it must be remembered that he was writing over 100 years ago, so that his 'modern' Western society was very different to ours. It is thus proposed to analyse his account of law and capitalism in three stages: as a theory in its own right; as a response to the writings of Marx and Engels; and as a theory in relation to Western society today.

Weber divided up the characteristics of a legal system as follows: a legal system characterised by irrationality (ie failure to apply general rules or principles) might be formally irrational or substantively irrational. The former description applies where decisions are made on the basis of tests beyond the control of human reasoning, such as trial by ordeal. The latter description applies where cases are merely decided individually on their own merits. Similarly, rational legal systems may be formally or substantively rational. A legal system is substantively rational when guided by principles other than law itself, such as morals. Only in formally rational legal systems are 'rules expressed by the use of abstract concepts created by legal thought itself and conceived of as constituting a complete system' (Lloyd, *An Introduction to Jurisprudence*). Weber claimed that such legal systems are a characteristic of Western developed society.

It is on the basis of this analysis that Weber rejected the Marxist view. He did not accept that law and the state was determined by economic factors – the relations of production. Instead, economic forces are just one of many factors; the growth of bureaucracy, for example, is highly important. Weber also rejected the Marxist version of 'class instrumentalism'. He spoke of legitimate authority rather than class domination: 'authority strives for acceptance not submission'. Legitimate authority is subdivided into three types: traditional, charismatic and legal-rational. The latter is central to Weber's account of law and its relationship to capitalism. Because there is a system of rationally made laws in developed society which stipulate the circumstances in which power may be exercised, that power is legitimate. Obedience is thus owed to the legal system rather than the person wielding the power. In making these points one might note the similarities between Weber and Hart on obligation to obey the law.

There is no doubting the richness of Weber's writings, both in sociological and jurisprudential terms generally, and in relation to his account of law and the modern capitalist society in particular. Furthermore, much of what he said was an effective response to the writings of Marx and Engels. But his theory is subject to limitations. Weber himself acknowledged problems with the example of England. Although his position has been defended, there is at least ambiguity in his assertion on the one hand that formal rational law assists the development of capitalism and his recognition on the other that capitalism emerged in England during a period of highly irrational law. Another limitation of Weber is that he was writing over 100 years ago: one might question the relevance of his response to 'traditional' Marxism today, for example. Despite these and other criticisms levelled at Weber, his analysis of the relationship between law and capitalism still provides much that is informative and thought-provoking.

QUESTION THREE

Examine the difference between sociological jurisprudence and the sociology of law.

University of London LLB Examination
(for External Students) Jurisprudence and Legal Theory June 1983 Q6

General Comment

It will be important to ensure that a comparison is actually undertaken. It would be all too easy to offer little more than a descriptive account of the studies of Pound and Durkheim.

Skeleton Solution

Techniques of social science – sociological factors in law – many concerns identical – Pound – Durkheim – distinction – research fields – chronological differences.

Suggested Solution

The growth in literature and thought on the relationship between law and society has been a marked feature of jurisprudence since the latter part of the nineteenth century. On a simplistic level, the 'sociological approach' can be split into two component parts: sociological jurisprudence and the sociology of law (or legal sociology). Both these components share many views and ideas – the importance of harnessing the techniques of social science in the legal area, the importance of sociological factors in law, the rejection of 'formalism' and scepticism about legal rules, and so on – but they are divided by others. It is not, as we shall see, possible to totally distinguish the two; basically, 'sociological jurisprudence' covers studies of how society affects law, and 'sociology of law' studies how law fits into society. The former takes law as an autonomous institution (even a necessary institution) in society, and concentrates on law and the role it plays in society and how that role affects it; the latter sees law as one among social institutions, and questions its role in society, and whether traditional legal rules and concepts adequately explain that. Rather than a distinct break between the two, we should see a spectrum of opinion between the starting points of law and society.

In fact, one of the main ways in which a theory is placed into one or other camp is the label it puts on itself, or at least the label put on its author. So Pound, Ihering, Ehrlich – all jurists – and the American Realists, several of whom were judges, of course, are seen as 'sociological jurisprudents', whereas sociologists who turn their attention to law, such as Weber, Durkheim are seen as 'legal sociologists'. This in spite of the fact that many of the concerns are identical. Both Pound and Durkheim, for example, consider the purpose or role law plays in society. Pound sees it as a form of 'social engineering', producing a balance from the interests which the law-making process weighs: judges' decisions balance these interests using 'jural postulates' to attach appropriate weight. Durkheim sees law as part of the cohesive matter of society, with repressive laws forming part of the bond of mechanical, homogenous societies, and restitutive laws part of heteregenous, organic societies. Many other views on the function of law have been expressed, on both sides of the divide.

However, we must not see this identity of interest as denying the reality of the distinction. Even in those views of the function of law in the last paragraph, we can I think see a different emphasis, as Pound looks to see what judges are doing with an eye on the social sanction, and Durkheim clearly using law as a support to his theory of mechanical and organic societies. (In fact, Durkheim is considering what can be seen as a classic sociology of law question: do different types of society have different sorts of law?) The different emphasis can also be seen as one looks at the research fields. The sociological approach as a whole stresses the importance of research as we noted above; not all sociological writing in law is about grand theory. The research on particular matters is divisible into the two strands of thought. On the one hand, there are what may be called 'socio-legal' studies, on areas of the judicial process etc. Attempting to see how the law works in practice – how legal aid, or bail, or sentencing, etc is decided, and whether the practice accords to the theory. This work, as Lloyd points out, is not related to any wider view of society, to any theory on society: rather, it concentrates on the law and legal system. Similar to these are the studies of judicial behaviouralism which follow the impetus of American Realism. On the other hand, some research into individual laws, etc actually tries to explain the social (and economic) context of that law: explaining how laws emerge or have emerged in the past from their backgrounds. Unlike in socio-legal studies, the focus here is on the fact of society which led to a specific piece of legislation.

Apart from labelling theorists in one or other camp, we can also, then, differentiate theories and pieces of research by considering where their main thrust and emphasis lies. Another aspect of the difference between sociological jurisprudence and the sociology of law is chronological: many writers have suggested that sociology of law will – or has – emerged from and after sociological jurisprudence. Hunt's *Sociological Movement in Law* identifies that movement as including the sociological jurisprudence of Pound etc, the American Realist Movement and the historically prior pioneer legal sociologists, Weber and Durkheim; it is followed after the Second World War by 'sociology and law'. Hunt is not impressed by the present output of the new 'school', no one (in his view) having yet produced a general theory in sociology or law to match Weber's. Selznick's developmental model has three stages rather than two; the first is the age of the pioneers, and the grand theories of Pound et al; the second the age of method, where jurists will learn sociological skills and sociologists will assist jurists in investigation of relevant questions; the third is the era of sociology of law, when questions such as law's function and the meaning of justice and legality will be answered.

In terms of our question, sociological jurisprudence would cover the first and still be involved in the second stage; while the sociologists in that second stage will be doing the sociological research referred to above. The third stage is when present research into sociology of law results in general theories; some do exist today (apart from Weber's): Selznick himself, Parsons and Bredemeier for example, have produced such theories. As this third stage takes over, the importance of the distinction considered in the question will be greatly diminished.

QUESTION FOUR

'Where the lawyer or the legal scholar talks about rights and expectations he does so with normative intentions. He purports to give directives to clients or to legal functionaries and he intends his analysis to form the basis of decisions, ultimately of action. The sociologist, on the other hand, uses the same terms without any directly normative purpose in an attempt to describe, reveal and explain.' (Vilhelm Aubert, *Sociology of Law*.) Discuss.

University of London LLB Examination
(for External Students) Jurisprudence and Legal Theory June 1985 Q5

General Comment

The following more complex 'quotation question' uses sociology as a starting point for a discussion of broader issues. Such questions are useful for the student as they demonstrate how to approach more difficult questions: by thinking first, high marks can be achieved.

Skeleton Solution

Normative statements – rules – committed or detached normative statements – Raz – lawyer – sociologist – Cotterrell – Hart – Ehrlich – common normative vocabulary.

Suggested Solution

Normative statements form a readily discernible part of social intercourse. Such statements, as Aubert correctly points out, are frequently associated with lawyers or legal scholars. Thus, where a lawyer advises that X has a right to inherit under Y's will or that he has a legitimate expectation so to do, such a statement is normative.

It would be a mistake, however, to confine normative statements to lawyers or legal scholars. The key to identifying a normative statement lies in the recognition that such a right or expectation is conferred pursuant to a rule. Rights and expectations do not exist 'in vacuo' but are the intended consequence of the enabling rule in question, and it is this intention of the rule that determines its normative character. Thus, in the above example, the rule in question is that the named beneficiary of a duly attested will has a right to inherit under that will.

Normative statements are curtailed by any rule-orientated activity. The most common activity of this type is the playing of games. The chess player who acknowledges that the bishop can only move diagonally across the board does so in recognition of the relevant rule of chess. Equally the footballer who accepts that the ball may only be handled under certain specified conditions does so for similar reasons. Both are making normative statements.

It is important to distinguish between the types of normative statement. Adopting Joseph Raz's formulation, normative statements may be said to be either 'committed' or 'detached'. 'Committed' normative statements are the most common. The maker of such a statement accepts that the rule in question is 'binding' on him. The rule may be binding in one of two ways. Firstly, it may be binding as a standard of conduct to which he must adhere. Thus the participant in a sport accepts that he is bound by the rules of the particular game he plays. Secondly, it may be binding as a standard to be applied in evaluating the conduct of those participating in the rule-based activity in question. The rule states that a footballer may not handle the ball is the same rule that the referee must apply in determining whether a free kick or a penalty should be awarded.

In a legal context, rules of law prescribe standards of conduct just as rules of a game do. Those subject to the law accept that legal rules are binding upon them in the conduct of their daily lives. Those same legal rules are binding upon the judiciary in the resolution of disputes and therefore form the basis of judicial adjudication.

The maker of a 'detached' normative statement, by contrast, does not accept that the rule in question is binding upon him. His statement describes in normative language a rule-governed activity from the point of view of those who accept the rules in question without himself sharing that view. Thus, a non vegetarian may say of vegetarians that the eating of meat is forbidden, whereas in the mouth of a vegetarian such a statement would be 'committed'. Both statements are normative – the difference lies in the intention of the maker of the statement.

A solicitor advising a client does so from the 'detached' point of view. Returning to the example used above, a solicitor who advises his client that the latter has a 'right' to inherit under Y's will is stating the application of the relevant legal rule without, of course, being subject to that rule himself. As Aubert correctly points out, such a statement may well also form a basis for action: in this case, an application by the client to be declared a beneficiary under Y's will. In this context Aubert's analysis accords closely with Raz's general theory of practical reasoning. It is a central tenet of Raz's theory that rules may be viewed as reasons for action. Thus, if there is a rule that 0 then that rule is a reason for doing 0. Perhaps the clearest example of rules, forming the basis of actions, or more especially of decisions, is that of a barrister making submissions in court. The barrister describes in normative language the rules of law applicable to the case before the court, with the aspiration that the judge will use those rules as the basis of his decision.

The legal scholar also talks about rights and experiences from the detached point of view. The textbook writer, for example, is concerned to state the law applicable in a given country as at the date of publication. His written statements are truly detached in that his task is purely descriptive without moral or other commitment to the rules of law which form the subject of his book. Indeed, he may violently disagree with those rules particularly if they are of a legal system to whose political régime he objects. His task is simply to state the law as it is.

Where Aubert's analysis may be subjected to criticism lies in his ascription to the legal scholar of the same normative intention as the lawyer. The lawyer intends his statements to form the basis of action or decision but the same cannot be said of the legal scholar (though he no doubt intends his analysis to be instructive). Take the example of the 'novel' point. The legal scholar who subjects a recent judicial authority to sophisticated analysis may reveal that the rule embodied in the precedent has a previously unsuspected application. Such a statement would still be normative as it describes the intended consequence of the rule but the legal scholar's intentions in making the statement would differ from those of a barrister making the same point in court. The latter would intend the statement to form the basis of judicial adjudication whereas the legal scholar may wish to highlight the absurdity of the rule or just make a clever point.

This example of the legal scholar illustrates the confusion in Aubert's analysis. A rule is normative in character if its intent is to form the basis of decision or action. Statements about rules, whether detached or committed, are normative in so far as they recognise this intended consequence of rules. But the 'intention' of the makers of such statements may vary and will not necessarily accord with the intention of the rules themselves.

That said, Aubert provides a useful insight into the lawyer's viewpoint and a ready basis of comparison with that of the sociologist. At a general level normative statements made by lawyers contain an implicit recognition of the law's claim to supremacy. Whilst a lawyer or indeed a legal scholar may disagree with a particular legal rule, he has no doubt concerning its intended effect. The law's primary concern is the governance of those under its sovereignty through the medium of rules, and lawyers (and to a lesser extent legal scholars) form an integral part of the machinery of government.

Not so the sociologist. He is, of course, concerned with the art of governance through the medium of rules but only to the extent that it is relevant to his broader enquiry viz, the nature of society. The sociologist's enquiry will therefore encompass the use of normative statements but it is not central to his purpose.

At this point it becomes pertinent to demarcate the respective fields of enquiry of the lawyer or legal scholar and the sociologist. Contrary to Aubert's claim, both are involved in a descriptive enterprise but the difference is that the lawyer's enquiry terminates at a comprehensive description of law. For the sociologist, a description of law from the lawyer's point of view may afford a starting point for further investigation of social phenomena.

The lawyer's point of view is particularly evidenced in the work of Eugen Ehrlich. Ehrlich identified the lawyer's primary concern as the resolution of legal disputes by the courts. His claim was that this constituted too insular a view of the social phenomenon of law. In the first place, Ehrlich argued, the resolution of legal disputes was often effected without recourse to the established legal institutions. Secondly, it was not true to suggest (as lawyers did) that the rules which governed the institutionalised dispute-settlement procedure were necessarily the same rules that regulated people's daily lives. In short, Ehrlich's view was that 'law' was a normative system embracing not only the courts but much wider vistas of social life.

In this context Ehrlich draws a distinction between 'norms for decision' and the 'living law'. The former may be categorised as lawyers' law, whereas the 'living law' consists of those norms governing conduct which lie wholly outside the ambit of the courts. The latter are regarded as 'binding' by those subject to them, just as norms for decisions are.

Empirical research has borne out Ehrlich's distinction. In the field of industrial relations shop floor practices are often regarded as rigid rules even though no legal sanction is attached. For example, the withdrawal of time allotted to the workforce by management for washing up has prompted industrial action even though it could not seriously be argued that such a withdrawal was illegal.

Ehrlich's point therefore is a good one. In the diverse range of human activity, lawyer's law plays but a minor role. Disputes arise every day in the governance of human affairs but recourse is rarely had to the official dispute settlement machinery. The reasons why this should be so are as varied as the activities in question. This field of enquiry is properly the sociologist's domain. As Aubert points out, the sociologist is concerned to explain why the law plays the part it does in human affairs. For this reason 'law', however it may be defined, provides a platform for further investigation.

The lawyer or legal scholar on the other hand, is not concerned primarily with the reasons why law plays the special role that it does in human affairs. He is merely concerned to know what that rule is. Thus, while the lawyer and sociologist may share a common normative vocabulary, they do so for different reasons.

Chapter 5
Realist Theories

A AMERICAN REALISM

5.1   Introduction

5.2   Key points

5.3   Questions and suggested solutions

B SCANDINAVIAN REALISM

5.4   Introduction

5.5   Key points

5.6   Questions and suggested solutions

A AMERICAN REALISM

5.1 Introduction

American Realism can be seen as a reaction to the theoretical school of formalism. Realism attempts to be more pragmatic than theoretical; the important issue is how law works in practice.

5.2 Key points

Rule-scepticism

a) There is more to law than the logical application of rules.

b) Rules are merely predictions of what the court will do.

c) Factors such as the background and upbringing of judges are more important in the settling of disputes than rules.

d) Llewellyn and his 'law-jobs' theory.

Fact-scepticism

a) The certainty of prediction which Llewellyn espouses is impossible in relation to lower courts.

b) The fact-finding process is inherently uncertain.

c) Jerome Frank.

Jurimetrics and judicial behaviouralism

a) Jurimetrics is the scientific investigation of legal problems using computers and symbolic logic.

b) Judicial behaviouralism involves research into the patterns of judges' behaviour (see J A G Griffith's *The Politics of the Judiciary*).

c) Note the connections with American Realism.

5.3 Questions and suggested solutions

QUESTION ONE

Discuss critically Llewellyn's 'law-jobs' theory.

University of London LLB Examination
(for External Students) Jurisprudence and Legal Theory June 1987 Q9

General Comment

A straightforward critical analysis of one theorist is called for here.

Skeleton Solution

Llewellyn – Realist – rule sceptic – identify the law jobs – functional analysis – ignores dimension of power – period style – fact sceptics criticism – over generalisations.

Suggested Solution

Llewellyn, one of the mainstream American Realist Rule Sceptics saw the basic function of law to be twofold. That it aid the survival of the group and that it engage in the quest for justice, efficacy and a richer life. To assist the law in fulfilling these functions the institution of law has a number of law jobs.

He saw an institution in terms of an organised activity which is built around doing a job. The important aim is to ensure that these jobs are well performed. These law jobs are then the basic functions which the law has to perform. He lists these law jobs in *My Philosophy of Law* as:

a) the disposition of trouble cases which he likened to garage repair work with the continuous effect of the remaking of the order of that society;

b) the preventative channelling of conduct and expectations so as to avoid trouble and looks not only at new legislation but at its purpose;

c) the allocation of authority and the arrangement of procedures which mark action as being authoritative;

d) the net organisation of society as a whole so as to provide integration, direction and incentive;

e) juristic method as used in law and the settlement of disputes.

The analysis of these is found in his *The Normative, the Legal and the Law Jobs: The Problem of Juristic Method* (1940) in which he identifies the bare bones aspect of law jobs and that these law jobs are implicit in the concept of a group. The first of these he sees as the most important yet he does not tell us about their interrelationship. He suggests that these law jobs are universal, yet this quest for universality has, as Lloyd and Freeman observe, led Llewellyn to concepts of a high level of abstraction.

Llewellyn was concerned to find the best way to handle 'legal tools to law job ends'. Although he suggests that his framework provides a general framework for the functional analysis of law, he suffers from a defect common to other functionalists in that he overlooks the dimensions and structure of power.

In his concept of juristic method developed in his *Common Law Tradition* he outlines his theory of craft. Here he identifies his period style of judicial reasoning. He identifies two polar positions within this period style and says that judges will fall within that spectrum. At the one pole is his Grand Style in which judges are less strictly self constrained by the rules of precedent and in his Formal Style the judge considers himself bound by the rules of precedent entirely. In the Grand Style the judge will follow what Llewellyn calls a 'situation sense' in order to ensure that a reasonable result is achieved. By identifying a judge's propensity then it may be possible to achieve the aim of the American Realists; namely the prediction of the outcome of the case. If we know what approach a judge takes we may be able to predict how he will approach a particular dispute.

Llewellyn has made an important point, namely that law is not just about rules and that the prediction of the outline of cases is an important and useful function. However, law is not solely concerned with the prediction of what the court will do about a particular dispute. It is also about behavioural guidance to individuals.

A fellow American Realist, although from the fact sceptic aspect, Judge Frank took the view that Llewellyn's work was focused on the appeal courts and took no real account of the work of the trial courts where it was not the application of the rule that was important in predicting the outcome but the uncertainty about the fact-finding process that was the key.

A strong criticism levelled at both the rule sceptics and the fact sceptics is that they engage in over-generalisations in order to make a valid point. Furthermore the judges do use rules to explain their decisions and the judge is judge by virtue of a rule that says he will decide disputes. These are relegated to virtual unimportance in Llewellyn's law jobs theory. To this extent that analysis is defective.

QUESTION TWO

'Realism on its own cannot provide the basis for a rounded theory of law.'

Do you agree?

University of London LLB Examination
(for External Students) Jurisprudence and Legal Theory June 1998 Q11

General Comment

Note that a question like this asks you to be engaged in what you are doing. The question does not require you to merely regurgitate your notes, but to tailor your material to suit the question. Ask yourself: what is a good theory of law? Is it one which only considers that the law is always judge-made?

Skeleton Solution

Teachings of American Realism – rule and fact scepticism schools – ideas of personalities of the movement – criticisms of the American Realism theory of law – conclusion.

Suggested Solution

The American Realist movement is anti-formalist and against any legal discourse which is not pragmatic. To the movement, a social phenomenon like law must be empirically centred and directed to the search for solutions to the practical problems in society. The image of the American Realist movement is one of a movement which is sceptical to regard rules as the 'be all and end all' of the legal system. This idea that law does not consist of rules historically made, but of the decisions of courts, is the key to understanding the position of the American Realists.

There are two schools in the American Realist movement – the rule sceptics and the fact sceptics. The rule sceptics are those who say that legal uncertainty is caused by the 'paper' rules of law, and who seek to look for uniformity and consistency in actual judicial behaviour. The fact sceptics, on the other hand, are those who believe that the unpredictability of court decisions rests mainly in the difficulty of discovering facts. The idea that even sound points of law often give way to decisions on the facts is presented by the movement to mean that courts can steer the law to fit what they perceive to be the merits of each case.

The personalities in the rule sceptic school include Justice Oliver Wendell Holmes (Justice Oliver Holmes, *The Path of the Law* (Collected Legal Papers, 1897)) and John Gray (John Gray, *The Nature and Sources of Law* (1902)). To Justice Holmes, the life of the law has not been logic: it has been experience. His view is that law is a prediction of what the courts will decide. He believes that rules laid down historically do not decide cases, but rather the rules laid down by courts as they decide cases form the law.

He argues that the true science of the law consists in the establishment of its postulates from within, upon accurately measured social desires instead of tradition.

Another rule sceptic who also echoed Justice Holmes regarding uncertainty in 'paper' rules is Gray, who says that statute is not law until interpreted by a court; it is merely a source of law. It seems strange that anyone would say an Act of Parliament is not law but only a source of law. If we take a look at s1 Theft Act 1968 we find a clear definition of the offence. To Gray, s1 of the Act is not law at all. It is no wonder that Cordoza, a critic of American Realism, says if Gray's thesis were to be accepted it would seem that 'law never is, but always about to be'.

The leading light in the American Realist movement is Karl Llewellyn (Karl Llewellyn, *The Common Tradition* (1960)) who saw law as an institution built around doing a job or a 'cluster' of jobs. The cluster of jobs an institution performs is to:

a) make group survival possible;

b) aid the search for justice, efficiency and richer life.

For the law jobs to be handled correctly Llewellyn developed the idea of 'craft' as a solution. A 'craft' is a 'know-how' among a body of specialists who are engaged in performing certain jobs within an institution. The important craft called juristic method is one such 'craft'. To Llewellyn there is a reasonable degree of prediction ('reckonability') in the appellate courts and there are a cluster of factors which make this possible. This cluster of factors includes the existence of law-conditioned officials; personnel who are all trained and experienced lawyers; the pressure of legal doctrine and known doctrinal techniques; the responsibility of the judiciary for justice; and a known bench and the general period style.

According to Llewellyn, the period style fluctuates between the formal style in real grounds, where decisions are hidden behind rationalisation, and the 'grand style', where the judges know that the roots of the law are in social needs. Judges do not slavishly follow precedent; their judgments try to relate the rules of law to the needs of the society that they have discovered. There is an appeal to reason in the grand style.

The extreme personality in the American Realist movement was Jerome Frank. He was a fact sceptic who said that in the majority of cases decided in the lower courts rules have little effect, in that courts are affected by issues like bias, beliefs and demeanour of witness, rendering the rules nothing more than pretty playthings. For any lay person, therefore, Frank says that with respect to any particular set of facts, the law is a decision of a court in so far as that decision affects that particular person. So until a court has passed a decision on those facts, no law on that subject is yet in existence.

This is a pretty cynical view of law. It beggars belief that anybody would disagree that the Companies Act 1985 is law. For example, if a person wants to form a new company he is given the procedures to follow to have the new company incorporated by the Act. There is no court procedure involved for a judge to give a decision. American

Realism can be held hostage to fortune. What is there to stop anyone saying that the decision of the Realist judge does not constitute a precedent to be followed in the future? What about existing laws which appoint the judges, establish courts and confer power on judges when appointed? Are they not law? Are the laws which establish the jurisdiction of each court not law?

We would join J W Harris (J W Harris, *Legal Philosophies* (2nd edn, 1997)) and ask if legal science is merely a science of prediction; what are judges supposed to do? Indeed, lawyers may predict judicial decisions but judges cannot. They must justify their decisions. Another point Harris makes is that rules matter both inside and outside the court room. Discrediting this belief will lead to cynicism about the law. This will in turn produce pessimism about the utility of law reform. Indeed, why bother changing the law? All we need to do is abolish Parliament and substitute people with the appropriate prejudices and biases. Judges will have absolute discretion because the rules to guide them are irrelevant. They do not need to assure themselves that they must have a shared and unified official acceptance of the rule of recognition of the system. After all, the rule of recognition is a pretty plaything.

This cynical view of law needs to be strongly repudiated. Law does not only concern the common law – the judge-made law. John Austin campaigned for codification because the common law alone does not provide a rounded view of law. Statutes made by Parliament are superior to the judge-made law. By ignoring this fact and claiming that statutes are only predictions about law, the American Realist school is in danger of establishing a false doctrine.

QUESTION THREE

'The prophecies of what the courts will do in fact are what I mean by law.' (Holmes)

What are the difficulties with this concept of law?

University of London LLB Examination
(for External Students) Jurisprudence and Legal Theory June 2000 Q6

General Comment

This question calls for a critique of the American Realist movement in order to provide an understanding of the distinctive features of their approach and their contribution. You should certainly explore their emphasis upon the judges and their interest in prediction, but you should also appreciate other themes, such as their opposition to black letter law and their interest in law in action.

Skeleton Solution

A diverse approach – revolt against formalism – emphasis on the courts – prediction techniques – law in action – fact and rule scepticism – the bad man technique – law jobs – grand and formal style of judges – Holmes – Llewellyn – critique.

Suggested Solution

Holmes was one of the leading advocates of American Realism. As a movement it is not easy to characterise as it has a range of features. It was, for example, similar to both analytical positivism and sociological jurisprudence. It sought a science of law based on a study of law in action – a very empirical approach. It engaged in a revolt against formalism as seen in abstract thinking – a desire to get to the facts. It was a reaction to black letter law approaches in which you apply legal principles to hypothetical fact situations, ie answering problem questions. It emphasises the role of judges and wants to be able to predict judicial behaviour – this aspect is clear from the quotation. The emphasis on the courts is made more understandable by noting that in the United States the courts have more power than in the United Kingdom. For example, the Supreme Court can declare legislation unconstitutional. Having said that the work of Dworkin does not leave the judges with much room for manoeuvre. The American Realists investigated the influences upon judicial decisions and questioned the impact of formal rules upon such decisions. Some were rule sceptics (keen to find out what the real rules were) whilst others were fact sceptics (they wanted to cast doubt on the ability of the courts to find facts). A recent manifestation of their thought has been jurimetrics, which uses computers to predict the decisions of the courts.

Llewellyn, another leading American Realist, identified some further features of the Realist approach. That it is concerned with the law in flux, ie its dynamic features with the judges as law makers: that law is a means to an end. Society can be in flux at a greater pace than law perhaps leading to a mismatch between them. They adhere to a separation of is and ought for the purposes of empirical observation, ie a value free approach, but they still have an interest in legal reform. There is scepticism as to traditional legal concepts and the impact of rules in court decisions. They stress the evaluation of law in terms of its effects. They use rationalisation in relation to law. Also important is a need to appreciate the differences in the type and importance of rules.

Gray was a forerunner of the approach and he emphasised the importance of the judges and the courts. Law is what the courts lay down though the judges are directed to certain sources for their law. Holmes wanted an objective approach that was not based on moral ideas. He saw the law as being the prophecies of what the courts will do in fact. The judges are presented as law makers. Holmes was a rule sceptic. He points to the flexibility in rules and he listed 64 techniques of precedent that provide for much uncertainty. Holmes invites us to take the fundamental question: what constitutes the law? His answer is in the following terms. You will find some text writers telling you that it is something different from what is decided by the courts of Massachusetts or England, that it is a system of reason, that it is a deduction from principles of ethics or admitted axioms or whatnot, which may or may not coincide with the decisions. But if we take the view of our friend the bad man we shall find that he does not care two straws for the axioms or deductions, but that he wants to know what the courts will do.

Frank stressed the uncertainty of the law and suggested that all the litigation that takes place indicates the large amount of uncertainty that in fact exists. He said that law only exists when judges make decisions. He pointed out the need to recognise the important role played by the lower courts. As a fact sceptic he in particular disputed the ability of the lower courts to uncover accurately the facts of cases. He points to the problems of the process, such as the unreliability of witnesses and the perception or lack of it on the part of the jury members. He also pointed to the role of personality and predjudice in judicial decisions. Frank challenged traditional legal assumptions, such as the following. That the personal element in the judicial process (witnesses, lawyers, jurors and judges) should not and usually does not have much effect on either legal rights or court decisions. That legal rules are the dominant factor in decision-making. That if the actual facts of two cases are the same, usually the decisions in those cases will be identical.

Llewellyn saw law as an institution which has law jobs. Examples are the preventative channelling of conduct and expectations and the allocation of authority and authoritative procedures. He was interested in the factors that influence judicial decisions and saw law as being what the officials do about disputes. He diluted this latter idea in his later writing. He developed the notion of grand and formal styles of judge. The former is more flexible, adventurous and less rule-bound. He contrasted the law in the books with the law in action. With Hoebel he carried out anthropological investigations into the law ways of the Cheyenne Indians. He used the case study method.

As with most other approaches they made an important point and over emphasised it, though they pointed to the weaknesses of other thinkers along the way. They over emphasised the role of the courts. Most people have little or nothing to do with the courts. They told us too little about the influences on judicial decisions. The judges may well feel bound to the law in different ways – Ross and Hart explore this. Llewelyn came up with only two styles of judge; as with other matters this is an oversimplification. They have had influence: perhaps we are all Realists now in that we know that law has a social context. On the other hand the law in the books does appear to be very useful. Generally the approach failed in that much remained as it was before as seen in the traditional style of legal education and its continued emphasis upon the appellate courts' decisions. We need to consider that perhaps there is more certainty as to the rules than they suggest – if they concentrate on the cases that go to court they will only ever see the cases that have been viewed as problematic; the certain rules are the least likely to go to court. In many cases the law (and indeed often the facts of criminal cases) may not be in issue. It is also possible to take a more positive view. For example, it is clear that they influenced such as the critical legal studies movement and the feminists and post modernists. Singer suggests that legal Realism has fundamentally altered our conceptions of legal reasoning and of the relationship between law and society. The Realists were, he believes, remarkably successful both in changing the terms of legal discourse and in undermining the idea of a self-regulating market system. He sees all major current schools of jurisprudential thought as products of legal Realism. Horwitz is similarly positive in his assessment. He sees the most important legacy of Realism in its challenge to the orthodox claim that legal thought was separate and autonomous from moral and political discourse. Their attack on deductive legal reasoning constituted, he argues, the Realists' most original and lasting contributions to legal thought.

B SCANDINAVIAN REALISM

5.4 Introduction

The Scandinavian school of Realism was more philosophical than the American school, with a broader interest in the legal system as a whole. The Scandinavian Realists rejected the 'metaphysical' and subscribed to the view that a statement was only meaningful if it could be proved by empirical evidence. The student might like to consider how much of the Scandinavian Realists' theories were based on empirical evidence. The psychological was used to explain laws; the normative effect of law exists as a psychological effect, and concepts like right and duty are explained as psychological feelings. In studying Scandinavian Realism the student should be astute enough to note the similarities and differences in comparison with American Realism.

5.5 Key points

Hagerstrom

a) Hagerstrom is regarded as the 'spiritual father' to the Scandinavian Realists.

b) The concepts of 'right' and 'duty' only have reality in terms of their actual effect in society.

Olivecrona

a) The legal rule has two elements – the 'ideatum' and the 'imperatum'.

b) The 'ideatum' is the conduct laws are meant to produce.

c) The 'imperatum' is the way the ideatum is expressed.

d) Olivecrona has been criticised for his lack of empirical research and for his overstatement of the importance of 'force' in the law.

Ross

a) Ross also attempts to use psychology to explain the normative effect of laws, but his explanation is superior to those of Hagerstrom and Olivecrona.

b) The similarities with Hart's *The Concept of Law* should be noted.

Is there a 'school' of Realism?

a) Both American and Scandinavian Realists tried to explain law in terms of 'cause and effect' and both emphasised research and empirical evidence.

b) Despite this, the Scandinavians concentrated on the verification of concepts like 'right' and 'duty' in a psychological way, whilst the Americans sought to show that legal decisions were not predictable if one merely looked at the logical application of legal rules.

c) The student should consider which, if either, of the American or Scandinavian brands of Realism is more convincing and illuminating.

5.6 Questions and suggested solutions

QUESTION ONE

'Kelsen and Olivecrona base their accounts of the nature of law on some kind of imperative element, but they differ very much in their basic conceptions of law as to the way in which the basic elements of law are to be arranged and explained in order to produce an adequate account of its nature.' (John Finch)

Discuss.

University of London LLB Examination
(for External Students) Jurisprudence and Legal Theory June 1983 Q9

General Comment

This question on Olivecrona calls for a comparison with Kelsen. Although this might seem a strange pairing, it provides a good exercise in thinking across topics.

Skeleton Solution

Legal rules as imperative – acceptance of constitution by officials – law as system of coercion – principal difference: why and how laws bind – but their arrangement of basic elements of law is closely comparable.

Suggested Solution

Finch's comment is incorrect. I hope to show that not only do Kelsen and Olivecrona agree as to an imperative element in law, they also show marked similarities in their discussions of the arrangements of a legal system. That there are important differences is clear; using the terms of the question it is only slightly oversimplifying to say that the argument I shall put forward is that in giving an account of the nature of law, they arrange the same basic elements of law in a similar way, but that they explain those elements differently.

They certainly do share the conception of legal rules as imperative. Moreover, they both suggest that this imperative element is unusual in that it derives not from the wish of any person or persons necessarily, but from the proper procedures of the system. Unlike Austin (criticised by both for supporting this element of a sovereign's volition 'commanding'), Olivecrona calls rules of law 'independent imperatives', and Kelsen 'depsychologised commands' to express this idea.

They have more in common than just that. For a start both see law's effect as emanating from acceptance of the constitution (authorising the creation of the laws) by officials. For Olivecrona, legislation is effective because it passes the procedure for promulgation of legislation authorised by the constitution. Officials of the system are interested to see that the necessary formalities have been carried out (although they are often prepared to accept the work of other officials); individual citizens are just concerned to follow rules given the appellation 'law' by the authorities. Legislators then, by virtue of their office under an accepted constitution, pass laws by following the rules thereof. Turning to Kelsen, his approach is more complex, it is true, but the basic points are there: legislation is valid, for him (we leave the difference between his 'validity' and Olivecrona's 'effective' until later; of both at this stage perhaps we should say the legislation 'takes effect') when it is passed following the procedure laid down by a higher norm, which eventually (in a chain of such norms) is authorised by the basic norm. This 'basic norm' is the presumption – by jurists – that the first constitution is valid: this first constitution in turn validates later constitutions including the present one; and that in turn lays down procedures for law-making by (inter alia, perhaps) the legislature. So, it is acceptance of the constitution (to put it simply) that accords effect to the legislation passed by the authorised procedure. The similarity to Olivecrona is striking (although Olivecrona concentrates on officials and on jurists – including judges, presumably).

Acceptance of constitution, proper procedure, legal rules. We have seen that for Olivecrona and Kelsen these rules resulting from the system are independent imperatives; we must now look at their joint view that law is a system of coercion, and that individual laws have coercive sanctions attached. Olivecrona says the law needs an organisation prepared to back up its rules by overwhelming force if necessary; law is properly seen as rules about the exercise of that force, and therefore as primarily addressed to officials informing them when to use such force. His 'primary' rules are to officials, and only the 'secondary' rules inform subjects how to behave; sometimes the latter are implicit, as when the legislation simply imposes a punishment for certain conduct. In the same way, Kelsen sees the law as a coercive system, and laws as including a coercive element. As with Olivecrona (particularly in his later work), he does see that the aim is to prescribe individuals' conduct by use of the sanction; again he considers that the 'primary norm' is the one that orders the sanction and so is addressed to officials; the norm which tells the subjects of the law what to do is secondary. This view of a law can be criticised, since it emphasises coercion and punishment rather than obedience, and particularly obedience out of respect for the law, not fear. Further, it seems to distort the function of those laws which confer powers on individuals and officials. These are seen by Kelsen as part of chains of norms with a sanction at the end (so, for example, the power to legislate is exercised to bring about general norms; the power to contract when used satisfied one of the conditions for the stipulation of a sanction – ie danger – by a judge); by Olivecrona, even civil laws are enforced sometimes by fines and imprisonment, and ultimately all civil laws – including contract etc – are backed by sanctions.

We can say then that Kelsen and Olivecrona's arrangement of the basic elements of law is similar: acceptance of a constitution causes acceptance of laws passed in the proper manner; both the system and these laws are coercive (Olivecrona possibly less insistent on each law being coercive), and the laws are primarily addressed to officials to stipulate sanctions.

However, Kelsen and Olivecrona's theories are by no means the same; the principal difference being the explanation of law – on the question of why and how laws bind. A foreshadowing of this was mentioned earlier, with Kelsen's 'valid' as against Olivecrona's 'effective'. Olivecrona followed the Scandinavian line of thought rejecting duties, rights etc, as 'metaphysical entities'. They only corresponded to reality on a psychological level. A duty was a feeling of being bound; the binding quality of law – its normativity, or 'oughtness' could be explained only as an aspect of the world of cause and effect. Because the constitution was accepted, law-makers appointed under it when they passed laws 'played on the minds' of the subjects, who as a result felt bound to obey. (Once a subject was what one might call legally grown-up, this process happened automatically, without fear of sanctions playing a direct part.) Logically then there was no duty if the subject did not feel bound; although officials would still feel bound to punish him.

Kelsen's theory is based on law being normative, and therefore in language at least being distinct from the world of 'causality', of cause and effect, and rather in the world of 'imputation' (if X, then Y ought to happen', as against 'if X, then Y happens). In his legal systems, rules are 'norms', which are valid because authorised by superior norms. Rules passed by legislatures are valid because passed under proper procedures authorised by a still higher norm, a constitution. It follows from this that one 'ought' to obey a legal rule even if one does not feel bound; if a sanction is stipulated for not doing so, one is under a 'legal duty' irrespective of fear of the sanction. For the 'validity', the first constitution must be accepted (by presupposition of the basic norm) and the system must generally work: social factors do have a role.

It is clear then that Kelsen's explanation of the nature of law – in terms of normativity within a system following acceptance of it and its general effectiveness – is not the same as Olivecrona's explanation – in terms of the psychological effects produced by an acceptance of the constitution. This should not stop us realising that the order in which they arranged the basic elements of law is closely comparable.

QUESTION TWO

'The juristic task is to observe the facts of human behaviour including judicial and other official behaviour, in all the circumstances of particular cases, and to interpret them scientifically without preconceptions.' (Julius Stone) How adequately does this statement portray the function of Realist jurisprudence?

University of London LLB Examination
(for External Students) Jurisprudence and Legal Theory June 1984 Q7

General Comment

This question is aimed at Realism in general and calls for a consideration of whether there is a Realist 'school'.

Skeleton Solution

There are two 'schools': American Realism – 'the facts of human behaviour' – emphasis on courts – Scandinavian Realism – reject concept of normativity – 'cause and effect' – more theoretical – less research.

Suggested Solution

This is a narrow question, calling for an analysis of the function which the Realist writers considered their work to be fulfilling; for, while it is possible to criticise what they said, and even to criticise the function which they chose to attempt to fulfil, what the function was – and whether the quotation given adequately portrays it – is a factual question. There were, of course, two 'schools' of Realist jurisprudence, termed American Realism and Scandinavian Realism respectively. I will look at each in turn, analysing the quotation to see if it is an appropriate statement of the 'function' of the school.

First, then, American Realism. As the name implies, Realists see themselves as explaining the position as it really is. In terms of explaining the legal experience, this involved stripping away the myths – principally those surrounding the central importance of legal rules – and setting out the reality.

Clearly, the American Realists wanted to look at 'the facts of human behaviour', and in particular at the behaviour of judges. Llewellyn expressly limits himself in some of his work to the appellate courts, in fact. This limitation was attacked by Frank, who thought that it was unrealistic to see the law from the viewpoint of the appellate courts when real legal experience, in fact, occurs in the first instance courts. The emphasis on the courts can be seen from the definition of law in terms of predictions of judicial decisions in particular cases. The 'offshoot' of American Realism, judicial behaviouralism, studies of how judges behave, also follows from this emphasis. Having observed, the Realists saw it as their function to interpret. Llewellyn wrote much about models of judicial behaviour and explained why – in his view – most legal decisions could be predicted with a fair degree of certainty. Frank, on the other hand, denied that such certainty existed because (at first instance) the centrally important task of fact-finding was inherently uncertain. We can see that though the function – to observe and explain – was the same for both, the conclusions of Llewellyn and Frank often differ. It might well be said that Frank far more than Llewellyn was concerned with 'particular cases', since he concentrated on lower courts and not the more rarefied atmosphere of appellate courts making legal – as against factual – decisions.

The scientific interpretation of the facts as observed by the Realists involved contradicting preconceptions based on the centrality of legal rules as the heavily operative factor in judicial decision making. At times, it seems, this rejection of preconceptions was itself the main function of Realism; indeed it might be said that it was the main legacy of the Realist school.

The American Realists did then, in general, see the function of their Realism in very much the same way set out by Stone. By investigating and looking at law in its social context and stripped of preconceived notions about rules, a greater understanding of law could be achieved; this investigation would take the form of studying particularly judicial behaviour.

Does Stone's quotation fit the Scandinavian Realists? They also wish to cut through preconceptions to reveal the true picture – that, after all, is why they are termed 'Realists'. In their case, the preconceptions which they wish to eradicate relate to the concept of normativity, which they reject: there is no such thing as an 'ought', and concepts such as rights and duties cannot be explained in terms of normativity. The Scandinavians do not, however, reject the notion of legal rules ('paper rules') as do the Americans: on the contrary, they clearly see such rules as guides to behaviour.

Much of the Scandinavians' writing is concerned with the attempt to show how legal rules work in the 'real' world of cause and effect other than the fictional realm of normativity. Why do people follow legal rules? It is clear, then, that they see their function as being partly to interpret the facts of human behaviour. Their explanation is in terms of a psychological effect of the rules in making people believe that something will and should happen.

Further, it is clear (still in the terms of the question) that the interpretation is principally of judicial and other behaviour. Alf Ross, for example, thinks that legal rules provide a scheme of interpretation to explain judicial behaviour; both he and Olivecrona explain legal rules as being principally rules about force addressed to officials, although both also see and explain the rules' function in guiding the behaviour of the law-subject.

However, the Scandinavians were not much concerned with observation of behaviour in particular cases. Their work was intensely theoretical and their explanation of the behaviour essentially abstract: they did not encourage research (as the Americans did) nor engage in it themselves.

With the small qualification mentioned in the last paragraph, Stone's statement is an adequate statement of the function of Realist jurisprudence and also provides a clue as to why two schools of thought with conclusions as different as those of the Scandinavians and Americans should both share the name 'Realist'.

QUESTION THREE

'The problem we all face is not whether to be realistic but how; not whether to portray law as a fact, rather than fiction, but what counts as a fact, and what therefore is a factual protrayal of it.' (D N MacCormick)

Discuss.

University of London LLB Examination
(for External Students) Jurisprudence and Legal Theory June 1988 Q5

General Comment

Quite a difficult general question on both American and Scandanavian Realism with elements of sociological movements also required.

Skeleton Solution

Basis of American Realist movement – examine reality of legal experience – lacking a technology – Glendon Schubert – judicial behaviouralism – Hunt – 'we are all Realists now' – problem identified in quotation – technology – Scandanavian Realism – rejection of metaphysics – concentration on world of cause and effect – the real world – problem to explain rights/duties etc – psychological explanation – Olivecrona – *Law as Fact* addressees of law – existence as a fact proved by reference to psychological factors – criticisms – Pound – law as fact – social phenomenon – but sociological jurisprudence developed from analytical model of law.

Suggested Solution

Whilst the movement that became known as American Realism sought to concentrate on the reality of the legal experience and move away from a mere logical application of legal rules as the sole method for the prediction of the likely outcome of a dispute, their important corrective to the method of pure analytical jurisprudence has now become conventional wisdom to the extent that Alan Hunt was able to write that whilst Realism is dead 'we are all Realists now'. What he had in mind was that legal scientists do now attempt to take 'the reality of the legal experience' into account; but as MacCormick has identified, the difficulty lies not in whether to look at such reality, but how. Herein MacCormick has isolated the very weakness of the American Realist movement.

Glendon Schubert, an ideological descendent of the American Realist movement, was of the opinion that the American Realists failed to achieve the objective that they set for themselves. He went so far as to say that they lacked both theory and method. That is somewhat of an overstatement. A preferable view would be that they did not fully develop their theory nor did they engage in the very matter that they so strongly advocated, namely a technology for the more accurate prediction of the outcome of the next dispute. As a judicial behaviouralist, Schubert was concerned with the motivations and the attitudes behind judicial decisions. That is exactly the area of interest for the American Realists. The real difficulty is not what to study as such but how to study it. How are jurists to scientifically study the motivations and attitudes that are so important to the Realists?

There have been attempts to deal with this both by American Realists and by those whom I have described as their ideological descendants. The most prolific Realist, Karl Llewellyn, through empirical research in the law reports, identified what he describes as the 'period style of judicial reasoning' by which he examined how a judge comes to a decision, but viewed this in different time periods. He identified that, through time, attitudes changed and that it was possible to outline two polar positions between the 'grand style' in which the judge feels less constrained by rules of precedent and rather adopts what Llewellyn termed 'situation sense' in order to ensure that a reasonable result is attained in a case. The judge would do this by reference to policy and principles. On the other pole, Llewellyn identified the 'formal style' in which a judge considers himself entirely bound by the rules of precedent, taking the view that rules of law decide cases and that policy is a matter for the legislature. As a technology this period style could be used to 'place' a judge in the spectrum between the grand and the formal styles and to use that placement in the prediction process by tailoring a dispute to fall within the area that he will decide in favour of. The difficulty with this as a method is, as Fuller observed, that it is to put consistency at a premium and to view the judicial process as a formalised game of 'snap'. Judges are no more nor less consistent than any other human being and that is quite inconsistent! Indeed Twining has described this period style as 'a relatively simple theoretical model'. It is submitted that as an attempt to answer the question of 'how', the period style is not helpful.

Another attempt to deal with the how question was developed by Loevinger and has become known as jurimetrics. This looks to the role of computers in the prediction process whereby the vast information which is of interest to the Realist is fed into the computer which will then presumably identify a 'pattern'.

Whilst this attempts to undertake in a scientific manner that which is currently dealt with through gossip and rumour – the preferences of judges – it suffers from the same drawback as Llewellyn's model, namely that it assumes a consistency of approach. Such computers will cope with data and identify a pattern. But the pattern that they identify may be of no use because of judicial inconsistency. The difficulty is increased when dealing with an appellate court bench with more than one judge. Then the Realist is interested in group relations among the members of the bench. Such membership may and does change, as do the interrelationships.

The judicial behaviouralists, among whom one could number Schubert and Griffith, seek to examine factors outside 'the law in books' such as the background and environmental conditions of the judge as an explanation for their decisions. Griffith does this with regard to what he sees as anti-Trade Union decisions among the English judiciary and which he explains by reference to the conservative background of the judiciary. This is flawed in that it is not the Conservative background of the judiciary that stands behind these decisions but the Conservative ideology of the legislature making the laws which the judiciary are then to enforce, eg sequestration of union assets.

The reality of the legal experience is such as to indicate that judges are not consistent in their approaches and the real problem is, as MacCormick has identified, that no one has yet developed a technology to explain that inconsistency.

The second part of the quotation addresses itself to the issue that concerned the Scandinavian Realists to the extent that it is accurate to so describe them. They were concerned to reject any realm of metaphysics which cannot be verified by empirical proof. Hence, rights and duties would be meaningless and fictional unless they are rooted in actual sense experience. That actual sense experience exists on the psychological level in that the meaning of a normative statement is psychological hence a right exists as a feeling of power and a duty as a feeling of obligation.

Olivecrona looked at the question of the addressees of law in *Law as Fact* in which he identified that if the subject is to have a psychological attitude towards a law then it must at least in the secondary sense be addressed to him. This was a variation from the work of Hans Kelsen which so heavily influenced Olivercrona initially. Alf Ross, who was perhaps the most sophisticated of the Scandinavian Realists, thought that jurisprudence should be rooted in an empirical study of official behaviour and not in norms that ought to be obeyed, but rather in norms likely to be applied by the court. The problem with much of the Scandinavian Realists is that they are not treated seriously, perhaps because much of their thesis is largely guesswork.

Roscoe Pound, as the main advocate for socio legal studies, saw law as a social phenomenon. He was concerned in the making, interpretation and application of laws to take account of law as a social fact. The problem with such an approach is as Hunt has identified, namely that Pound used sociology when it suited him. Harris argues that the socio legal research that seeks to identify law as a fact and to offer a factual portrayal of law engages the same concept of law as analytical jurisprudence. Harris doubts whether anyone has succeeded in identifying a sociological conception of law which transcends or replaces conceptions arrived at in the analytical mode. Hence, while the socio-legal studies attempt to study law in action, their starting point is taken from law in books. There is a merging of the 'fact' and of the 'fiction'.

On such a perspective, indeed, MacCormick is correct. There appears to be little dispute as to whether to portray law as fact. Who would want to portray it as fiction? The difficulty is in identifying what is fact. That difficulty is not resolved by sociological jurisprudence.

Chapter 6

The Historical School

6.1 Introduction

6.2 Key points

6.3 Questions and suggested solutions

6.1 Introduction

As with Realism, the issue of whether there is a 'school' is pressing. The divergent theories of Maine and von Savigny suggest that 'school' may not be a particularly apt term. Von Savigny and Maine both, however, reacted against the natural law doctrines which espoused unchanging principles and lacked historical perspective. Today, the importance of these writers (most particularly Maine) lies in their influence on anthropological and sociological studies of law.

6.2 Key points

Maine – the 'organic' theory

a) The development of legal systems passes through six stages: royal judgments; custom; codes; legal fictions; equity; legislation.

b) Static societies move through the first three stages only; progessive societies move through some or all of the latter three.

c) Maine's methods have influenced much in modern jurisprudence and sociology.

Von Savigny – the 'mystical' theory

a) Law is an expression of the will of the people – it develops from the 'Volksgeist' (character and spirit of a nation's people).

b) Law will thus develop gradually, as reflected in judicial decisions and legislature. Eventually juristic skills will be added and codification will take place.

c) Although von Savigny grasped an important point in that a country's values and history do manifest themselves within the law, his concept of 'Volksgeist' was imperfect.

6.3 Questions and suggested solutions

QUESTION ONE

'Maine's thesis was always – as he himself recognised – subject to important limitations.' (W Friedmann)

Discuss.

University of London LLB Examination
(for External Students) Jurisprudence and Legal Theory June 1986 Q9

General Comment

This calls for a critical evaluation of the theory of Maine. There will be some overlap with his contribution to anthropological jurisprudence.

Skeleton Solution

Maine investigated law's social and historical context – method followed by sociologists and anthropologists – development of legal systems – considered limited range of societies – *The Cheyenne Way* – significant contribution.

Suggested Solution

Critical reaction to Maine's work falls into two parts – an admission of the great impact he and his scientific method have had on later studies of law from various standpoints, together with a realisation of the shortcomings of his own particular studies and conclusions. In looking at these shortcomings and limitations, we should not ignore the more general impact; nor, of course, should we forget that our criticisms are made with the benefit of hindsight.

It is, I think, fair to put Maine's limitations in perspective by dealing first with the overall effect of his writings. He saw that law could not be understood without an investigation into and understanding of its historical and social context. In his endeavours to produce a theory of how law develops with society through history, he based his ideas on research into the materials at his disposal. This investigative, scientific method has since been followed by many anthropologists and sociologists who have developed legal anthropology and legal sociology, following Maine's emphasis on careful study of records of communities and investigations of surviving primitive communities. Maine might be said to be the father of these two disciplines, particularly the former. Also, comparative law studies such as his now form part of many university law courses.

Having said that, Maine's precise conclusions can be rejected in many respects. His main thesis concerned the development of legal systems. From his knowledge of English and Roman law and from his studies of some primitive Indian peoples, he concluded that law developed in stages. All societies passed through the first three such stages (kingly judgments divinely inspired; customary law in the hands of an aristocratic elite and codes, or written laws) but only progressive (as against static, primitive) societies pass to the further three stages of legal development (by fictions, equity (an alternative body of rules) and finally legislation).

It is not clear how far Maine meant this development sequence to be either rigidly followed in each case or indeed to be universal at all. The range of societies which he considered was very limited. If he had had more material at his disposal, his conclusions would have been very different. For example, it is clear from more modern anthropological studies that primitive societies do have methods of legislation, deliberate law-making processes (see eg Llewellyn and Hoebel's study *The Cheyenne Way*) and many societies do not have the equivalents of fictions and equity in their development. The laws of primitive societies and of societies generally show more variety than Maine allowed for – although it must be remembered that he would probably have been the first to predict that further research would invalidate his detailed views in this way.

Maine also touched upon the development of the content of laws in developed societies; he claimed that the laws of such societies had 'hitherto shown a movement from status to contract'. This movement is one from laws based on a position in family or household – for example, the privileges of a husband and father and the incapacity from a contractual viewpoint of a wife – to laws based on freedom to contract irrespective of status.

It has been claimed that this development has not been continued, but rather that the reverse has occurred. Legal relations are again dictated by status as employees, consumers, tenants, etc – it is said. There is an argument about whether this further movement is in fact a reverse, or an onward development towards a more real freedom of contract; in any case, the claim of a reverse cannot constitute an objection to Maine's theory, since he was simply pointing to the development to that time, 'hitherto' as he put it.

One suggested limitation on Maine's thesis is, therefore, misplaced. More generally, the limitations which I have identified in Maine's work must not be allowed to overshadow the significant and continuing contribution which that work made to the study of jurisprudence.

QUESTION TWO

'Maine's theory ... is ... free from the abstract and unreal romanticism which vitiates much of von Savigny's theory about the evaluation of law.' (Friedmann)

Discuss.

Written by the Editor

General Comment

An evaluative comparison of the theories and differing approaches of von Savigny and Maine.

Skeleton Solution

'Mystical' – 'organic' – von Savigny – 'Volksgeist' – custom – juristic skills – decay – criticism of the theory – Maine – six stage development of legal system – scientific empirical techniques – nonetheless flawed.

Suggested Solution

Von Savigny's theory has been described by some writers as 'mystical', whilst Maine's is 'organic'. This points at the differences between their theories; although both reacted against natural law and its lack of historical perspective, their approaches were largely separate. The quotation suggests that Maine's theory is superior to that of von Savigny in that it is free from 'abstract and unreal romanticism'. The two theorists will be examined in turn to ascertain whether this is in fact the case.

Von Savigny saw the development of law as an expression of the will of the nation; it emerged from the 'Volksgeist' (spirit of the people). Thus the concept of a universal natural law was incorrect. He saw the development of law in the following terms.

a) The first stage of law is custom, originating from the values of the people.

b) The second stage is the addition of juristic skills which codify the expression of the 'Volksgeist'. Eventually law dies away as 'the nation loses its nationality'; that is, its national identity.

It is useful to consider at this point the extent to which von Savigny's theory succumbs to 'abstract and unreal romanticism'. Perhaps a good definition of 'romanticism' is that which is 'remote from experience', or even imaginary. Many have criticised the notion of 'Volksgeist' as being just that – it is simply not true that every 'people' has a corporate spirit or identity. One only has to think of the variety of racial, cultural and political groups in the United Kingdom today to be convinced that 'Volksgeist' is an unreal concept. Furthermore, there is much technical law which does not really fit into von Savigny's pattern of development. It does seem therefore, that von Savigny's theory was to an extent vitiated by romanticism. Perhaps his real problem was that he took a legitimate idea (that national character does have an influence on the development of law) to fanciful extremes.

Having thus accepted the criticism which Friedmann levels at von Savigny, it is necessary to consider whether Maine's theory avoids the same criticism. Maine shared von Savigny's rejection of natural law, but his approach lacked von Savigny's 'mysticism'. He was greatly influenced by Darwin's *Origin of Species* and studied the historical development of legal systems. He concluded that legal systems followed a six stage pattern of development: royal judgments; custom; codes; legal fictions; equity; legislation. According to Maine, static societies pass through the first three stages only, whereas progressive societies pass through some or all of the latter three. The fact that Maine adopted scientific empirical techniques to reach his conclusions does go some way to support the view that his theory was free from 'abstract and unreal romanticism'. Indeed his method is now influential in modern sociology and anthropology.

Despite this, Maine's conclusions are not without their critics. Studies such as Malinowski's *Crime and Custom in Savage Society* throw doubt on the sequential development of law espoused by Maine. In all probability the research Maine carried out was inadequate to support his theories. It is thus clear that, despite being free from the defects inherent in von Savigny's theory, Maine's theory was itself flawed.

QUESTION THREE

Of what value today is the historical approach to jurisprudence?

University of London LLB Examination
(for External Students) Jurisprudence and Legal Theory June 1983 Q4

General Comment

A straightforward question on the historical approach with the added requirement of an application to contemporary conditions.

Skeleton Solution

Laws in their historical context – von Savigny – Volksgeist – uniqueness in each society – contrast Maine – Marxism – legal anthropology – sociology – valuable approach.

Suggested Solution

Stated simply, the historical approach to jurisprudence stresses that laws cannot be understood properly unless they are placed in context, specifically their historical context. This insight was shared by two very different scholars of the nineteenth century, von Savigny and Maine, whose viewpoints have the appellation 'historical school' or 'historical approach'. For von Savigny the reason history was so important was that over time a society or law developed from the Volksgeist or spirit of the people; unless this process and the importance of the historical and social factors were recognised, the law could not be understood or explained and attempts at reform would fail. The Volksgeist theory was one of the uniqueness of law in each society as a result of its own unique history and customs; in this respect it can be contrasted with Maine's exposition of the relevance of history, since he pointed to a developmental sequence in the form of the law (six stages from kingly order to legislation) and in its context (from status of contract) which were common (at least in the former case) to all legal systems.

A brief survey of those views comprising the historical approach is required as an introduction, to precede the general line of my answer to the question. This is that the 'Maine-line' has been influential in several major directions and is still influential today; the 'Volksgeist' approach is generally rejected although it does have some influence on Marxism, and that the general insight with which we started is an accepted factor in the study and practice of law.

Although few write about historical jurisprudence any more, three 'schools' of jurisprudential thought which are very productive at the present day can be said to be, to different extents, off-shoots of the historical approach. First, Marxism. Because Marx was writing at about the same time as Maine, we cannot claim a conscious influence of Maine on Marx, although the influence of Maine and later anthropological and sociological writings on later Marxists is clear. However, Marx and Engels clearly viewed law – to the extent that they considered it at all – in the historical context, and like Maine were much influenced by ideas of evaluation so prevalent in mid nineteenth century thought.

Marxist theory as a whole is historical. Man is emerging through a series of class conflicts, to the ultimate classless state; the law reflects the present situation (the economic 'base' of the relations of production) at each stage. At present, for example, the UK is a capitalist society in which the class conflict is between the owners of the means of production (the bourgeoisie) and the working class. The law is an instrument of the bourgeoisie to oppress the working class, and can only be understood as such; it reflects the present relations of production (eg strict laws of ownership, laws of contract and conveyance to allow for freedom of commerce, etc). The view of law reflecting the particular stage of development of society is one which is very similar to Maine's view; reflections of von Savigny's thought can be seen in the idea of law reflecting the particular economic position of the society. The present day importance of Marxism need not be argued.

Second, Maine is directly responsible for one of the booming fields of jurisprudential study, that of legal anthropology. While Maine's own work *Ancient Law* can be criticised both for lack of research and for over-generalised conclusions, there is no doubt that his innovation in attempting to trace developmental factors relevant to our own law through study of records of old and observations of present primitive societies has been of great value. Studies such as Malinowski's on why Trobriand Islanders followed assessable 'rules' in the absence of visible enforcement mechanisms, Gluckman's on the judicial processes of the Northern Rhodesian Barotse tribe and Llewellyn and Hoebel's on the dispute settlement of the Cheyenne widen our knowledge and perception of social control and dispute settlement. These and wider-based studies on social control generally enable us to question ethnocentric positions on the value of rules, institutions such as courts and police, and coercion: we can learn much about our own legal systems by seeing, for example, that in many primitive societies negotiation and conciliation are more important in settling disputes than is an authoritative decision-taking body.

There are some parallels to be drawn between legal anthropology and the third area in which Maine's views have been influential. This area is the sociological one; like anthropology a discipline in itself outside law, where gradually widening perspectives can tell us much about our legal systems and a proper definition of law. Maine and von Savigny pointed the way to considering not only law as it is laid down in books, but as it relates to the society; this and the growth of sociology outside law have caused a great amount of work and writing on the subject of law and society. The sociological jurisprudence associated with Pound, the earlier sociology of Weber and Durkheim, the work of the Realists in America, and modern writers like Selznick, are all examples of this.

Maine, then, has had influence, and his line of thought has had influence, in several directions in which much valuable work is still being undertaken today. Even von Savigny's approach and emphasis on national factors has left its mark, although as a theory it is long since rejected. Indirectly, too, the historical approach has permeated through much writing in analytical jurisprudence; the historical approach ran counter to the imperative theory of Austin and Bentham, since the command-sovereign model sees law-making as the outcome of an individual's will, rather than of a historical process.

Recent positivist theories such as Kelsen's and Hart's are not guilty of this fault: Hart develops his idea of a legal system from a primitive society, and Kelsen's norm chains go back to a first constitution, for example. Both realise the importance of historical factors in law.

Directly and indirectly the historical approach to jurisprudence remains a valuable one.

QUESTION FOUR

'Undoubtedly the historical approach contributed an important insight to modern legal thinking by grasping the valuable truth that law is not just an abstract set of rules imposed on society but is an integral part of that society deeply rooted in the social and economic order in which it functions and embodying traditional value – systems which confer meaning and purpose upon the given society.' (Lloyd: *The Idea of Law*.)

Discuss.

University of London LLB Examination
(for External Students) Jurisprudence and Legal Theory June 1985 Q8

General Comment

The main theorists to examine are von Savigny, Maine and Marx. The methodology of their work needs to be examined.

Skeleton Solution

New insight – von Savigny – Maine – latter pioneered scientific methodology – legal anthropology and sociology – Marxist view of society – historical school was major advance.

Suggested Solution

My answer falls naturally into three parts. First I will try to show why it was an insight to see that law was more than an abstract set of rules, by looking briefly at the theories which had prevailed before the historical school. Second will come an explanation of how the historical school (in its disparate forms) grasped and analysed the new contribution, and third will be a discussion of how this 'valuable truth' has been important to modern legal thinking. In a sense, my answer puts the historical school in its own historical context!

Two schools of thought were prevalent up to and at the first half of the nineteenth century when the historical school came to the fore: natural law and the early positivists. Both in their different ways looked at law in terms of an abstract set of rules; for the natural lawyers, human law was controlled by the natural law dictates of reason, so that a large part of that human law was in the form of absolute principles imposed from outside. Human law-givers did have a discretion apart from the rules laid down by natural law, but the concentration was on the imposition of the external, objective (and common to all societies) principles. Positivism in the form propounded by Austin and Bentham also concentrated on the imposition of rules, this time by a sovereign within the society. Laws were not uniform from society to society, but there was no need for laws to be reflective of the society's values; rather, they reflected one person's will.

It was then a breakthrough, a new insight, when historians such as von Savigny and the other German romantics and Maine wrote of law from a different standpoint. Of course, the 'historical school' really consists of two parts, since the work of von Savigny differs from that of Maine in radical respects and it must be said that whilst Savigny focused on the uniqueness of each society (a feature of the insight as presented in the quotation), Maine was more concerned to point to common strands in the development of law in different societies.

Von Savigny's works match the 'valuable truth' as stated in the question almost absolutely. For him, each society's law was an expression of the 'Volksgeist', or will of the people. In each century, the shared values of the populace were reflected in law at its primitive stage; this law was then honed into perfect shape by judicial skills and if the proper course was followed it would then be codified and preserved before the third stage, that of decay, set in. Hence, law was both an integral part of the society and deeply rooted in its traditional value-systems: indeed, to try to force foreign or external law on the people would not succeed, since it would not fit with the 'Volksgeist' and would be rejected.

Maine, as I have said, was more concerned with the development of law in different societies. He looked at various societies and formulated a developmental sequence common to all legal systems. 'Static' societies passed through three stages of development and 'progressive' societies through three further stages. The developmental stages, particularly the first three (divine judgment of kings, aristocracy, codes), match a development in society away from kingly authority and on to the age of writing: to this extent law is deeply rooted in the economic and social order in which it functions. Maine, though, emphasises similarity rather than different value systems unique and central to varying societies.

The insight which we are discussing was, therefore, more the work of von Savigny and his followers than of Maine. Maine, though, pioneered the scientific methodology which has been taken up by two of the movements in modern legal thinking which most benefited from the fresh and wider perspective gained from studying not just the rules which make up law, but also the social background. These two movements are legal anthropology and sociology. Maine was, in fact, the first legal anthropologist. An anthropologist must look at law in wide perspective, simply because often the narrower 'landmarks' which he would look for in a developed legal system (courts, statutes, legislature) are missing. Anthropology looks at traditional folk-ways in the context of the particular community to see what lessons can be learnt.

Sociologists obviously are interested in the part played by law in society. From the earliest days of sociology, both sociologists such as Weber and 'sociological jurisprudents' such as Pound attempted to explain law's place in society. Weber, Durkheim and others tried to show how different types of law were to be found in different types of society and Pound tried to point to the way in which law, by balancing interests, tried to accommodate the varying values and choices of different groups in society.

More modern sociologists, heavily influenced by Marxist thought, might reject the first part of the historical insight ('law … is an integral part of that society') as only partially true. It is the case that law is an integral part of most modern societies, since it is used by those in power in a society to keep them in power at the expense of the majority. However, law is not a necessary part of society: in a Marxist or communist state, law would have withered away. On this sort of ('conflict') viewpoint, the traditional value-system which law embodies is very much a one-sided system which sees the function and purpose of the society totally from the ruling classes' viewpoint.

Indeed, the Marxist analysis of history and how the law changes to meet the needs of the dominant class at each stage is very much akin to the 'truth' we are considering, although (as with Maine) the Marxist view is one which looks at similarities between different societies rather than their uniqueness.

Chapter 7

The Anthropological School

7.1   Introduction

7.2   Key points

7.3   Question and suggested solution

7.1 Introduction

This topic has obvious links with the sociology of law (Chapter 9) and the historical school (Chapter 6) and the student would be sensible to revise these topics in conjunction with each other. Clearly, revision of the anthropological school will have to be selective, since the subject encompasses many writers and viewpoints. The most helpful starting point for the student is to consider whether the study of 'law' in primitive societies throws any light on our own concept(s) of law and the legal system. Such an approach can be combined with a general overview of anthropologists and detailed reference to a few interesting contributors – for instance, Malinowski's study of the Trobriand Islanders.

7.2 Key points

An overview

a) Law is merely a small part of anthropology as a whole.

b) Anthropology involves looking at other societies and then attempting to use the information gained to enhance our understanding of our own society.

Criticisms

a) It is affected by ethnocentrism – in simple terms, studying others by reference to concepts developed in our own society. This has a distorting effect.

b) 'Law-centred' studies may be contrasted with wider studies of dispute processes. The latter are more successful at avoiding the distortion produced by ethnocentricity.

The value of anthropology for the law student

See the suggested solution below.

7.3 Question and suggested solution

'Anthropology has little to offer the student of jurisprudence.' Do you agree?

University of London LLB Examination
(for External Students) Jurisprudence and Legal Theory June 1987 Q7

General Comment

This is typical of questions posed about anthropology. The student must adopt an evaluative approach rather than just provide an account of some of the empirical work that has been undertaken. An in depth account of a few researchers, rather than a mention of many, is the best tactic to adopt.

Skeleton Solution

Anthropology – legitimacy of cross cultural comparisons – ethnocentricity – different studies – usefulness – problem of language – micro level understanding – relevance of conclusions of anthropological studies – development of heuristic devices – conclusion – anthropological study of our own society.

Suggested Solution

I would answer this question through an assessment of the legitimacy of cross cultural comparisons and the adequacy of drawing conclusions for our own society from anthropological studies. It is on this premise that I will assess whether anthropological studies do have much to offer the student of jurisprudence.

At a funeral oration for the Athenians who died fighting for Athens, Pericles said, 'Our institutions are not borrowed from those around us; they are our own, the creation of Athenian Statesmen; an example and not a copy'. I would take the view that that quotation has a lot to offer on the legitimacy of the application of 'lessons' from anthropological studies to our own society. I take Pericles to say that a conclusion about cheese will not assist in an understanding of wine. I will however indicate those areas where it is my view that anthropological studies may contribute to a greater understanding of our own society, including the legal system.

One of the main difficulties with anthropological studies is the tendency that they have towards ethnocentricity. This involves the study of others through concepts developed by ourselves. On the other hand it could be said that on the micro level at least phenomena in our society also occur in primitive societies. In primitive society the study of these common phenomena may be more simple since they are less likely to be complicated and obscured by the complexities of an advanced industrial society. This view looks to the study of primitive society as if it were a laboratory for the understanding of our own society. The validity of this approach in itself is highly suspect.

Even if the 'laboratory thesis' is accepted, then the scientist/anthropologist will still have to develop a mechanism for the avoidance of the tendency towards ethnocentrism by which the scientist will largely invalidate his study as he takes law out of its context and arranges his observations according to preconceived yet inapplicable notions. Malinowski attempted to get around this defect in his study *Crime and Custom in Savage Society*. Perhaps the only effective way is through the avoidance of translation! In his study of the Barotse of Northern Rhodesia (now Zambia), Max Gluckman came across the notion of 'the reasonable man' which he observed was employed in the same way as in our courts to arrive at an objective test by which to assess the conduct of the defendant. Bohannon isolated the problem as being one of language, hence the point above about translations. He claimed that Gluckman analysed the Barotse according to the doctrines of the common law which is clearly not applicable to them. Bohannan insists that if there is to be any potential for anthropology to truly understand any tribe then it must use tribal terms and not Western concepts. The solution proposed of developing a computer language is unsatisfactory as it would have to be programmed by someone who has his own notions and certainly more importantly, it would be read and understood by comparison with already existing notions in the original language of the reader.

I do not think that our advanced industrial society developed tribunals because Laura Nader found that the Zapatec Indians had developed something performing a similar task to what she identified as a tribunal, anymore than I would think that becase the Eskimos resolve disputes through 'song contests', by which the person who uses the best insults wins, would be an appropriate method of dispute resolution in our society. Yet it clearly is adequate for their society.

Some of the approaches adopted in the anthropological studies may be of use in an understanding of our own society but these could well have developed without engaging in anthropological studies.

Although Durkheim tried to make a distinction between mechanical solidarity and organic solidarity-type societies, it has to be observed that Western industrial society has both restitutive and repressive laws and that both of these are expanding. That fact does not necessarily defeat the usefulness of Durkheim's model in helping us to understand the difference between the two types of laws, but the conclusion drawn by Durkheim has been proved wrong.

If the models used in the anthropological method from primitive societies are applied to advanced industrial society then that exercise may well enhance our understanding of our own society through sociological inquiry. It is my view though that the conclusions reached in the anthropological studies are inapplicable to our own society so far as the institution of law is concerned and I take it that that must be the prime area of interest of the jurisprudence student. In *The Law of Primitive Man* Hoebel said that 'the more civilised man becomes, the greater men's need for law – law is but a response to social needs'. He thought that the institution of law was a necessity. He observed that without a sense of community there is no law and that without law there cannot for long be a community. For example, the Andaman Islanders (in the Indian Ocean) have no suprafamilial authority. Social control is exercised by and within the family. However, in our society the individual is independent of both the family and the clan. Such a mechanism as is applied in the Andaman Islands would be wholly inadequate here.

It ought to be said that anthropological studies can show us that conclusions that are relevant to primitive societies are not relevant in our advanced society. Felsteiner's study, *Influences of Social Organisation and Dispute Processing* shows that the form of dispute settlement flows from the social organisation. He distinguished between TCRS ('technologically complex, rich society') and TSPS ('technologically simple, poor society') and observes that cross comparisons between these are of very limited value. Perhaps von Savigny had a point in this regard when he noted that each society develops the law it needs and that, indeed, law is a reflection of the particularities of each society (the 'Volksgeist').

Anthropological studies do have certain advantages, not least of which is that it provides us with an understanding of law in societies other than our own. Certain heuristic devices have also been developed through anthropological studies and these may well be useful models for a study of law in our own society. At the micro level anthropological studies have pointed to the working of some aspects of our own society. Gluckman's model of testing not only cases – which undergo a transformation when taken to court – but also looking at rules and praxis (the way people act under the law) does not however explain the purpose of law but is useful as far as it goes.

Rather than focus considerable attention and resources on anthropological studies, it would be preferable to pay greater attention to sociological inquiry into our own society from the point of view of the needs of the jurisprudence student. In particular one would look for an inquiry into the nature of our state; the form and function of law; the source, distribution and location of power in our society and the study of conflict in our society. Admittedly, these are rather parochial issues; however they represent a view that although lessons can be drawn from primitive societies such as that coercive law is not always the best dispute resolution technique, these lessons are already drawn and these anthropological studies merely cloak a conclusion in a robe of authority. Our society had already 'invented' tribunals long before Nader told us that they were a good way of resolving certain disputes.

I would conclude that the only really interesting anthropological study would be one carried out by a person from another type of society. His findings would tell us more about our own society than any anthropological study we would carry out on his society. I am therefore drawn to a conclusion that the insights to be gained from anthropological studies are of little advantage to the student of jurisprudence who is interested in studying the law in his own society.

Chapter 8

Marxism

8.1   Introduction

8.2   Key points

8.3   Questions and suggested solutions

8.1 Introduction

With the developments in the Soviet Union and Eastern Europe, resulting in the overthrow of the regimes claiming a communist ideology based upon Marxist-Leninist doctrine, Marxism has become a topic in flux.

8.2 Key points

Base and superstructure

According to Marxist theory, society's base is formed by the relations of production. The state, law and all other social institutions form part of the superstructure built on to the base and reflect that base.

Class instrumentalism

In Marxist theory the law is the tool of the ruling class. Since the state and other social institutions depend upon the relations of production, the law will, in a capitalist society, reflect the fact that the means of productions are controlled by a small ruling class. The law both legitimises this situation and oppresses the working classes.

Marxism in reality

Marxist theory on the post capitalist society is often crudely described in terms of state and law 'withering away'. In fact, a more sophisticated version of this theory allows for a post-revolutionary period where the bourgeois state is replaced by proletariat power. This state will remain until communism is achieved, at which stage the state and law will disintegrate. Students should consider, however, whether this reflects reality; and whether the so-called Marxist societies were really Marxist at all, or merely very crude approximations.

8.3 Questions and suggested solutions

QUESTION ONE

'The downfall of most of the world's supposedly communist states has not weakened the Marxist analysis of law.'

Discuss.

University of London LLB Examination
(for External Students) Jurisprudence and Legal Theory June 1999 Q11

General Comment

This question requires a level of knowledge of current affairs. The 1990s witnessed the collapse of communist states in Eastern Europe, culminating in the re-unification of Germany and the collapse of the former Union of Soviet Socialist Republic. Did the collapse of these countries mean the collapse or weakening of the Marxist theory of law?

Skeleton Solution

Marxist theory of law – the base and superstructure – the prophecy/revolution/dictatorship of the proletariat – analysis of the fall of previous communist states – summary and conclusion.

Suggested Solution

The teachings of Marx regarding the nature of law and the division of classes in society (who live in an antagonistic relationship) may hold no fear for us in the modern world, particularly with the failure of Marxist teachings in previously communist countries in Eastern Europe and the collapse of the former USSR. Although it may be improbable that there will ever be a communist state on the strength of Marxist teachings, we must, however, recognise that the tools of analysis that the theory provide are still powerful and relevant in the modern world.

Marx believed that the history of all hitherto societies was a history of class struggle (Collins, *Marxism and Law* (7th edn, 1995)). So, throughout history every epoch was divided into classes. From the hunter gathering era through to slavery, feudalism and capitalism, each society was polarised into the 'haves' and the 'have-nots'. There comes a time when the current mode of production comes into conflict with the social structure; this process is the 'economic determinism' which leads on to the next epoch.

Marx took a look at evolution in capitalist society, and concluded that capitalism was in crisis. It was a system where the bourgeoisie (who are the owners of the means of production, that is, land, capital and factories) exploited the proletariat (or the working class), who had nothing but their labour to sell.

These two classes live in the economic base. This relationship is known as the relations of production. Because the working class have only their labour to sell, the ruling class can decide what to pay for their labour. Today, laws have introduced the minimum wage in Britain, but the Marxist will argue that the minimum wage is still a poverty wage. The bourgeoisie are able to exploit the labouring class, and the profit they make represents the surplus value of the working class' labour.

According to Marx, the exploitation of the working class is possible because of the law, which is a superstructure built upon the base. The law is able to regulate the ownership of property, and criminalise any attempt or actual stealing of these properties. In this way, according to Marx, the law becomes a tool of oppression in the hands of the bourgeoisie to keep the working class down. The law is used through the state, which is a construct of the ruling class to give that class a semblance of neutrality.

However, this state of affairs (where one class exploits the other class) cannot continue forever: a time will come when there will be a revolution by the proletariat. This will lead to the overthrowing of the bourgeoisie and the establishment of a dictatorship by the proletariat. The state will then wither away.

No one is really anxious about this prophecy, because it has failed to materialise. However, the analysis that the theory provides us with is still very relevant to our world. The analysis concerns the co-existence of two classes, one dominant and one subservient. The dominant class rules over the subordinate class.

It is said that the collapse of the world's so-called communist states has proved that the analysis of Marx is false. It is argued that the failure of such societies proves that Marx was an idealist in that there could never be a perfect communist society. Marx claimed that when communism was established, law would wither away and there would be only the administration of things. This argument leaves people speechless, because given what human nature is, it is inconceivable that there could ever be such a society without law.

It is arguable that no perfect communist state in the manner envisaged by Marx ever existed before the collapse of the former Eastern European Socialist countries and the USSR, which was itself not yet a communist state but merely in the advanced stage of socialism. Laws were still used in all of these former so-called communist states, and so evidently they were not yet communist per se.

We must therefore understand that the existence of this superstructure (law) reflected the conditions in the economic base. If we take the former Yugoslavia as an example, we can understand the dynamics better. We have the forces of production who exist in the base. If these forces, who constitute the owners of the dominant instrument in society (power) are members of a particular tribe, we have a classic example of two unequal classes. Those who enjoy the levers of power turned themselves into the dominant force to coerce and suppress the minority tribe. The recent events in Bosnia (between Croats, Serbs and Muslims) are a classic case of class dynamics. The same is true of the situation in Kosovo between the Serbs and the ethnic Albanians. To some extent, the same class struggle occurred in the former Czechoslovakia between the Czechs and the Slovaks, leading to the so-called velvet revolution which established the two republics of Czech and Slovakia.

Marx's tool of analysis is therefore still powerful in analysing the world today (Lloyd and Freeman, *Introduction to Jurisprudence* (6th edn, 1994)). If we stop to ponder over the issues raised, we can see that the collapse of the former so-called communist states has not discredited Marxist analysis of law. In all of these countries that collapsed, we can see that laws were still being used, and that these laws were in the hands of the majority tribe. The minority tribe was still oppressed, and in classical Marxian terms this led to the explosion of revolutions throughout the so-called communist countries in the late 1980s through the 1990s to early 2000.

If we take a look at our own societies in the western world we can see the relevance of the tools of analysis of Marxian theory much more clearly. We still have classes in society. The bourgeoisie still own the means of production. The only difference is that in modern times the working class is better educated, and so members of that class do not have only their physical labour to sell. Today, people sell their skills and are better paid. We have accountants, teachers, lawyers, doctors, all employed by the big multinationals and conglomerates. These big institutions still have the say when it comes to policy-making, despite their efforts to aspire to equality through the lie that is 'share democracy', which the Marxist would call false consciousness. The ruling class still dictates power over the working class.

The superstructure still plays its ideological role through advertising, which lulls people into assuming that their situation is the norm of any functional society. Marx would argue that advertising laws are there to propagate the values of the ruling class to the working class as good values, and this enables the products of the ruling class to be patronised by the working class.

The law allows employers to insert clauses into the contracts of employees, enabling the employer to claim the rights to any intellectual property that the worker creates while using work facilities or while at the work place. Certainly, Marx would view this as a means by which the ruling class prevent the working class from gaining any leverage of power vis-à-vis the ruling class.

The conclusion we can draw from the above discussion is that, irrespective of the collapse of the so-called former communist states, we must be aware that the power of Marx's analysis of law has not suffered in the slightest. It is still a powerful tool for analysing the classes in modern society.

QUESTION TWO

What insights, if any, does Marxism have for our contemporary understanding of law?

University of London LLB Examination
(for External Students) Jurisprudence and Legal Theory June 1998 Q9

General Comment

Questions about Marxism are often asked in one form or another. The pity is that many candidates fail to appreciate the moral insight of Marx's theory of law and are thus unable to attempt such questions. A little more attention paid to reading up on Marx's theory of law will help immensely.

Skeleton Solution

The work of Karl Marx – Marx's nineteenth century observation – Marxist theory of law and state.

Suggested Solution

Karl Marx's view of law was influenced by his observations of the harsh realities of life in the Lancashire cotton mills during the nineteenth century. These observations led him to believe that capitalism is an exploitative system. It is a system where one class, the ruling class, dominates over the working class.

The idea is borne that society is polarised between two classes – the ruling class and the working class. In fact, Marx believed that the history of all hitherto societies was a history of class struggles. This conjures up the image of two polarised classes who have always had an antagonistic relationship over the years. Marx explains that we find these polarised classes in every era, from the feudal era to the slave-trading era through to the industrialised (capitalist) era. In all of these eras, one is able to determine what type of society it is by studying how that society produces its goods and services.

The building block of any society, therefore, is the economic base. In this economic base exists the human relations. The owners of the means of production (the bourgeoisie) co-exist with the workers (the proletariat). The bourgeoisie are able to use their economic power to hire the labour of the proletariat. The proletariat have only their labour to sell. This is the relations of production which exists in the economic base.

With specific relevance to the capitalist society, the owners of the means of production exploit the working class in the sense that they take advantage of these people who have only their physical labour to sell. They pay the workers little money, creaming off the surplus value generated by their labour, and keeping it for themselves.

With the nature of this exploitative relationship, which is all to the benefit of the ruling class, the status quo must be maintained: the way for the ruling class to maintain its grip over the labouring class (and perpetuate its harmony) is to erect the superstructure over the base. Included in the superstructure are law, politics, ideology and religion. Law as part of the superstructure is needed to perform a dual role – to legitimise ownership and control over the working class, and to perform an ideological role to mystify the reality and make the working class take things for granted, believing that 'that is the way things work'. Marx called this false consciousness.

The Marxist view of law is that law is part of the institutional framework, used by the bourgeoisie both as a means of control and to mystify the proletariats' reality. Marxists believe that law is used as a means or a tool of domination in two senses. One is based on coercion and the other on ideology – that is the transfer of the values of the dominant class to the lower class. As far as coercion is concerned, the legal system of the capitalist society is able to call upon a network of other organisations of the state (such as the police and prisons) to protect and maintain the status quo. With these organisations in place to protect the interests of the ruling class, the law is able to project its false consciousness onto the working class, making them believe that the law is there to protect the interests of all. Marxist critique of property law is that it is presented as a testament to the fundamental right of everyone to own property, while in reality it operates in the interests of the ruling class. Although landlord and tenant laws give some protection to tenants, these same laws give mandatory grounds upon which landlords can easily evict their tenants.

Interestingly, the relationship between the landlord and tenant in the economic base makes the tenant believe and accept that this use of the superstructure is normal, the natural order of things. The superstructure is needed to regulate the relationship between the landlord and the tenant. So the superstructure must also be used to evict the tenant. The tenant is served a statutory notice of eviction and he takes it for granted that this is the normal way things work. The Marxist will argue that this is how the tenant has been mystified into accepting the reality (in this case, that being made homeless is normal).

Again we see the control that the ruling class exert over the working class in numerous public order laws. If members of the working class congregate at a place in large numbers without permission, this will soon attract the attention of the law enforcement authorities, who will use the superstructure to disperse the crowd. Anybody who refuses to leave voluntarily may find himself charged with a public order offence. It is difficult not to see that the superstructure is used to control these people, who mostly belong to the labouring class.

Since the ruling class cannot be seen to be too authoritarian, it also uses ideology to control the working class. This entails selling the values of the ruling class to the working class. In order for the ruling class to keep making their money, they must project into the consciousness of the working class the idea that the goods the working class makes are good for their consumption. To this end the law allows advertising of the products of these multinational corporations. The airwaves of both radio and TV are saturated with commercials which relate to the relations of production in the economic base. The superstructure is then used as a tool to whip and dominate the minds of the working class into thinking that the commercials are to be taken as a matter of course. In this way the law is used in an ideological way to mystify the reality, which is that the ruling class wants to manipulate the working classes' minds into following a particular trend. One only has to consider commercials for political parties and candidates during electioneering to understand the subtle control such advertising laws exert on people.

However, the law in capitalist societies has made many strides towards protecting the worker. There are examples such as share ownership, where workers have become shareholders in the company in which they work. The Marxist, however, would scorn this and argue that this is done to mystify the reality. Real power is still in the hands of the large conglomerates, pension funds whose collective voting power will always crush the voice of the large collection of members who are the working class. Such is the reality. Workers may own shares in their companies, but the ruling and powerful class holds the ace, which it plays during any decision-making with its enormous voting power. The control the ruling class has over the working class is thus absolute.

Let the working class to go law and attempt to argue that the law is loaded in the interest of the bourgeoisie. If, as Hart says, the officials of the legal system (which is the superstructure) have a shared and unified acceptance of the rule of recognition of the system, all they have to do is to identify the law to show the existence of the rule of recognition, and thus dismiss the case of the workers. The status quo is thus maintained by the superstructure. The point to note here is that the Marxist sees the legal system as a reflection of the base, where owners of the means of production control everything and call all the shots. The legal system maintains this state of affairs by using the weapon of the law to control the working class.

Although Marx prophesied that the exploitation of the working class would lead to a revolution, resulting in a dictatorship by the proletariat, we are wiser that it has failed to materialise (Lloyd and Freeman, *Introduction to Jurisprudence* (6th edn, 1994)). This is because of the capitalist society's ability to undergo law reform. Marxist theory of law provides very useful insights into the nasty and brutal class relationship which exists in contemporary capitalist society. This relationship is one of control, sanctioned by the law which, for example, allows people to be dismissed by an employer when he wants to downsize to make more profit (couched in the term of efficiency). The theory allows us to understand the law better, possibly encouraging us to construct arguments to bring about improved legislation.

QUESTION THREE

'While the specific predictions and empirical statements of Marx and Engels on law were rooted in the nineteenth century and have been largely disproved by history, many of the concepts and tools of analysis they created remain of vital importance for our understanding of law in society today.'

Discuss.

University of London LLB Examination
(for External Students) Jurisprudence and Legal Theory June 1996 Q10

General Comment

It is a big mistake to assume that the demise of communism in the former Soviet Union is synonymous with the demise of Marxist theory of law as a political tool. Think carefully about the theory. The predictive element in the theory may have been disproved by history but the theory itself is largely a powerful tool.

Skeleton Solution

Work of Marx and Engels – nineteenth century observation – Marxist theory of law and society – relevance of theory to our understanding of law in modern society.

Suggested Solution

The work of Marx and Engels on law was influenced by Marx's observation of the harsh realities of life under capitalism in Lancashire cotton mills in the nineteenth century; this led Marx to conclude that capitalism was in crisis. This led to his 'historical materialism' theory which says that social phenomena do not exist in isolation; rather they are interconnected, and any analysis of institutions must be done to include looking at their historical developments and contradictions in order to reconcile them. Human relations in society must be approached in this light. The observations of Marx and Engels led to their work which is a critique of capitalism. It is a conflict theory of law.

The Marxist theory sees law as a superstructure imposed on a sub-structure; the human relations, in society. The law serves the interests of the owners of the means of production – the bourgeoisie.The workers – the proletariat – are exploited by the bourgeoisie, but this dialectic between the two groups will reach a resolution when the oppressed class overthrows the ruling class through a revolution to establish a dictatorship of the proletatiat, leading to a classless society. The state will wither away and there will be administration of things.

From the above, it is seen that Marxist critique of capitalism sees the exploitation in society that is based on the efforts of the bourgeoisie to earn profit from the labour of the proletariat. How is this done? Workers are employed by a capitalist. They produce goods and services that enable the capitalist to make a profit after paying the workers' wages. The profit the capitalist makes is the 'surplus value' of the workers' labour. The state is constructed to use the superstructure – law – built on the relations between the owners of the means of production and the workers, to control the proleteriat and maintain their dominance of the proletariat. The state is a creation of the exploiting class to facilitate this end.

The state is presented as a detached entity exposing the interest of the whole society, and law and the legal system are presented as being objective as described in the concept of the rule of law which says the law applies equally and is non discriminatory. The law is presented as seeking everyone's interests. This, in Marxist ideology, is to mystify the reality of law as an instrument of oppression in the hands of the ruling class. The Marxist view of law says that law is a means of social control used by the ruling class to dominate the working class. Two types of domination are isolated; one based on coercion and the other based on ideology.

Coercion is used through the legal system. The legal system relies on institutions like the police and the prisons to control the lower class and to protect the interests of the capitalist class – in particular, to protect the property of the capitalist class. Property is seen as a fundamental right, and there is a line drawn between lawful and unlawful acquisition or appropriation of property belonging to another. The criminal law is seen as an instrument used to facilitate this end.

The second function of law is ideological. The ideological nature of law is that it is supposed to be a matrix of complex values and beliefs. The values and beliefs are those of the dominant class, and they underpin the existing social order. Thus laws on private property, the employer/employee relationship and the institution of family are seen by the ruling class as a useful and productive unit for the worker, thus allowing the bourgeoisie to maintain their hegemony over the working class.

The Marxist view of law recognises that consent is likely to be achieved through ideological means, as greater coercion would mean a breakdown of the relationship between the bourgeoisie and the proletariat that may hasten the predicted revolution of the masses. To will the proletariat into false consciousness, the capitalist state constantly renews itself and undertakes law reform to forestall the uprising of the masses. The welfare state, for example, was established to guarantee the minimum subsistence which the state gives each poor person as a ploy to hoodwink the worker into thinking the capitalist society seeks his/her interests.

In Marxist analysis, therefore, the law is a bourgeois law. The concept of the rule of law is used as a smokescreen, to convey the impression of democracy where fair liberal values are promoted. In Marxist ideology this image of law is illusory and largely symbolic in its practice. Bankowski and Mungham (Bankowski and Mungham, *Images of Law* (1976)) say that the welfare laws are still bourgeois laws promulgated to induce false consciousness among the proletariat. The law is always the superstructure that reflects the relations between the owners of the means of production and the workers.

The criticism of capitalist society by Marxist theory of law can be analysed by looking at a society like Britain to see whether there is some credibility in the theory. We can say that in a modern society like Britain the conditions that existed in the nineteenth century no longer apply. The welfare state has provided a huge cushion between the ruling class and the working class. We can also mention the property-owning democracy introduced by the Thatcher Government in the 1980s where workers were integrated into the mainstream of the British economy. Then there is the share ownership in privatised utilities – employees own shares in their companies. This is a kind of 'stakeholding' policy introduced to make the worker feel part of the enterprise. Some miners have joined hands to buy out the collieries where they work. It can, therefore, be said that in modern-day Britain the distinction between the capitalist and working-class person is very much blurred.

It follows from the above that the Marxist theory of law presented as a conflict theory of law seems inappropriate in modern-day Britain, and that the theory is best understood in its historical context – as an observation on the nature of law as it existed in the nineteenth century under capitalism.

However, to understand the value of the Marxist theory of law we need to concentrate on the coercive and ideological functions of the law as espoused. For example, as long as the criminal law is used to regulated the activities of the lower class and the civil law is used to regulate the activities of the ruling class, a case can be made that Marxist of theory of law is useful in our understanding of today's society. For example, many poor working-class people are brought within the purview of the criminal law for stealing and possession, convicted and sentenced into imprisonment, whereas the civil law is used to regulate companies and their bosses, who may commit horrendous offences like environmental pollution and escape with a fine. Similarly the boss who installs unsafe machinery which kills workers also escapes with a fine.

The ideological nature of the law is that it seeks to establish values that are somehow seen as values of the elite. Parliament makes laws because Members believe they are needed by society to solve problems; some people may say Members of Parliament belong to an elitist class and that, therefore, they reflect the values of their class. Although the present trend in law reform has made Marx's prediction of revolution false, the theory itself has a core value which is helpful to understand the nature of relationships that exist in society. Our understanding of law in society today is immensely enriched by Marxist theory of law.

QUESTION FOUR

'The ideas of the ruling class are in every epoch the ruling ideas: ie the class which is the ruling material force of society is at the same time its ruling intellectual force.' (Marx and Engels)

Does this help us to understand law?

University of London LLB Examination
(for External Students) Jurisprudence and Legal Theory 1990 Q7

General Comment

The Marxist account of society and the role of law and ideology therein needs to be explained and commented upon.

Skeleton Solution

Is and ought – Marxist view of ideology – base and superstructure – Althusser – Hay – the complex view of ideology (Summers) – content of ruling ideology – Thompson's defence of the 'Rule of Law' – critique of Marxist ideological theory.

Suggested Solution

The statement reflects a central tenet of Marxist thought about the structure of society, and more particularly the role of ideology. This view has important implications for how we understand law, but its claim that law is merely ideology may be said to be inaccurate and extreme. These two allegations can be assessed when one lays out the main elements of Marxist ideological theory.

Essentially Marx and Engels claimed that 'is' determined 'ought'. That the 'material conditions' of people's lives, which consisted of the conditions under which they worked (the 'relations of production') and the economic resources of society (the 'forces of production') both constructed and determined the ideas that persisted within society. These economically determined ideas include law. Not only do Marxists claim that ideas and consciousness result from the economic structure of society, they also assert that the ideas within society reflect the ideas and dominance of the 'ruling class'. This class (frequently termed 'capitalists') controls the economic structure of society and as a result are able to present their ideology to the rest of society as the 'dominant ideology'.

Crucial to Marx was a distinction between the 'economic base' and the 'superstructure' of society. The former consisted in the relations of production and the forces of production. Over and above this was the superstructure (which included religion, politics, law and morality) which was merely a product of the economic base. The ideology of capitalism, Marx claimed, became the dominant ideology because capitalists controlled the economic base. Law is reduced to a mere creation of the ruling class whose function is to serve the capitalistic interests of that class. The process by which the ideas of this class become transmitted to the rest of the population and why they should accept it was not fully explained by Marx and Engels. One must, therefore, turn to other Marxist theorists in search of an answer.

Althusser claimed that the intellectual force of the ruling class became dominant by utilising the superstructural institutions such as family, church, media and law. Law was in his term an 'ideological state apparatus'. Althusser claims that it is because the ruling class have the greatest economic power within society that it can use, inter alia, law to force its ideas on the rest of society. Hay presents a similar analysis, claiming that the ability of the ruling class to successfully enforce an increasing number of criminal offences without an accompanied increase in enforcement mechanisms was due to use of legal ideology. This ideology presented law as both terrifying and merciful, more importantly it claimed that law was neutral and the product of people's (the 'proletariat's') own minds.

Hill, Abercrombie and Turner doubt the efficiency of this transmission of ideology. They claim that the ideology is not completely accepted and often not at all. How can Marxists account for civil disobedience and criticism of the law if they wish to present the proletariat as blinded into obedience by ideology? No attempt is made to isolate the reasons why people obey laws; sometimes they might refute the ideology but obey for prudent reasons. Summers presents a more sophisticated explanation of the workings of legal ideology. For him, the superstructure consists of a pluralism of different ideologies which reflects the complexity of the power structure of society. However, one class tends to dominate; it can use its power to make its own ideology dominant. The law is both ideology and tool for securing this dominant position. We may feel that this paints a truer picture of law by including its instrumental aspect.

Despite these criticisms, Marxist theory has increased our understanding of the law by providing a possible explanation of the nature of law within Western society. Marx claimed that all ideology was the result of 'praxis' – what people experienced in their everyday lives was reflected in their ideas. This being so, Marx claimed that the economic structure of capitalist society saw people as individuals in a conflict with each other as to who could produce and exchange the greatest amount. This is reflected in the ruling ideology of law as a neutral mediator of individual interests; this view has much in common with that of Hobbes. Marx denounced this view as false consciousness. In order to achieve revolution, the workers had to see themselves in the world as they really were (an aim of both Realist and critical legal studies theorising). It was felt that this could be achieved by piercing through the dominant ideology and seeing workers (ie the proletariat) as a class (not isolated individuals) in relation to the material conditions of production.

Marxist analysis of the ideology of law has been criticised as crude economic instrumentalism, as such it distorts the true and important functions of the law by terming these aspects illusory ideology. An example of such criticism is EP Thompson's defence of the rule of law as an 'unqualified good'. He claims that legal ideology does not always justify dominance. Often it protects the weak and restrains the social elite. Modern examples can be said to be maternity (and now paternity) rights in the employment law field as well as the recent mushrooming in the review of the exercise of public power by the courts. The Marxist response that such functions of law are bribes and concessions to 'buy-off' the working class must be supported by empirical evidence otherwise they fall victim to a charge of conspiratorial paranoia.

Marx and Engels were unclear as to just how much the superstructure was determined by the base. If all the ideas within a given society were the products of its material conditions (as Marx and Engels often seem to claim) this would undermine their own theories of revolution and social change. Engels acknowledged as much, asking 'Why do we fight for the political dictatorship of the proletariat if political power is economically impotent?'

As a result of an unwillingness to have their own theories dismissed as merely economic constructs, Marx and Engels seem sometimes to claim that the superstructure also affected the economic base! Therefore, ideology and law could also be a determinative factor upon the economic relations within society. For example, the inheritance laws in England were seen by Engels as not only the result of economic causes but also of tradition.

Horwitz has expanded this complex (and on the face of it contradictory) view of ideology by looking at how the law, as one particular ideological mechanism within the superstructure, was systematically used by the American judiciary to facilitate and legitimate industrial capitalism. Thus it was an independent institution. It could effect tangible economic change and a recognition of this better fits our everyday experience of the law. Indeed it avoids not taking the law at 'face-value' (to use a Dworkinian term) by not seeing in law illusion.

QUESTION FIVE

How critical of the ideal of the rule of law is the Marxist approach?

University of London LLB Examination
(for External Students) Jurisprudence and Legal Theory June 1994 Q4

General Comment

This is a hard question and the answer requires a reasoned understanding of what Marx left for us as a philosophy, with specific reference to the rule of law and where it operates to continue and reinforce class divisions in society. It also requires an examination of Marxist theories of law because there is no separate treatise on law. Therefore, the question of how critical the ideal of the rule of law is must be judged against the overall Marxist approach.

Skeleton Solution

Marxist theories of law – no separate treatise on law – law and ideology – conclusion.

Suggested Solution

Marxism is in essence a political and social ideology because Karl Marx considered the economic system to be the base for all systems in society, including a legal system. Both Marx and Engels based their philosophies on the insights of Hegel, who saw civilisation as having a defined place in the progress of freedom based on the concept of the dialectic. The Hegelian dialectic is a theory where progress is a result of a clash of theses and antitheses which result in a compromise named 'synthesis'. Through the process of such conflict, a society will progress towards the truth.

Law is not defined in Marx's writings as a specific treatise, although law is considered as a manifestation of 'ideology' which is a central element of Marxist theory. History, to Marx, was a record of conflict of class against class, with the law 'taking sides', where society is divided into base and superstructure. Here, the base is the actual relationship between people who are involved in 'production' which is seen as the economic structure of society. The exploiter of such economic relationships is described as the dominant class.

A superstructure is made up of:

a) a reflection of these relationships in legal and political forms;

b) the dominant class view of the world; and

c) the development of awareness of social conflict which allows a critique of (a) and (b).

To Marxists, law represents a mirror of inequalities in society which are often obscured by the ruling classes' presentation of it as impartial and detached. Marx suggests that a judge, whilst believing he is working with objective categories, is merely working with categories which are the product of economic forces so that law becomes a false consciousness.

Engels analysed the tension between material forces and ideology in a letter to Conrad Schmidt by suggesting that law can exert itself on the base by:

a) having a crystallising effect which maintains traditions, customs and religious concepts. Such an effect is restrictive on the achievement of awareness of class struggles and, as such, holds up the inevitable process of history;

b) the more antagonistic forces there are in society, the more the law seeks to achieve a compromise of conflicting interests; and

c) the demystification of law has a critical effect on raising class consciousness necessary for revolution.

Thus, Marx and Engels see law as having a relative degree of autonomy, seeing it as an ideological cloak which hides the truth about social conflict through compromise or conservatism and an aspect of state control. Therefore, the Marxist perspective of law is dependent on the Marxist concept of the state which determines how critical the ideal of the rule of law is to Marxism.

Marx identifies the state as an intermediary in the foundation of all communal institutions, which gives them a political form. He considers that there is an illusion of the law being based on will, ie a will cut off from its real basis of free will. The state is viewed by Marxists as no more than an aspect of superstructure which does not exist before the emergence of the classes – the state's consequential growth mirrors the burgeoning of a class system.

To Marxists, the state is 'the executive committee' of the bourgeoisie within capitalism which rules on its own behalf, utilising the legal apparatus, with the threat of coercive action against those who seek to overturn the existing order.

Marxists have prophesied that the state, being affected by change and decay, will wither away when a triumphant revolution replaces 'the government of persons by the administration of things'. If classes disappear, post-revolution, there is no need for a legal apparatus in which to express class rule, so that poverty and exploitation, seen as the root causes of crime, will vanish within the new, classless society. People will develop into 'group creatures' having no need for codes and rules so that the need for an institutionalised law vanishes.

Vyshinsky, and other Soviet jurists, found such a doctrine difficult to accept, relying on the view that the construction of a socialist society would make it necessary to consolidate law and the State. Vyshinsky considered it as essential to retain law as an administrative law as a means of regulating social relationships. However, Pashukanis held that 'all law is bourgeois law', denouncing Soviet law as a relic of the former bourgeois state. To counter such a view, Vyshinsky defined law as the totality of rules of conduct which express the will of the ruling class being laid down in a legislative manner. This, together with the rules and practices of communal life, would be sanctioned by the power of the state.

Excesses within the legal systems fashioned from Marxist theory occurred in political situations where the rule of law and the rights of the accused were banished as 'remnants of bourgeois dominance'. The result saw a denial of human dignity and the growth of legal theories which merely justified the state's political practices. The collapse of some Marxist regimes in recent years illustrates what is widely held to be an essentially flawed theory of law.

Chaper 9
Feminist Jurisprudence

9.1   Introduction

9.2   Key points

9.3   Questions and suggested solutions

9.1 Introduction

Feminist jurisprudence is a relatively new topic and it has its most obvious roots in Marxist theories of law and in the Critical Legal Studies movement. It often refers to itself as 'critiquing' male values inherent in the legal system and so it is natural that its adherents are not accepting of what passes for orthodox legal doctrine. The secret to answering questions is to try to adopt a committed role in which you imagine the existing legal structures (or the 'gendered justice system' or 'gendered discourse') from the point of view of the oppressed. Like the CLS movement, there are a wide range of writers to write about and so answers have wide scope. Nevertheless, it is vital to inject your own views about the position of women within legal systems.

9.2 Key points

a) The 'critical' position to be adopted, as for Marxism and CLS. It is important to specify why this position differs from more orthodox positions.

b) The description of the theories of law and justice held by at least two feminist jurists.

c) The attitude adopted by the student towards feminine 'justice' in general, linking that attitude to reading.

9.3 Questions and suggested solutions

QUESTION ONE

What distinctive insights have feminists to offer to the theory of law?

University of London LLB Examination
(for External Students) Jurisprudence and Legal Theory June 1999 Q8

General Comment

This is another straightforward question about the feminist movement's ideas as they relate to law. You must be very careful that you discuss the question relative to the legal system, and not become bogged down with the politics of the movement.

Skeleton Solution

Origins of feminist jurisprudence – description of feminist jurisprudence – the claims made by feminist legal scholarship – insights regarding the law – conclusion.

Suggested Solution

Feminist legal scholarship could be said to have developed in this country between the late 1960s and the early 1970s. The principal reason for the rise of the feminist movement in law was the perceived injustice and inequality between the male and female genders (as seen by the movement) with regard to the law. For example, many women enrolled on law courses in the 1960s and became aware that insufficient attention was paid in the syllabus to issues of concern to women, such as rape, domestic violence, sexual harassment, sex discrimination and inequality of pay between the genders.

Feminist legal scholarship is seen as an enquiry into the law's contribution in building, sustaining and embellishing patriarchy, and seeks ways to undermine this contribution and eventually eliminate it.

Clare Dalton ((1987) 38 Syracuse Law Review 1129) is one such feminist who argues that their scholarship explores womens' subordination (both its nature and extent), and is dedicated to discovering the origins of this subordination, and initiating a course of action for change. It focuses on the legal system, its scholarship is based on womens' experiences and its goal is to seek (through raising awareness) to influence revision of the law. To Clare Dalton, women must not merely learn about the effect of law and local institutions, but must also challenge the structure of legal theory, which is essentially male-orientated, in order to agitate for radical changes.

Lucinda Finley (Finley, Lucinda, 'Breaking Women's Silence in Law: the Dilemma of the Gendered Nature of Legal Reasoning' (1989) 64 Notre Dame Law Review 886) states that the language of the law is inherently male. Examining the relationship between language, power and the law, she claims that the law embodies a conception of 'male equality' which matches the gender of its male architects. Legal theory and legal language are patriarchal in a normative sense, and reflect only a male-based perspective. She argues that the law uses only privileged white men as the norm of equality in the law, as well as for assessing the reasonable man.

She, however, points out that, just because the law is patriarchal, it does not follow that women have been totally ignored by the law. Women are the targets or subjects of many laws; however, womens' nature, capacity and experience is seen through the male eye, rather than through womens own definitions and experiences informing the law.

For example, the legal definition of rape is made from the male perspective. The issue of consent is seen from the male perspective. Whether force is used or any resistance shown is from the male perspective, and the definition of sex as the penetration of the vagina by the penis is from the male perspective. It is not the woman's experience of sexual violation which defines the crime.

The crucial point in all this criticism of the traditional legal norm is that it does not sufficiently address the female/male problem of equality. Employment law places an obligation on employers to treat all employees equally, and yet if the employer can show that the nature of the work is such that he must only employ males, then the employer will escape any sanctions. The notion of equality becomes farcical if the law does not insist on it and ensure that all laws treat both genders equally.

If it is possible for females to be allowed to serve in the armed forces of the United Kingdom, for example, it is argued that there is no justification why women should not be allowed to fight on the front line just like men. A point is also raised regarding the inequality of pay in the work place. Although the law stresses equality, it is argued that this is only skin deep when it comes to equal pay between the genders. It is argued that employers assume that, since a woman may take time out to raise children, she cannot demonstrate loyalty to the establishment and so her prospects are rather diminished relative to the male gender. Added to this is the absence of many women in positions of authority. The same argument used above is employed to sustain this point. To the feminist, the law can do better. It can place a duty on employers to ensure parity between the two genders in the work place. Where there is a duty to conform the employer may be more inclined think differently.

Feminists further argue that the law dispenses male-orientated justice. Women have a different make-up to men. Men are, arguably, hard, uncaring and distant; women on the other hand are caring, and do not react with white-hot rage as men do. Thus the definition of provocation as a defence to murder does not take into account this difference in women. The notion that everybody is susceptible to sudden and temporary losses of self-control is not true of the female psyche. Women are generally slow to anger, and it may take cumulative occurrences for them to lose self-control. The failure to recognise this difference between the genders is itself an injustice in the law.

It must be said that certain case law has addressed some of these concerns. The cases of *R v R* [1992] 1 AC 599 on marital rape and *R v Thornton* [1992] 1 All ER 306 on the concept of the 'battered woman's syndrome' have sought to address some of the problems revealed by feminine legal scholarships. Indeed, to the extent that the law has changed at all to accommodate such issues we can make the point that feminists have provided good insights to the theory of law.

QUESTION TWO

'Feminist jurisprudence does not so much claim that traditional jurisprudence was wrong, but demonstrates that women have been in a radically different social relation to the law than men.'

Discuss.

University of London LLB Examination
(for External Students) Jurisprudence and Legal Theory June 1996 Q11

General Comment

Since feminist jurisprudence is now a strong element in the study of law, questions on issues raised by the topic can be given the attention they deserve by the candidate. With many women now involved in the study and practice of law, there are bound to be critical questions asked about some 'received wisdom' and ideas about how the law looks at men and women. Attempt the question only if you are confident about the point which feminist thought about the law makes.

Skeleton Solution

Origins of feminist jurisprudence – description of feminist jurisprudence – the claim made by feminist jurisprudence – Lucinda Finley as a paradigm – summary and conclusion.

Suggested Solution

Feminist jurisprudence can be said to have developed from the general women's movement in the late 1960s and early 1970s. Ashe says the development of feminist jurisprudence was an inevitable 'extension of the engagement of female reflection and speech to one more area of discourse' ((1987) 38 Syracuse Law Review 1129).

From the latter part of the 1960s onwards many women enrolled on law courses, and questioned the neglect in law curriculums of issues of concern to women like rape, inequality in pay among the sexes, domestic violence, sexual harassment and sex discrimination. Feminist jurisprudence is a broad church and reflects different strands of feminist thought, but the unifying theme is that society and in particular the legal system is patriarchal. It is, then, an inquiry into the law's contribution to building, sustaining, underlying and embellishing patriarchy, and seeks to find ways whereby this patriarchy can be undermined and eventually eliminated. This aim is what distinguishes feminist jurisprudence from traditional jurisprudence.

Dalton ((1987) 3 Berkeley Women's Law Journal 1) says that feminist jurisprudence explores women's subordination, its nature and extent, and is dedicated to finding the how and why of this subordination, and to finding a course of action for change. Its methodology is to concentrate on the legal system. It is feminist because it is based on women's experiences, and it seeks through awareness-raising to achieve the goal of law revision. Wishik says traditional jurisprudence is patriarchal and has not the spaces within which to 'create visions of feminist futures' ((1985) 1 Berkeley Women's Law Journal 64), and Dalton opines that women cannot only learn about the effect the law and legal institutions have on the lives of women but also how to challenge the structure of legal thought which in a culturally specific sense is 'male' oriented and calls for radical changes. In other words, feminists have found the 'maleness' of traditional jurisprudence worrying and want a change.

Finley ('Breaking Women's Silence in Law: The Dilemma of the Gendered Nature of Legal Reasoning' (1989) 64 Notre Dame Law Review 886) concentrates on legal language, which she says is gendered, to prove the inherent 'maleness' of the law. She says this is seen in legal reasoning and its language of expression. According to Finley, throughout the history of Anglo-American jurisprudence, the primary linguists of the law have been almost exclusively male. She says the history of traditional jurisprudence is such that it has been shaped, defined, interpreted and given meanings consistent with men's understandings of the world and people who are considered different from them. Because of this, law has excluded or marginalised the voices of those 'others', who happen to be women.

Finley says the men of law have societal power and are oblivious competing terms; they are insulated from challenges to their language and have come to accept their language as natural, inevitable, complete, objective and neutral. Finley's work is an examination of the relationship between language, power and the law. Her thesis is that legal language and legal reasoning is gendered and that this gender matches the male gender of its linguistic architects. Law is seen as a patriarchal form of reasoning as the philosophy of liberalism of which law is part. Finley's claim that legal reasoning and language are patriarchal has normative sense in that male-based perspectives, images and experience are often taken as the norm in law. It is instructive as Finley says that the law uses privileged white men as the norm for equality law, for assessing the reasonable person, the way men would react is the norm for self-defence law, and the male worker is the prototype for labour law. Legal language draws heavily on men's experiences and the powerful social situation of men relative to women.

According to Finley the fact that many women are trained lawyers and are adept at male thinking does not mean legal language is androgynous – it just means that women have learned male language. She stresses, however, that the claim that law is patriarchal does not mean women have been totally ignored by the law. Women are the targets or subjects of many laws, but the point being made is that women's nature, capacities and experiences are seen through the male eye, rather than women's own definitions informing law. Finley, therefore, argues that feminist jurisprudence does not claim that traditional jurisprudence was wrong but that women have been in a radically different social relation to the law than men.

She gives several examples drawn from mainstream law that prove that the law is defined by male experience rather than the woman's. The legal definition of rage is an example at male perspective. It is the male's view of whether the woman has consented that determines the issue of consent; it is the male view of what are force and resistance in situations other than rape that defines whether force has been used against a woman and she has resisted. As far as sex is concerned, it is the male definition of sex – penetration of the vagina by the penis – that is accepted rather than the woman's experience of sexual violation that defines the crime.

According to Finley, in order for feminists to use the law to agitate for change, women must be able to talk about the complex relationship between power, gender and knowledge. Feminists must accept this connection in order to demystify the 'neutrality' of the law, to bring an awareness to the law that women's definitions have been excluded and marginalised; this will show that the law's 'neutrality' is one of the tools for silencing women.

Is there any chance that when feminists speak of the connection of power, history and domination they are employing politics and passion not law? Consider this. In legal language, experience and perspective are deemed to be biased. Having no experience or prior knowledge of something is equated with neutrality. This is relevant to jury selection. A woman who has been raped is more likely to be excluded from jury selection for a rape trial, the assumption being that her experience will render her incapable of being objective. Can it be said that her experience, rather than making her vindictive and biased, will give her critical understanding, making her more able to challenge the male-created vision of the crime? Is it possible that her experience leads her invariably to think of legal language as patriarchal? Is Finley right that the woman with personal experience of rape is more objective? This is very doubtful and Finley is not convincing here. She has a point though in saying that legal reasoning is embedded in a patriarchal framework that equates abstraction and universalisation from one group's experiences as neutrality. In so doing, legal reasoning views male experiences and perspectives as the universal norm around which terms and areas of law are defined. This is what feminist jurisprudence seeks to change.

Touching on labour law, Finley says that the meaning of work is gendered to mean work done for usages outside the home. This focus does not take into account women's work at home as wives which is unregulated by law. Why not pay women for housework? Is housework not 'work' in the conventional sense because the male architects of legal language say so?

On tort law, Finley says that the law defines injuries and compensation primarily by reference to what has kept people out at work and what their work is worth. She says in this framework damages for non-economic loss, pain and suffering, and nervous shock are seen as marginal and expendable. The most obvious cases of nervous shock to be cited are *Bourhill* v *Young* [1943] AC 92 and *McLoughlin* v *O'Brian* [1983] 1 AC 410. Did the court in these two cases think of the submissions of the plaintiffs as marginal and expendable because the law considers physical attributes of women as the same as men? This is a difficult point Finley makes. It is easy to dismiss the law on nervous shock as patriarchal because women consider nervous shock a crucial area of recovery. I do not think it is entirely correct to say if women are denied recovery for nervous shock it is because the law sees them as suspect and expendable.

Another area of the law on which Finley comments is the criminal law. The language of criminal law makes the paradigmatic criminal male. The female criminal is deemed doubly deviant, first for not conforming to the stereotypical view of the woman as a mother, and second for being a criminal (Chesney-Lind and Daly, 'Feminism and Criminology' (1987) 5 Just Q 497; Heidensohn, 'Models of Justice: Portia or Persephone? Some Thoughts on Equality, Fairness and Gender in the Field of Criminal Justice' (1986) 14 International J Soc of Law 287). This is about the conflict aspect of language. The language of conflict means there will be winners and losers, and in a patriarchal system, it will often be women and their concerns that are devalued, overlooked and lost in the race to set priorities and choose sides.

Similarly the law on provocation is seen from male experience. Because women do not react with a sudden white-hot rage they are denied the defence of provocation. The agitation of women for a change in abortion law is explained on the basis of the autonomy of the woman. Denying women a right to abortion is denying them rights over their own bodies, and this is seen through male eyes not the woman's.

Having considered the limitations of legal reasoning and the connection between power, gender and legal knowledge, feminist jurisprudence looks at the multiple experiences and voices of women as the frame of reference. It asks us to look at things in their historical, social and political context. It distrusts abstractions and universal rules because 'objectivity' hides biases; it questions norms and assumptions in traditional jurisprudence, questioning its content and pushing its boundaries. This is all based on the fact that experiences of men and women are many, different, and diverse but they also overlap, so difference may not be a relevant legal criterion.

To Finley, therefore, the answer does not lie in the French feminists' argument for creation of a new language. Women cannot create their own separate legal language, but since their voices must be heard the only possiblility is to speak the same legal language as men in order to try to bring women's experiences, perspectives, and voices into law, and help to empower women and legitimate their experiences. She acknowledges that there has been development in language change. The term 'sexual harassment' is now in vogue, as is the term 'battering' used for domestic violence. The effect of change in legal reasoning and language has been felt in the United Kingdom. As the case of *R v R* [1992] 1 AC 599 shows, the concept of rape has been broadened to cover rape in marriage. On the law of provocation, the law has, as in *R v Thornton* [1992] 1 All ER 306, recognised the concept of the 'battered woman syndrome' as an acceptable defence. This recognises that sudden loss of self-control is not in the make-up of women as it is for men, and the case of *Roe v Wade* 410 US 113 (1973) shows the law recognising the autonomy of women over their bodies.

Feminist jurisprudence has made enormous strides. It has succeeded in pushing the boundaries of law and legal language to the extent that the law has now come to recognise that women in the past have been in a radically different social relation to the law than men. It is not that traditional jurisprudence is wrong and must be abolished. It is just that women's experiences and expectations were not sufficiently recognised by the definitions of law which traditional jurisprudence offered.

QUESTION THREE

'Since all previous jurisprudence has been written by men who have laid down the rules of what is acceptable to write, the idea of a feminist jurisprudence is a contradiction in terms.'

Do you agree?

University of London LLB Examination
(for External Students) Jurisprudence and Legal Theory June 1995 Q6

General Comment

This type of question has started to appear regularly because the concept of feminist jurisprudence is now recognised by academics as a philosophy in its own right. The range of reference materials covering the subject has increased and students must use the most contemporary sources. Whether there is, or is not, a feminist jurisprudence will continue to be debated for years to come. However, the student should not be afraid to express a view either way and justify such a view.

Skeleton Solution

Introduction: broad concepts and historical development – the women's movement and female law students – equal treatment – conclusion: the opening of the debate.

Suggested Solution

If the ideal of a feminist jurisprudence is 'a contradiction in terms' as the question suggests, then a great deal of paper and printers' ink has been expended needlessly in the last 15 years upon what some commentators apparently dismiss as a 'contradiction'.

Those who support the idea of a feminist jurisprudence as a 'contradiction in terms' ignore reality and jurisprudence itself, which cannot but reflect the social context from which it springs. As the twentieth century draws to a close, feminist jurisprudence has evolved as a branch of jurisprudential theory which deals with the reality of women's emergence as active participants in the intellectual, commercial and professional life, primarily of western societies, namely the United States, Canada, Australia and, latterly and belatedly, the United Kingdom.

Not unexpectedly, the feminist jurisprudential mainstream has migrated across the Atlantic in much the same way as the women's movement itself. The mere fact of a 'feminist jurisprudence' reflects a vast new paradigm shift, or new movement, which re-examines and challenges current jurisprudential orthodoxy, which undeniably has been sustained by men. Nonetheless, to say unequivocally that men have somehow 'laid down rules of what is acceptable to write' in jurisprudence is a remarkable irrelevancy.

It is submitted that a body of 'rules of what is acceptable to write' does not exist and that therefore the statement is a nonsense. The statement is, however, interesting in that it is perhaps an indicator of the uncertainty, intellectual confusion, even overt hostility and derision which feminist jurisprudence has attracted until very recently. Nonetheless, feminist jurisprudence has successfully pushed back horizons and extended jurisprudential perspectives. As Katherine Bartlett argues in *Feminist Legal Methods* (1990), 'knowledge is located in a social context and reflects different experiences'. The key therefore lies 'in the effort to extend one's limited perspective'.

It could be extrapolated from this that, prior to the emergence of feminist jurisprudence, jurisprudential perspectives were indeed limited by experiences that were exclusively male. It is doubtful though that such an exclusive male perspective will continue to prevail in jurisprudence into the next century.

Contemporary feminist literature is the products of the women's movement of the late 1960s and early 1970s. Its most vociferous and influential exponent, Simone de Beauvoir (with her seminal work, *The Second Sex* (1949)), was followed by other feminist writers including Betty Friedan, Kate Millet and Germaine Greer.

The women's movement coincided with, or perhaps led to, a dramatic increase in the number of women students in law schools in the 1960s and 1970s, particularly in North America – a trend which has been mirrored in the United Kingdom. Interestingly the Council of Legal Education in 1996 turned out more women than men who qualified for the Bar. It is now perhaps safer than ever to claim that far from remaining a curiosity, feminist jurisprudence will almost inevitably take its place as part of the jurisprudential mainstream. (How likely is it that an examination question in the year 2020 will even suggest that feminist jurisprudence is 'a contradiction in terms'?) Twining's Hamlyn lecture entitled *Blackstone's Tower: The English Law School* (1994) examines the increase in the number of female law students with no definite conclusion as to its effect on the profession.

Despite the dismissive comment which it still attracts, feminist jurisprudence has become both a cause and a result of consciousness-raising in areas of law that were hitherto neglected, including sex discrimination, domestic violence and sexual harassment, issues which have been brought to the fore largely by the increased number of female law students. When such students qualify as practising lawyers, the litigation they undertake on behalf of women does, it is suggested, influence both scholarship and opinion within jurisprudence.

Feminist jurisprudence existed de facto at least a decade before it was labelled as such. The term 'feminist jurisprudence' was not identified, nor recognised as a separate (or separated) branch of jurisprudence, until legal theorists like Ann Scales first used the term at Harvard in 1978, followed by Catharine MacKinnon in 1983. Both regarded feminist legal theory as a belief that 'society and necessarily legal order is patriarchal'. Feminist jurisprudence, therefore, seeks to undermine and eliminate such patriarchy.

Subsequently, feminists have carried on the enquiry, focussing on the politics of law and on 'the law's role', as Wishik says (1985) 'in perpetuating patriarchal hegemony'. The goal of such analysis is change, or 'revision', as Adrienne Rich puts it in *On Lies, Secrets and Silence: Selected Prose 1966–1978* (1986). Clare Dalton, however, seeks to challenge the structure of legal thought as, in Lloyd's words, 'contingent and in some culturally specific sense "male"'. Here, the need for radical rather than ameliorative change is implied, particularly as the assertion under discussion that 'all previous jurisprudence has been written by men' is unarguable (if 'previous' means prior to 1980).

Although it may be a matter of dispute that 'men ... have laid down rules of what is acceptable to write', Scales' criticism ('The Emergence of Feminist Jurisprudence: An Essay' (1986) 95 Yale LJ 1373) that, for example, the US Supreme Court's equal protection approach to sex discrimination 'makes maleness the norm of what is human' is less easily argued. 'It is necessary', she says, 'to reconstruct the legal system which 'usurps women's language in order to further define the world in the male image'. 'Domination', Scales says, 'is the injustice of sexism, not irrationality'. Scales, as Lloyd explains (see *Introduction to Jurisprudence* (6th ed 1994)), looks to a feminist jurisprudence which will focus on domination, disadvantage and disempowerment, rather than one which merely examines differences between men and women.

In a 1985 article ((1984–85) 13 NYU Rev L and Soc Change 325), the liberal feminist Wendy Williams dismissed the concept of 'equal treatment' as being beneficial only to women who 'meet male norms' rather than those who engage in female activities such as childbearing or child rearing. Employment practices which continue to place women at a disadvantage if they pursue a maternal role would only tend to confirm Williams' observation. In *Feminism Unmodified* (1987), MacKinnon pursued much the same argument, asserting that feminists should concentrate on identifying dominance, in which social inequalities arise as the result of the subordination of women by men.

These views, however, have come in for criticism. All women cannot be said to be subordinate to all men. Therefore, what is seen as an overemphasis on male dominance is perhaps misleading. Post-modern feminism obliquely attempts to deal with this objection, denying that there is a single theory of equality that will benefit all women. Equality itself is seen as a product of patriarchy and therefore in need of feminist reconstruction. Post-modern feminism thus contributes usefully to the feminist jurisprudential debate as one of the four schools of feminist theory identified by Cain who classifies them as post-modern, liberal, radical and cultural feminism.

The liberal feminist, according to Cain, sees equality as equality of opportunity. Radical feminists such as Christine Littleton and MacKinnon vociferously support alternative measures to challenge such equality, while cultural feminists like Carol Gilligan and

Robin West view male/female differences in a more positive light, advocating change which supports the underlying values of this difference, like 'caring' and 'connectedness'.

Cultural feminism probably lies at the heart of Lucinda Finley's examination of the relationship between language, power and the law. Even less conspicuous areas of law like tort reveal (in Lloyd's summary of Finley's views) 'the law's cognition of women refracted through the male eye, rather than through women's experiences and definitions' and cites as just one example, the traditional prejudice of assessing damages for non-economic loss, pain, suffering and nervous shock as 'marginal and expendable' (see Lloyd and Freeman, *Introduction to Jurisprudence* (6th ed 1994)).

Matters like these, of course, occupy the personal sphere. Feminist jurisprudence nevertheless insists that they be taken no less seriously than so-called 'public' questions, involving all people, which in the past have been the major concern of jurisprudence – once an exclusively male preserve, but no longer.

Since the commentaries on feminist jurisprudence were first published, events and subsequent legislation have moved forward, notably in the tabling of legislation which allows for the prosecution of sexual offences against children by British citizens, even when these offences have been committed abroad. Female genital mutilation is, of course, illegal in western countries. That it is a traditional practice in many other areas of the world is a matter for feminist jurisprudence to address, now and in the future, together with other issues which can be categorised as 'human rights' rather than specifically 'feminist' concerns.

Far from being 'a contradiction in terms', feminist jurisprudence has opened up useful areas of debate from which to re-examine and reassess a wide range of issues, issues which, while not necessarily ignored by jurisprudence 'because all previous jurisprudence has been written by men', have been undeniably neglected. It is in redressing this neglect that feminist jurisprudence has revealed its value.

QUESTION FOUR

'The strength of the feminist work so far lies in the critique that has been mounted of the foundations of traditional jurisprudence rather than any suggestions for radical improvement.'

Do you agree?

University of London LLB Examination
(for External Students) Jurisprudence and Legal Theory June 1994 Q6

General Comment

This question is a relatively modern innovation for the jurisprudence course. The subject matter of women's rights is of growing importance, being seen as a rights movement which parallels to some degree the rise of natural law. The answer requires examples from commentators who have compared natural rights and women's rights on the basis of principle.

Case law on marital rape and the defence of provocation continue to suggest a building on the foundation of traditional jurisprudence rather than issues of radical improvement, though individual judgments, such as the decision in *R v R* [1992] 1 AC 599, point a clear path towards equal rights rather than separate rights.

Skeleton Solution

Natural rights and women's rights – equal rights versus separate rights – sexual discrimination: rape and the defence of provocation – conclusion: wives with equal rights.

Suggested Solution

While many primitive societies are essentially matriarchal, considerable evidence has suggested that over the centuries women have been treated in an unequal fashion when compared with men. J S Mill questioned the traditional position of women in society in his work *On the Subjection of Women in the Nineteenth Century*. The inferior position of women, where for example in the old marriage service they were obliged to obey their husbands, and the rule that a woman's property belonged to her husband, did not begin to change significantly until the Married Women's Property Act 1882 came into force.

By the beginning of the twentieth century, writers such as Engels (*The Origins of the Family*) and Safiotti (*Women and Class Society*) began to influence the historic view of the male capitalist being perceived as the villain, and women and workers being oppressed and exploited. The rise of the suffragette movement and the opening of career and educational opportunities enabled women's rights to appear on the political agenda for the first time.

Dworkin's view (in *Taking Rights Seriously*) establishes that there are principles which underlie laws which the courts will apply and include rights which should be respected because of race, sex, language or religion. He cites the 14th Amendment of the Constitution of the United States to justify his view, stating that all people should be treated as equals.

Around the same time, Rawls (in *A Theory of Justice*) suggested that there are principles of equal rights which go to the heart of equal basic liberties for all. His view was that social and economic inequalities should be arranged in order that they are both of greatest benefit to the least advantaged and 'attached to offices open to all in conditions of fair equality of opportunity'.

Nearly 20 years later, the House of Lords reviewed several appeals dealing specifically with male and female rights. In *C v S* [1987] 2 WLR 1108, it held that, concerning the request for an abortion, a father has no rights. Commentators have criticised the protection of such rights towards a female because they involve the denial of rights to a father or the unborn male or female child.

The House of Lords in *R v R* [1992] 1 AC 599, held that a husband may be convicted of rape against his wife. The justification is that today's marriages are fundamentally different from those of previous generations. In this context, Dworkin and others acknowledge the principles which indicate that a law may change as society develops, with the principle of equal concern and respect requiring free and continuing consent to exist within marriage, so that the relationship is one between equals.

Iris Young (in *Justice and the Politics of Difference*) postulates a modern thesis for feminist jurisprudence. She observes that the law's insistence on treating like cases alike creates the pretence that important differences in people, such as black, disadvantaged women, or white advantaged men, are not real differences because such laws merely reinforce the unjustified differences in the way in which people are treated.

If morality is to be part of the law (as natural law suggests), there will be differences between men and women which are morally relevant in defences raised such as provocation. In *DPP* v *Camplin* [1978] 2 All ER 168, the action of a 'reasonable man' requirement was interpreted to include not only a man but a boy who was both retarded and sensitive. However, legal argument today is not so thinly applied as to disallow the extension of the 'reasonable man' test to include (for provocation defences concerning domestic abuse) a 'reasonable women' requirement.

The mainstream attitude on women's rights today remains in favour of equal rights based on a principle of equal concern and respect. Whilst Phillips (in *Feminism and Equality*) has adopted the widely accepted view that gender will not preclude equal treatment of either sex, positive discrimination in favour of women is also discussed within the foundations of traditional jurisprudence. Feminist writers such as Germaine Greer and Simone de Beauvoir have achieved, with others, many legislative changes (Sex Discrimination Acts, Equal Opportunities Act) which may be termed a 'radical improvement' for women.

It is perhaps important to note also the work of Alice Walker. She takes a view akin to certain civil rights activists who argue a more radical stance. Walker advocates that women are not the same and that separation is the solution if they so choose. It is submitted that true radical improvement would consist of separate societies, achieved by ending economic, social, domestic and legal dependence, though, to many people, the principle of visiting one another solely to reproduce is questionable.

Chapter 10

Utilitarianism

10.1   **Introduction**

10.2   **Key points**

10.3   **Questions and suggested solutions**

10.1 Introduction

Utilitarianism is famously known in terms of the 'greatest happiness principle', the idea first mooted by Jeremy Bentham and his immediate mentors (in particular, James Mill). The idea is simple and appealing: governments should act, by legislation, to produce, amongst all other choices open to them, a state of affairs where the maximum happiness could be enjoyed by the greatest number of people. The appeal lies in the idea that everyone is to count; you do not discount some people because of some contempt for them or the way they live. But it is most important to realise that utilitarianism has come a long way since Bentham's principle. The main difference between Benthamic (or, as it is sometimes called, 'hedonistic') utilitarianism and modern doctrines of utilitarianism is that the idea of pleasure, or happiness, both highly subjective terms, are replaced by the idea of 'welfare' as measured by the satisfaction of declared wants. Modern utilitarianism thus is seen to be much more closely linked to economic analysis – it is only a short step to equate welfare with wealth (they are not the same; just try comparing penniless Tiny Tim, who was happy, with rich Ebenezer Scrooge, who was unhappy, in Dickens's *A Christmas Carol*). The advantage of the modern approach, besides being more realistic (how do you judge whether a person is made happier by some policy?), is that it nods in the direction of endorsing the value of personal autonomy by making a person's declaration conclusive of what is good for him.

A student preparing for an examination must be aware of the following points: the difference between 'rule' and 'act' utilitarianism (only rule utilitarianism – the view that the right act is the one that is in accordance with the rule that, if followed, will be productive of the most happiness – makes any sense of the law because the law consists of injunctions to rule following); the difference between 'pleasure' and 'happiness'; the weak position of minorities in utilitarian calculations; the problem of the 'incommensurability of values' (how do you inter-personally measure people's pleasures or 'happinesses'?); and the problem of rights (eg Dworkin's argument that rights based arguments 'trump' arguments of policy).

Utilitarianism is an excellent subject to write an examination answer on because it is a topic full of examples and you can wax lyrical about them with pretty much a free hand! Make sure, however, you thoroughly grasp what utilitarianism is about; it is no use just writing what you hope will sound good to an examiner because understanding the basic idea has some difficulties. Once these are grasped, then the essay will write itself. One good way to find examples is to notice just how frequently politicians use utilitarian arguments sometimes to justify otherwise rather shady arguments; note, too, the relationship between the economic analysis of law and utilitarianism. The latter is particularly important given the question because there is a large group of people, known as the 'law and economics' school, who would think that this sort of reasoning (basically cost-benefit analysis) is entirely appropriate for law.

10.2 Key points

This is used by many theorists as a starting point for advancing their own theories of justice. In broad terms utilitarianists regard as just that which maximises 'welfare' or happiness. The student might wish to consider the theories of Bentham and Mill in particular.

10.3 Questions and suggested solutions

QUESTION ONE

State what, in your view, is the most convincing form of utilitarianism. Can it account adequately for the existence of moral rights? Does it have to?

University of London LLB Examination
(for External Students) Jurisprudence and Legal Theory June 1996 Q6

General Comment

This is a straightforward question on utilitarianism. To gain good marks, however, the candidate has to demonstrate an understanding of the utilitarian principle and its practical meaning. What does it mean to say a particular law has a utility value either for the majority or minority members of community?

Skeleton Solution

Classical utilitarian doctrine – theory in perspective – individual rights as moral rights – Dworkin's rights thesis – conclusion.

Suggested Solution

The father of utilitarianism, Jeremy Bentham, says in his book *An Introduction to the Principles of Morals and Legislation* (1823) that:

'... nature has placed mankind under the governance of two sovereign masters, pain and pleasure. It is for them alone to point out what we ought to do, as well as determine what we shall do.'

Bentham advances the principle that the proper basis for morality and legislation is to use the felicific calculus to test the rightness or wrongness of any action private or public.

He says the maxim 'the greatest happiness of the greatest number' provides the criterion for testing the morality of the utilitarian principle. This principle, therefore, is about seeking the greatest or highest welfare of the greatest number of people. To achieve this he recommends that:

a) since men want happiness they must approve a principle which says that they ought to have what they want;

b) acceptance of the principle of utility reduces disagreements about future matters of fact, thereby making morals and legislation scientific;

c) given that men are motivated by pain and pleasure, properly drafted legislation can produce a coincidence between the interest of the individual and the interest of the community. Recognising the rewards and punishments laid down by the law, a person will be able to draw the necessary conclusions about the rightness or wrongness of any proposed actions, that is, the effects of his or her actions upon his or her own happiness as well as that of the entire community.

With these recommendations in mind, Bentham advocates that the obligation to obey the law is based on the promotion of the collective good. He says, therefore, that 'the evil of punishment must exceed the profit of the offence'.

The attractiveness of the moral principle enshrined in the principle of utilitarianism is instructive. The jurist sees the law as a mechanism which operates for the good of the whole society. If the good of the whole society is of the essence, then the utilitarian will argue that the moral worth of the principle in recognising that action be taken in the interest of the moral rights of the majority is worthy of attention.

Professor Dworkin in *Taking Rights Seriously* (1978) says the moral appeal of utilitarianism rests on the fact that in coming to a judgment about general welfare, each person's interest counts equally. To Dworkin, people must be treated with equal concern and respect when political decisions are taken that will affect them. This idea finds expression in utilitarianism in the sense that each person's interest counts equally in the utility calculations. However, Dworkin favours a version of utilitarianism which allows an individual's rights to trump general welfare.

Dworkin's position follows from the criticism that even though classical utilitarianism is said to be a moral principle in that the rights of the majority are protected and promoted, the rights of the minority are sacrificed in the process. It becomes a question of the rights of the majority against the rights of the minority.

The flows in the utilitarian doctrine can be stated to lie in the felicific calculus used to measure pleasure and pain. How does one measure pleasure and pain using a felicific calculus? We are dealing with intangibles which are subjective elements, and it is difficult to measure pain and pleasure in any objective way. Having said this one is conscious of the fact that legislation made by legislatures is based on a utility calculation, using the greatest happiness of the greatest number maxim of Bentham. To Bentham good legislation can be made using the felicific calculus. It is arguable that if the motive behind law making is to seek the interest of the whole community, then utilitarianism accounts for the moral rights of the majority of citizens, say the right to life of everyone.

The very idea that classical utilitarianism accounts for the moral rights of the majority throws into question the moral rights of the minority. If the majority has a moral right to life, does it mean the sacrificing of the moral right of the minority to achieve a similar end? Because of this, classical utilitarianism is criticised for not catering adequately for individual moral rights as against the collective moral rights.

An argument can be raised on the moral worth and autonomy of the individual which means that people should not be treated merely as aggregate numbers in some grand calculus of general social benefits. According to Kant, human beings are not means to an end but ends in themselves. John Rawls' idea (Rawls, *A Theory of Justice* (1972)) of trading one person's welfare for another's offends peoples' moral intuition. For Rawls, classical utilitarianism cannot satisfy the requirement of moral justice because of its ability to sacrifice the interests of the individual for the collective welfare.

This idea that the individual is an autonomous moral agent is questioned by Nicola Lacey (Lacey, *State Punishment* (1988), p36), who says this view must be modified in order to account for an adequate conception of political society. She asks whether the total integrity of individuals in an imaginary state of nature can really be preserved on the transition to a political society, and that whether it is enough to view society merely as the sum of the individuals within it, its creation forming no extra or incompatible rights or obligations as Robert Nozick suggests in *State, Anarchy and Utopia* (1974) (Lacey, ibid, p38).

A response to Lacey's argument is that although an individual is a member of a political society, the individual has a moral right to be treated with equal concern and respect, and exemplary sentences, eg 'sacrificing' one offender in the hope of deterring others, are morally objectionable, as they condemn an individual in order to achieve a social goal.

Professor Hart (Hart, *Prolegomenon to Principles of Punishment: In Sentencing* Eds Gross and Von Hirsch), in tracing the utilitarian value in sentencing, says the primary operation of criminal punishment consists of announcing certain standards of behaviour and attaching penalties for deviation, and leaving the individual to choose (just as Bentham advocated with the felicific calculus in calculating pain and pleasure). Hart says this is a method of social control which maximises individual freedom – which itself has a moral worth – within the framework of the law. That classical utilitarianism is not satisfactorily convincing, in that it does not adequately account for individual moral rights, is shown by Hart's call that the state must forbid the use of one human being for the benefit of others except for the individual's voluntary actions against them (Hart, ibid).

The arguments marshalled above accept that the classical utilitarian doctrine is convincing and show that classical utilitarianism, as espoused by Jeremy Bentham, is a moral doctrine. It considers the moral rights of the whole community, not individuals. This is as far as it goes. It has also been shown that the moral rights which the principle recognises are the moral rights which the majority enjoys, and that in achieving this the moral rights of the minority are sacrificed. However, it is arguable that the moral rights of the individual must be protected. This places the moral rights of the majority in conflict with those of the minority. It cannot be right that a theory can be made to apply unequally to people in a society. Whether it is for better or for worse, the classical utilitarian doctrine does account for the existence of moral rights.

However, I am of the view that the classical doctrine does not adequately account for moral rights if it trades off the welfare of some people for the benefit of others. If we accept that apartheid is an evil system it cannot be justified that a law will enshrine the right of the majority to treat the minority who are of different racial background obnoxiously simply because it increases the general happiness or welfare of the majority. Is the end a good in itself? What about the misery of the minority? This is why classical utilitarianism cannot adequately account for the moral rights of people.

But does it have to account for moral rights at all? Indeed it does – since human beings are autonomous moral agents any theory that seeks to promote their general interests and welfare must recognise the moral worth of the individual. Professor Dworkin advocates that in a majoriterian democracy where decisions are taken in the interests of the majority, the rights of the minority must be protected and the interests of the majority must be subjected to considerations of individual rights. To Dworkin, rights are species of moral rights, and respecting them is consistent with treating people with concern and respect. I agree totally with this view.

QUESTION TWO

Are the values of equality and freedom opposed to utilitarian values?

University of London LLB Examination
(for External Students) Jurisprudence and Legal Theory June 1998 Q10(a)

General Comment

This question appears to be a difficult one at face value because many candidates might think it is about abstract concepts like rights and freedoms. This is understandable, but such questions enable you to demonstrate your views about issues like equality and freedom and consider whether such issues are opposed to a consequentialist theory like utilitarianism.

Skeleton Solution

The values of freedom and equality – J S Mill's harm principle – utilitarianism and limitation to the harm principle – summary and conclusion.

Suggested Solution

John Stuart Mill (J S Mill, *Utilitarianism, Liberty and Representative Government* (1910)) states that freedom of speech is essential in the pursuit of truth. If people are denied free speech to dispute opinion and articulate their ideas, then they are denied the most important instrument for discerning between truth and falsehood. The reality is that the truth of our beliefs can only be vindicated if we are allowed the freedom to air our views and express ourselves.

This is based on the assumption that everybody in a society is equal and has equal access to this right of free speech. The importance of this right can be seen when we consider that there is no way of considering the competence and impartiality of the government (as arbiter of good conduct and truth) if all we can expect is a government which stifles and censors opinion. On this basis, it is arguable that equality and freedom are utilitarian values, because with the shared interest everybody has for the promotion of welfare in society, there is a beneficial collorary for society as a whole.

Bearing in mind the importance of the values of equality and freedom, J S Mill has provided a yardstick for measuring these values. His harm principle, which provides this yardstick, says 'The only purpose for which power can rightly be exercised over any member of a civilised community against his will, is to prevent harm to others. His own good, either physical or moral, is not a sufficient warrant'. The harm principle encapsulates Mill's idea that individuals must be allowed to develop their own distinct identities and modes of life. Mill's book (J S Mill, *On Liberty* (1985)) has certainly become the most celebrated defence of individual freedom in the English language.

However, because Mill disclaimed the idea that his views rest on any abstract right, and that his belief in utility was unshakeable because the ultimate appeal on all ethical questions rests on utility, we would be right to argue that the strength of his commitment to individual freedom makes his loyalty to utilitarianism questionable.

This point is made in the knowledge that, since utilitarianism seeks to increase happiness and welfare and is consequentialist per se, its values are at variance with the values of equality and freedom. Jeremy Bentham (Jeremy Bentham, *An Introduction to the Principles of Morals and Legislation* (1823)) recommends that in order to achieve the goal of increased welfare, men must:

a) approve a principle which says they ought to have what they want;

b) accept the principle of utility which reduces disagreements about future matters of fact, thereby making morals and legislation scientific.

In order to achieve the above aspirations, the means of achieving them are inconsequential because it is the end (the consequence) which matters. We would be right, therefore, to say that if the utilitarian believes that sacrificing the freedom and equality of some few people to achieve the desired increase in welfare and happiness, then that is a sacrifice worth making.

This means that there is a limitation to Mill's harm principle. For example, having freedom and equality will not entitle one to equal treatment when one is sick, because a health authority may well argue that scarce resources are to be expended on a large number of people rather than to be spent on one sick person. The one sick person will be sacrificed to achieve the welfare of many. Similarly one's entitlement to equality and freedom does not entitle one to help oneself to property belonging to one's neighbour.

Support for the view that freedom and equality cannot be taken literally, and that the limitation to Mill's harm principle is provided for the benefit of others, is explained by Dworkin's theory of rights. Dworkin (Ronald Dworkin, *Taking Rights Seriously* (1977)) has argued that unlimited freedom makes no sense in that, where freedom is understood in the 'strong sense', the individual's freedom must be interfered with in order to protect the freedom of others. This means that, like the harm principle, Dworkin's argument looks at the situations when the law must limit freedom to bring about equality. For example, A is not free to murder B, and C is not free to libel D. We would be inclined to look upon laws preventing murder and libel as upholding the rights of others. Laws such as these have utilitarian ends.

We may argue that there is a contradiction between freedom and equality and utilitarianism. How is this contradiction reconciled? The argument one needs to make here is that the moral effect of ascribing rights of personal freedom and equality to individuals is to limit the extent to which the conduct of those rights-holders is governed by duties. The point here is this: if our every action becomes the subject of a duty to act to increase happiness in society at large would we then be morally at liberty to do only those acts required by duty? The objection to this state of affairs is that there would be no moral space within which we would be free to act as we chose. Morally speaking, if we say we have freedom and equality, we make the statement that within these areas, we are without duties to act in specific ways.

However, the utilitarian would say that this state of affairs must be conceived as an area of total arbitrariness, because there may still be good reasons why we should use our freedom and equality in some ways rather than in others. Although we may believe that freedom and equality are values we cannot compromise, we must recognise that others are entitled to equal concern and respect, and so our freedom and equality may be curtailed to protect the equal freedom and equality of others. To Mill, protecting such freedom has utility.

QUESTION THREE

Are you a utilitarian?

University of London LLB Examination
(for External Students) Jurisprudence and Legal Theory June 1998 Q10(b)

General Comment

This is not as difficult as it looks at first glance. This question demands that you take a position on utilitarianism. It is a straightforward question, easily answered with some careful thought. Be aware that a lot of people accept that utilitarianism is the most appropriate doctrine for any society, so do not be too dismissive of the theory. Look at it objectively.

Skeleton Solution

Jeremy Bentham's classical theory – consequentialist nature of utilitarianism – act and rule utilitarianism – attractions and criticisms – conclusion.

Suggested Solution

Jeremy Bentham (Jeremy Bentham, *An Introduction to the Principles of Morals and Legislation* (1823)) argues that 'nature has placed mankind under governance of two sovereign masters, pain and pleasure. It is for them alone to point out what we ought to do, as well as determine what we shall do'. Based on this notion, utilitarianism holds that in considering what to do we must aim at actions which meet the requirement that happiness must be promoted and suffering minimised. According to Bentham, the right action is the one which promotes utility or maximises welfare. This is explained by his maxim: 'the greatest happiness of the greatest number'.

Utilitarianism is an important theory because it has profound influence and reflection on our moral beliefs. An example is necessary: imagine that commuters have been experiencing daily frustrations with problems due to signal failures and breakdowns on the national railway network. Say these problems are traceable to insufficient attention paid by the managers of the railway network. We all assume that it is our business to subject the performance of the railway bosses to scrutiny. We do this because we feel that keeping an efficient and well-maintained railway system is the moral responsibility of the railway bosses. Their duties have utility; to seek the increase in welfare or happiness of train commuters. The purpose of our scrutiny is to make the rail network a safer environment for all of us. This welfare maximisation is considered a neat idea, a moral standard worth achieving.

Utilitarianism is a consequentialist theory in that it looks at the consequences of an action. For example, every health authority in the United Kingdom has the responsibility for managing its budget relative to the total population in its catchment area. In trying to allocate its resources equitably, the health authority is mindful of the utilitarian maxim 'everyone counts as one and no one for more than one', and decide how much can be spent on drugs, equipment and logistics. Presume that a sick child needs a very expensive treatment which will bite deeply into the resources at the disposal of the health authority. Considering that it had decided to spend X amount per head relative to the population in its catchment area, it decides to refuse to fund the treatment of this sick child. In taking its decision the health authority considered the consequences of spending Y amount to fund the treatment of the sick child: it would mean suffering would increase for others. The right action is the one which will promote the welfare of the many.

Imagine I have agreed to be a caretaker of the house of a friend, who is going away on a sabbatical. A week later I change my mind when I receive another offer to manage an orphanage. I do that because I think managing the orphanage has more utility value – many people will benefit from the experience. However, the utilitarian will not be happy about my behaviour because of the adverse effects it could have. I gave a promise which I later broke. Society would be in danger if people kept breaking promises.

The difficulty for opponents of utilitarianism here is that they must bear in mind that the morality of keeping promises is based on a calculation of the consequences. Even if it was simply that my promise had to be overridden by a sudden emergency, the utilitarian insists that we must always remember that the promise-breaking relates to a past fact.

As a consequentialist theory, utilitarianism looks only at the end and not the means by which this end is achieved. Let us assume that members of the intelligence service have received a tip off that a terrorist group has planted a bomb, primed to be detonated when a prominent member of the Government rises to speak at a rally. If this were allowed to happen, many people would die. The intelligence service decides to evacuate people from the rally and from nearby homes. They forcibly remove people who refuse to budge, thereby infringing their liberty. The utilitarian will argue that, as long as the lives of many people are saved, the means by which the intelligence service achieves this aim is not important.

There are different versions of utilitarianism, such as act and rule utilitarianism. Act utilitarianism states that, where a person has a choice between two courses of action, the right action to choose is the one which produces the most happiness not for the person himself but for all who are in any way affected by the act. 'The greatest happiness of the greatest number' is the benchmark for the right action, and this happiness is usually interpreted to mean a balance of pleasure over pain. It is suggested that for each alternative course of action, it is possible to weigh the amounts of pleasure it produces for some people and add these up. We then add up all the amounts of pain and subtract the sum of pain from the sum of pleasure; the correct action is that which produces the greatest positive or least negative medium of pleasure over pain.

Rule utilitarianism differs from act utilitarianism in the sense that it makes general happiness the benchmark for the right action, but only through an indirect two-stage procedure. Imagine a rule says that act A is of higher utility than any alternative but is banned by rule Y because it is of the kind F, the performance of which will decrease happiness. There must be something about act A to explain the contrast. Rule utilitarianism will find a happy medium with act utilitarianism and incorporate F1 instead of F and thereby allow for the prescription of A. For example, if allowing 1,000 people to cross a weak bridge at a time will cause the bridge to collapse and everybody to be injured, rule utilitarianism can agree with act utilitarianism for a rule which will prescribe that only X number of people must cross the bridge at any one time.

The attractions of utilitarianism is that it is a moral theory. Happiness is said to be the foundation of morality, and so many people are attracted by a theory which espouses the welfare and happiness of people.

There have been many criticisms of utilitarianism (M E Simmonds, *Central Issues in Jurisprudence, Justice, Law and Rights* (1994)). It is an aspirational theory and as such cannot lay claim to be a moral theory. The happinesses of people are not the same, so it is difficult to subscribe to a theory which is aspirational but cannot measure the consequence of any act before it happens.

Utilitarianism can be criticised for trading-off the happiness of one person for the happiness of another. It has no independent method of distribution of welfare, so it has only instrumental concern for welfare. It is impossible to trade-off the misery of slaves for the happiness of slave owners.

Further, the theory cannot explain its disdain for rights, since to the utilitarian the end justifies the means, even if one human life is sacrificed in the process of saving one hundred people. What is important to the utilitarian is that there is average utility in terms of happiness as a result.

Utilitarianism is said to be a moral theory, but its disregard for rights and freedom makes one question the basis of its morality. It seems crude to say that a sadist's happiness has a utility value when happiness is at the expense of the misery of others. John Rawls is right to say that such happiness, the right to do it, cannot be defined in terms of the good. Justice is always prior to such a right. We are reminded by the philosopher Immanuel Kant that human beings are ends in themselves not means to an end. This moral philosophy impels me to reject utilitarianism.

QUESTION FOUR

What is utilitarianism? Is it a good guide to judicial decision-making?

University of London LLB Examination
(for External Students) Jurisprudence and Legal Theory June 1993 Q9

General Comment

The question can be answered in many ways, and it is not necessary to go into the economic analysis of law to provide an excellent answer. Nevertheless it is one very fruitful way of doing so as the answer below takes this line.

Skeleton Solution

Bentham's doctrine and act and rule-utilitarianism – general problems with utilitarianism: its inability to identify the dignity of individuals and its wrong assumption that values are commensurable – the connection with economics: the Pareto criterion of measuring welfare and the Kaldor-Hicks criterion – application of economic analysis to law – conclusion that individual dignity, in the form of rights, cannot be measured or protected in money terms.

Suggested Solution

Jeremy Bentham proclaimed that political acts (eg those of the officials in a legal system) should be morally adjudged according to whether they produced consequences for the maximum happiness (or pleasure) for the maximum number of people; a political action, say, of legislative enactment, was therefore right if there were no alternative action which would produce even better consequences. The important things was that everybody's potential happiness had to be assessed and added together and seen as a consequential state of affairs. The idea did not allow room for the 'act that is right in itself' or the idea that an act could be judged independently of the consequences it produced (assuming, of course, that a clear distinction could be drawn between a description of 'the act' and 'the consequences').

Later utilitarians, predominantly legal thinkers, refined this 'act' utilitarianism to what became known as 'rule' utilitarianism, which said that an act was utilitarianly right if it supported, or was in accordance with, a rule which, if followed in general, would bring about the greatest happiness of the greatest number. This idea was developed to meet the criticism of utilitarianism that it could not account for the way we think that it would be wrong to overturn rights that people have acquired through the application of rules such as those in legal systems, or in useful social institutions such as the institution of promise-keeping, just because it would be 'useful' to do so. Rule utilitarianism thus purported to say that people have rights, to have their valid contracts enforced, for example, because, in the long run, having contracts in society is more conducive to happiness than not having, even although in the short term greater utility would be achieved. It is easy to see, however, that rule-utilitarianism is not the slightest bit different from act-utilitarianism; it just says that you do some acts with the long term in mind! That is the only extra explanation it gives about the nature of those acts which consist of conforming to a rule. The rule utilitarians therefore come nowhere near explaining our strong moral belief that certain acts are right in themselves and that situations should never arise in which human beings might be treated as means to ends rather than as ends in themselves.

This idea that individuals don't have their own inherent rights to be treated as 'ends in themselves', as having their own individual dignity is matched by another equally unsavoury idea of utilitarianism, that all happiness and pleasure (or 'welfare' as modern utilitarians describe it) is inter-measurable. Think about it; if the injunction is to go for the greatest happiness of the greatest number, you have to make calculations such as the following: if we raise interest rates, that will make a further one per cent unemployed and that creates a certain amount of unhappiness; on the other hand, it will increase the amount of interest that those with savings receive and will make them happy and it will keep inflation down which will ensure more overseas investment here which in the long run will get the economy going and that will make people happy. This seems very practical, but it amounts to saying that the unhappiness of those about to be thrown on to the dole queue can be 'traded off' against those who will gain from higher interest payments. Is this really possible – apart from whether it is just? Take two people, one of whom likes to drink two pints of beer each evening, another of whom prefers to make leather sandals each evening. Can we measure in any way the relative worth of these activities, such that we could trade them off?

Here is where the connection with economics comes in. We can imagine the drinker and the sandal maker to strike a bargain in money terms. If only one of the two activities could be carried out, the person who was prepared to pay the most money for the activity would be the one who would value it most and thus the greatest happiness of the greatest number (in this case, two) would be served by allowing the person who values it most, in money terms, to do it. Simply put, because money is a fungible, the commensurability of value, when converted into money terms, seems perfectly feasible, indeed, practically sensible. (Although, note that to ensure a fair system, both participants in this mini-market would have start off with roughly equal amounts of money in order to make the assumption that the value of each activity is properly measured.)

The law and economics movement seizes on this idea and says that people's legal rights are best determined by reference to a hypothetical market. If in this ideal world, the two litigants would have bargained, in money terms again, for a particular outcome, but it is only the real world that is preventing them from doing so, perhaps because of transaction costs, the courts should impose the ideal solution. This would have the advantage of either bypassing a number of expenses that would otherwise have to be met, or by coming closer to a solution that could not otherwise have been reached. In other words, the law and economics movement would have judges making a cost-benefit analysis of legal decision-making. Give Mrs McLoughlin damages only if giving them to her will first deter in future people like Mr O'Brian doing what he did and so prevent hospital costs, and second, not require a disproportionately high increase in traffic insurance premiums.

But the problem with this approach is that it can give no sense to Mrs McLoughlin having a right to damages, whatever the rule utilitarians say. Why? Because whether she is paid damages or not is entirely dependent upon the current economic climate; sometimes people in her position will be paid damages, other times not. That sense of her being injured through someone else's negligence and that being in itself the reason for her receiving compensation is notably missing. I conclude, therefore, that utilitarianism in its modern 'economics and law' form is wholly inadequate for dealing with problems arising in legal reasoning; legal systems are about fairness, justice and people's rights and not just about increasing the gross domestic product.

Chapter 11

Critical Legal Studies

11.1   Introduction

11.2   Key points

11.3   Questions and suggested solutions

11.1 Introduction

The Critical Legal Studies movement is a recent development of the Realist movement, especially in the United States, but also in England.

11.2 Key points

a) This is on the frontier of legal development.

b) It has still not run its course.

c) It incorporates ideas from American Realism, the social sciences, political studies etc.

d) It is essentially destructive, rather than constructive.

11.3 Questions and suggested solutions

QUESTION ONE

'Critical Legal Studies are now a spent force.'

Assess the extent to which the CLS movement has attained its objectives.

University of London LLB Examination
(for External Students) Jurisprudence and Legal Theory June 1999 Q10

General Comment

The Critical Legal Studies movement (CLS) is not a favourite topic of many candidates. Perhaps many feel that the movement is already a spent force! This is not a particularly intellectual movement in the sense of one which offers a substantive (either empirical or analytical) theory about the law. It is only by paying attention to what the movement says that you will be able to make up your mind about it.

Skeleton Solution

Background of the CLS movement – thesis of leading lights of the movement – the individualism versus collectivism dilemma – conclusion.

Suggested Solution

The CLS writers are not united behind a single body of thought, and so it is difficult to gauge the CLS position on any particular issue. There are some points of general agreement which can be explained, however.

The first critique of the law from CLS writings rejects the view that legal doctrines can determine the outcome of cases. This point refutes the claim of traditional legal scholarship that law is a coherent and rational body of rules and principles. The very idea that established rules and principles guide us is rejected. The argument of the CLS is that law is not an autonomous system that can claim to be objective, because human and social realities provide input into the legal process. This is a repudiation of received notions that courts apply clear and predictable rules through an impartial procedure called 'legal reasoning'. To the CLS, there are choices before the courts which are not predetermined by any existing rules.

This view characterises the law as indeterminate, arguing that 'legal reasoning' is nothing but an exercise in the use of abstract doctrines, with no way of proving which side is right or wrong. Lawyers and judges can manipulate doctrines to suit any purpose: thus a judge could reach a decision either way using the same doctrine. Roberto Unger (Roberto Unger, 'The Critical Legal Studies Movement' (1983) 96 Harvard Law Review 563) states that 'a doctrinal practice that puts its hope in the contrast of legal reasoning to ideology, philosophy, and political prophesy ends up as a collection of makeshift apologies'.

It is true that many lawyers believe that legal rules determine the result of a case, even though the nature of the adversarial legal system makes it possible to argue for both sides in a case. For example, the same lawyer who can prosecute a person for tax avoidance can also advise clients on VAT, tax laws, insurance and regulating one's business within the law. The lawyer can do this because he believes in the regularity and certainty that the law provides in both the short and long term.

The second general theme we can decipher from CLS writings regards the contradiction thesis, which rejects any notion that the legal system contains a single, coherent and justifiable view of human relations; rather, CLS authors see doctrine as reflecting two or even more different (and often competing) views, none of which are either coherent or persuasive enough to be called dominant. Roberto Unger adds to this by saying:

> 'The generalisation of contract theory revealed, alongside the dominant principles of freedom to choose the partner and the terms, the counter principles; that freedom to contract would not be allowed to undermine the communal aspects of social life and that grossly unfair bargains would not be enforced. Though the counter principles might be pressed to the corner, they could neither be driven out completely nor subjected to a

system of metaprinciples that would settle, once and for all, their relation to the dominant principles.'

The main point that CLS writers such as Roberto Unger want to make is that the recognition of the contradictory principles inherent in legal doctrine is a danger to the established order. By explicating contradictions, a lawyer can easily negate the ability of a doctrine to serve its purpose. Roberto Unger argues that doctrine can be seen as legitimate only if it embodies a 'coherent and justifiable view of human relations'.

Unger is of the view that legal rules must be interpreted and extended to express a more coherent order, rather than appear as a disconnected series of trophies with which different factions mark their victories in an effort to enlist government power in the service of private advantage.

Unger's diatribe against the law is unpersuasive. Who really believes that the law is a 'disconnected series of trophies with which different factions mark their victories'? Unger is to be answered with Dworkin's theory (Ronald Dworkin, *Law's Empire* (2nd edn, 1991)) of 'law as integrity'. Law as integrity requires judges to assume that the community's practice is structured on the principles of justice, fairness and procedural due process, and that in all fresh cases that come before them, they are to make each person's situation as fair and just by the same standards.

Law as integrity sees the law as a coherent whole, and requires judges to go through the entirety of the law (which is assumed to have an integral life of its own) in order to justify the decisions they make. The CLS writers must know that law as integrity is an aid to the interpretation of the law, to be used by the judge during adjudication, rather than a pre-existing feature of the law itself. The fact that legal rules are contradictory should not cause anyone to despair of the law. As law as integrity illustrates, the laws of a community are always the product of great division; this is why law as integrity offers a scheme to judges which allows them to be bold, and not be afraid to use their convictions to interpret the law in order to make it speak with one voice – to treat people equally.

The CLS movement also offers a view of modern western society, claiming that individualism in the modern society must be replaced by communitarianism, so that people would be more inclined towards a collectivist goal. Unger argues that we need this collective society, and a jurisprudence which will ask searching questions about the inequalities in society.

One may find this idea regarding society a throwback to the Marxian model of a moral society – communism. The collapse of communism elsewhere may make this idea unattractive, but generally one can make the point that the CLS idea says more about our society, which is not the same as an analysis of the role that law plays in society.

On the CLS groups' general view of the law, one cannot find anything attractive about what it espouses. The views are all nihilistic; without some substantial input we cannot even recognise it as a good theory. It merely trashes the law without suggesting alternatives to replace it. More the pity. To me, the group peddles a false doctrine about the law which is dangerous.

QUESTION TWO

'We are all critical legal scholars today.'

Do you agree?

University of London LLB Examination
(for External Students) Jurisprudence and Legal Theory June 1998 Q5

General Comment

Questions about the critical legal scholars are popular in the examination papers these days. It is wrong, however, to suppose that one can obtain good marks by merely giving a historical account of the Critical Legal Studies movement (CLS). Marks are gained by showing that a legal system, like the one we have, has inbuilt prejudices which support the contentions of the CLS writers. Use examples to illustrate your answer.

Skeleton Solution

Background to the CLS movement – Roberto Unger's thesis – Duncan Kennedy's thesis – individualism versus collectivism dilemma – conclusion.

Suggested Solution

The Critical Legal Studies movement (CLS) originated in the United States in the 1970s. The movement's main thesis regarding the law is seen to be subversive in nature. Roberto Unger (Roberto Unger, 'The Critical Legal Studies Movement' (1983) 96 Harvard Law Review 563), who founded the movement with Duncan Kennedy in Harvard Law School, claims that the movement has undermined the principal viewpoints of traditional legal philosophy and put another conception of law in their place.

The CLS thesis refutes the claim that traditional legal scholarship produces rules and principles of law which guide our behaviour. Both legal formalism and positivism, which look upon law as a system of rules which are rationally made, are repudiated. Like American Legal Realism before it, the CLS does not consider law and the legal system as autonomous. Traditional legal scholarship treats the law as objective and neutral. The CLS claims that law cannot be objective because human and social realities always manifest themselves in the legal discourse. This is a complete rejection of received wisdom, which informs us that courts apply clear and predictable rules through an impartial procedure called 'legal reasoning'. The CLS points out that, in so far as judges have choices which are not predetermined, it cannot be true that their decisions are logically deduced purely from only historically made rules.

This is a view of law made famous by American Realism. This theory sees law as indeterminate, and it characterises 'legal reasoning' as nothing other than an exercise in the use of abstract doctrines, with no way of proving which side is right or wrong. If lawyers and judges are influenced by social realities then they are able to manipulate legal doctrines to reach any conclusion which they desire.

Roberto Unger criticises the objectivism and formalism in the law in his work. To him, any claim that the law is right and legitimate is only possible if it embodies 'a coherent and justifiable view of human relations'. He targets the law of contract and property law. Of property law, he says that it has its own inbuilt legal market which is a constitutional interest with its own legal structure in a democracy. To him, the situation is fraught with ambiguity and indeterminacy, because of the abstract nature of the concept of rights.

With respect to contract law, Unger explains that contract law allows freedom to contract, but that this is promptly contradicted by other principles which say that people can only bind themselves in contract for what the law allows. Unger presents an argument on formalism which states that every doctrine relies on some view of human associations which are 'right and realistic' in social life. The lawyer needs a theory as his guiding vision, which prevents him from seeing legal reasoning as a game of analogies. To Unger, reliance on analogies leads to analogy-mongering, and this must stop. He claims that this received wisdom is challengeable as wrong, and to do this we must rely on a normative theory of a branch of law supplied by the CLS. This is Unger's 'deviation doctrine', which I must say embellishes the CLS's nihilistic view about law. He says that his views push the liberal ideas about the state and society, freedom from dependence and governance of social relations by the will:

> 'To the point at which they merge into a larger ambition: the building of a social world less alien to a self that can always violate the generative rules of its own mental or social constructs and puts other constructs in their place.'

The CLS also present an instrumentalist view of the law which states that the law is oppressive. It allows the powerful to maintain their hold on the class divide. Law is used as a tool by the powerful, who form the elite, to control the working class. This is a well rehearsed passage from Marxist literature about law in a capitalist society. The working class has been induced to believe that the economic base, which concerns the relations of production, is there to work in its interest. The working class takes this for granted, believing that since the system works to generate more profit, it benefits them in the long run. This to the CLS is the 'false consciousness' found in Marxist theory. This 'false consciousness' mystifies the reality. As Duncan Kennedy points out (Duncan Kennedy, 'A Bibliography of Critical Legal Studies' (1984) 94 Yale Law Journal 461) 'the legal system acts as a "defence mechanism" shielding the harsh realities from our understanding and thereby legitimising the legal system in our eyes'. The pretence that the base will generate prosperity for all leads the unsuspecting public to wholly embrace capitalism, believing that happy days are ahead.

Ultimately the CLS believes that it offers us hope in jettisoning the society we know of – the post-industrial western society which is seen as individualistic. Modern society is divided into 'haves' and 'have-nots', and this leads to alienation. CLS writers argue for a society where communitarianism will replace the rampant individualism created by capitalism. With the communitarian ethos, individualism is replaced by collectivism. This involves pooling resources in society. To Roberto Unger we need a jurisprudence which will ask searching questions about the inequalities which exist in society.

If, for example, employers install unsafe machinery which kills or damages workers, the CLS would ask why they (the directors of the company) should be controlled by regulatory laws enforced by the Health and Safety Executive? Why should such employers escape serious punishment and receive only a small fine? If there was a law such as corporate manslaughter, then these employers would pay more attention to the safety of the systems which they provide in the work place.

The CLS are nihilistic about the law, in that they are unable to find a replacement for the law that they trash; it would be asking too much to agree with this question, which claims we are all critical legal scholars today. Some of us still believe that the law is certain and determinate; therefore we reject the CLS thesis.

However, it would be unfair to be wholly dismissive about the entire CLS thesis, especially if we consider that there is some sense in a thesis which challenges the class division existing in society today. If nothing else, we have become aware of how the law seeks to perpetuate the status quo regarding the interests of the elite, and how it mystifies this reality by convincing the public that the law is there to work for the general interest.

QUESTION THREE

'Although the Critical Legal Studies movement may appear nihilist, it offers scepticism, and scepticism is always a necessary first step towards positive transformation. This is often misunderstood by the movement's opponents.'

Discuss.

University of London LLB Examination
(for External Students) Jurisprudence and Legal Theory June 1992 Q10

General Comment

A general question on the nature of, and impact of, the Critical Legal Studies movement.

Skeleton Solution

Critical Legal Studies movement – Unger – Scandinavian Realism – Alf Ross – scepticism – Hume – excessive scepticism versus mitigated scepticism – discussion of the quotation – scepticism as the basis for all new theories.

Suggested Solution

The Critical Legal Studies movement came to the fore in the 1970s. It is a radical theoretical movement which rejects the distinction between law and politics and the notion that law can be neutral and value free. The movement proposes the integration of law and social theory. The existing social order is not accepted as an immutable state but rather as a state of affairs which represents a compromise of conflicting interests. Law and legal reasoning are seen as elements in the creation of a particular social order. In attempting to demonstrate that existing forms of legal consciousness merely serve certain interests in society, critical legal theorists claim to facilitate greater freedom for the individual.

The rejection by the movement of immutable legal standards has led to the criticism that the movement is nihilistic, that is that it rejects the existence of any values. This is also a criticism which has been levelled at the Scandinavian Realist movement which adopts a liberal approach somewhat similar to the Critical Legal Studies approach. Roberto Unger, a proponent of the Critical Legal Studies movement, says that a regime of rights would be necessary in the 'non-structural structure' which he proposes. Thus he suggests that four broad types of right would be necessary, namely immunity rights, destabilisation rights, market rights and solidarity rights. Unger's acceptance of the necessity for such rights is a movement away from pure nihilism. Alf Ross, a proponent of Scandinavian Realism, argued that the concept of justice is devoid of meaning, merely an emotional expression which does not postulate any material requirement as to the content of law. Thus, he argues, all wars and social conflicts have been fought in the name of some notion of justice. However, he admits that the words 'just' or 'unjust' can be used to indicate conformity or non-conformity to a rule or a set of rules existing at a particular time which suggests that he too moves away from an entirely nihilistic approach.

If it is accepted, therefore, as the quotation for discussion suggests, that the Critical Legal Studies movement is sceptical rather than nihilistic one must question whether scepticism is indeed a worthwhile standpoint as 'a necessary first step towards positive transformation'. David Hume rejected what he called 'excessive scepticism' or 'pyrrhonism'. He argued that such scepticism was an essentially academic pursuit which had no place in the real world. In *Enquiries Concerning the Human Understanding and Concerning the Principles of Morals* Hume argues that no benefit to society can result from such scepticism. If the theory were to be accepted, he argued, all human discourse and action would cease and man would be left in a state of lethargy. Instead, Hume suggested the reality was that even the most trivial event in life would banish such a theory because it is in man's nature to act and reason and believe. The only advantage which scepticism could offer, in Hume's opinion, would be to show the 'whimsical' tendency of mankind, namely that the basis of actions, reasoning and belief cannot always be explained. The excessive scepticism which Hume criticises is basically nihilistic insofar as it is a destructive theory offering no alternative to existing legal thought and values.

Hume also considered the merits of a more mitigated form of scepticism which perhaps flowed from 'pyrrhonism'. Mitigated scepticism might, according to Hume, have the advantage of alerting individuals to the inherent deficiency in their understanding and thereby curb natural dogmatism and intolerance of antagonists. Such mitigated scepticism might serve to demonstrate that human understanding is minute in comparison with the enormous perplexity and confusion which Hume saw as being inherent in human nature. In Hume's view the humility which such limited scepticism would produce would be a characteristic of the just reasoner. In this sense the quotation under discussion identifies what must be viewed as a benefit of scepticism if one accepts that tolerance of opposing viewpoints is an essential prerequisite for constructive discussion. Any philosophical standpoint which denies the immutability of particular values is stultifying. Theorists such as Bentham saw claims to 'absolute' validity as merely a cloak to lend credence to regimes which preserved an unjust status quo. The first step towards setting such absolute values aside, therefore, must result from a sceptical standpoint which questions the claims to validity of a particular order.

In conclusion, therefore, it must be said that by refusing to accept without question the validity of the existing legal order the Critical Legal Studies movement, like Scandinavian Realism, provides a useful starting point for further discussion. It must be said, however, that a limited form of scepticism might fairly be said to be the starting point of every new legal theory, because the basis for offering a replacement for existing legal theory is a criticism of the existing accepted theory. The essential question, therefore, is whether scepticism alone is enough. For my part I see sense in the views put forward by Hume and discussed above, namely that scepticism alone is neither a useful nor a realistic basis for practical discussion since it essentially denies the validity of any of the fruits of discussion. However, as the Critical Legal Studies movement progresses it may develop from the basically sceptical standpoint into a practical and workable theory. The beginnings of this more constructive approach can be seen in Unger's work which acknowledges the necessity for substantive elements such as the broad rights mentioned above.

QUESTION FOUR

How challenging to jurisprudence are the perspectives of the Critical Legal Studies movement?

University of London LLB Examination
(for External Students) Jurisprudence and Legal Theory June 1993 Q10(a)

General Comment

Candidates are either too dismissive of the Critical Legal Studies Movement (CLS) or are too accepting; make up your own mind about it. A good way is to meet a committed CLS teacher. You will find him – if he is good – exciting and innovative (Duncan Kennedy is a very good example), with a refreshing 'anti-solicitor with 2.4 children and mortgage' attitude. He will make you re-think your ideas about accepting the legal system as it is. But you may also find, after a while, that there is not much of deep intellectual interest in what he says; that in the heat the light becomes dim! There is a lot that is exciting and a lot that just does not stand up to rational analysis. Don't be taken in by nonsense talk; that, for example, 'rational' talk is only a way of 'covering up' 'real' 'contradictions'; 'rational', as you know, does not mean that. In other words, keep a clear head: see the good, see the bad.

Skeleton Solution

History and background – methodology – politics of CLS theorists – Liberalism's contingency and contradiction – philosophical background – positive political programme (Unger) – self-undermining – prioritising of contradictions – contingent nature of human existence – conclusion that not clear what political programme the CLS movement would support.

Suggested Solution

Since the Critical Legal Studies movement is relatively new, its value as a theory of law is still being assessed, but despite its continual development it has given much of interest to thinking about the law. Indeed, like other sceptical theories it may undermine the coherent world of law which legal academics and practitioners tend to portray.

The Critical Legal Studies movement is a body of like-minded thinkers who claim to attack the virtues that they say are proclaimed by the liberal legal system. This attack is mounted from different points; contract (Unger); property laws (Hay); the Rule of Law (Kennedy and Horwitz); Race and Sex Discrimination Law (Freeman); Employment and the Criminal Law (Kelman) to name but a few of the areas of the application of so-called 'critical' theory.

A word can be added here about the idea of a 'critical' theory. The idea is often bandied about rather proudly, as though the Critical Legal Studies scholars were the first to look at the law critically, while clearly the positivists, led by Bentham most famously and effectively, not only built the intellectual framework for that idea, but also carried it out with plans for legislative reform. No, the idea of a 'critical' theory is that it aims to criticise the idea of 'theorising about the law in the first place'; hence, CLS's understanding of positivism is based on a mistake about what positivism was trying to do. Positivism is not trying to make the law appear better than it 'really' is; it is attempting to build a way into the idea of law of criticism from outside the law. This is a point which the CLS movement has utterly ignored.

The common themes that run through their work is a view that law and legal reasoning is an illusion (although practically all of them teach in law schools!). They also claim that the practice and reasoning of law is riddled with contradiction. They claim, like Dworkin, that there is no distinction between law and politics although Dworkin, for them, is dangerously liberal. For them, values (both social and legal) come from within the community. Therefore, they say, although very unclearly, that truth and justice are mere social constructs, and as a consequence, law is tainted with a false consciousness which pervades the practitioners, law schools and the other institutions which organise the law.

A second area of value is the methodology that is applied by CLS theorists. Much of this represents a kind of mixture of French 'deconstruction', sceptical jurisprudential theories (especially Marxism and Realism) with the language philosophy of Derrida and the social theory of Habermas, Marcuse and Mannheim. But this shouldn't be taken too seriously. The message is: explore all the assumptions that you make and never take any as God-given (but this message has been around since Aristotle; Plato made a fine art of it). The reference to these philosophers really provides a modern basis of this 'assumption seeking' and is called by the CLS 'trashing,' or 'deviation,' to use Unger's term. Note this: it is interesting that the CLS, despite its dismissal of objectivity and truth (inherent in its sceptical claims), claims that its own claims are true.

CLS, as its name suggests, is critical. It criticises a liberal view of law as presented by American law schools and American legal practice. It castigates such liberal notions as the rule of law, equality before the law, justice, fairness; in short the values that some might claim underpin the legal system. Like Realism, this attack seeks to liberate the individual's mind in order to expose what is really going on. However, the CLS attack is more radical, more sceptical and more far reaching.

Kelman has denied that CLS is merely Neo-Realism; he asserts that a new departure from the Realist movement is a belief that the indeterminacy of legal rules and argument cannot be overcome, that it is an inherent part of the system. CLS also insists that the liberal legal system is 'committed' to indeterminacy.

Few CLS theorists have formulated positive programmes to fill in the gap left by the deconstruction of liberal law. An exception is Unger who claims that he is seeking to restructure law without a structure so that society can evolve a 'super-liberalism' which will truly reflect the traditional aspirations of liberalism (and so he is presumably a liberal who would join with Rawls, Dworkin and so on, although he rather notably does not). He sees liberalism as consisting of the principles of individual freedom, equal claims to social wealth, interactions between people based on love and mutual respect (how, for goodness' sake, it this general programme different from Dworkin's political philosophy?). He claims that we should return to a tribalist form of society which will curb industrial interests in favour of the communitarian interests of mutual co-operation.

Unger raises more questions than he answers. His programme is subject to the self-undermining that will affect any CLS theorist who puts forward any positive proposals. Unger's programme is, of course, susceptible to criticisms of indeterminacy, arbitrariness and contradiction itself.

The value of CLS thought is reduced by the inability thus far to be a programme for action. However, there is much which is of interest in the CLS movement; its energetic urge to modern jurisprudence to examine its assumptions and the assumptions upon which our modern legal system is based must be healthy.

QUESTION FIVE

Using the perspectives of the CLS movement, what changes to the content and style of legal education would you suggest?

University of London LLB Examination
(for External Students) Jurisprudence and Legal Theory June 1993 Q10(b)

General Comment

The general gist to this type of answer should be gleaned from the answer to part (a) (Question Four, above). If the candidate is not 'fired up' with the Critical Legal Studies Movement (CLS), he or she is probably best advised to shy away from this question. But it is a question that could be done extremely well – with relatively little knowledge. Be anarchic! Think of your own law course! Is it satisfactory, in the light of what you think is good about the CLS movement (it is doubtful that you could say anything with any verve or interest to an examiner if there was nothing about the CLS movement of which you approved). What about the assumptions that your lecturer makes? Does he smugly assume that Commercial law is the be-all and end-all? That nothing is worth while unless it can be reduced to a bill of sale, or a statement which reduces to rights over chattels? Does he ever say anything critical about, not just particular laws (because positivists would advocate that, and CLS does not like positivism), but about the whole process of law altogether? If you disapprove here, you probably have a CLS bent. Use it; you will write something good. Don't be cowered by the view that there is a 'right way' to answer the question. The suggested answer below attempts to be as creative as possible.

Skeleton Solution

Origins of the CLS movement – what CLS says that is of importance – English law schools as compared to the US – 'black-letter law' – case-method – approaching a case 'from a critical perspective' – 'trashing' – overall conclusion that there are advantages seeing the law from a new perspective but with rider that the 'trashing' approach is fundamentally nihilistic if it has nothing to offer in its place.

Suggested Solution

The CLS movement began in the US after the great expansion of the universities with the coming of the post-war 'baby boom'. It was also a time of increased economic prosperity, although the stability that this encouraged amongst the middle classes was being eroded through the rise of demands for civil rights by black people and the escalation of the Vietnam war. Young people in universities had a degree of both economic power and a political say for the first time in generations, if ever. It was fun to be in universities then, since there was a strong consensus, fuelled by the economic stability, that studying at a university was an achievement in itself, entirely unrelated to the commercial prospects of the degree. This was admirable but would be regarded as an idea wasteful of resources by many in England and the US today.

CLS grew out of this climate and, in short, brought the attitude of 'independent, critical study' to the law schools. Why did this occur in the US and not in the UK until later (although it is not clear that CLS has ever really caught on here)? One of the reasons is the vast difference between US and UK law schools; the great Realist movement in the US law schools of the late nineteenth century and beyond has already led to a more questioning approach. Endowed with more funds, too, the law schools could bring about reforms that have barely begun yet to reach the UK; the case law method, properly paid teachers, law taught primarily as a postgraduate degree, properly equipped libraries and so on; the differences are well-known.

These factors combined to produce, to mention only the more famous, law teachers of the calibre of Roberto Unger and Duncan Kennedy. They were (and are) Sixties-appointed law professors who 'took on' the profession of law teaching. You can see what they were getting at; there is such an animal, as we all know, called the 'black-letter lawyer'; we should focus on him (he is predominantly male) because he is precisely the target of the CLS movement. In fact, if you see the CLS movement as having its origins in this attack, a number of seemingly mysterious points about CLS are solved. It explains its prevalence in law schools (practitioners have nothing to do with it), its being a 'movement' as opposed to a distinctive philosophy and, above all, it explains why it is that there seems to be little depth in many of the things that CLS people claim. Indeed, the idea of Critical Legal Scholarship appears odd; there is nothing especially scholarly about what they do.

The 'black letter lawyer' has wreaked havoc on the minds of many lawyers, those who expect that there is an 'answer' somewhere, if only they could find the particular word or phrase buried in a casebook somewhere. You know the kind of lawyer; he is the one who craves the certainty of the law (and is probably must better suited to property law and the Chancery chambers than anywhere else) and never questions the whole set-up – the legal system – that puts him into the position that he is in. One reason for the creation of this kind of lawyer is the teaching; the teacher who has a set of notes, slightly updated from year to year and who reads these notes out to a large group of students who dutifully write them down and regurgitate them in an examination. What else would these students – future lawyers – know about the law?

Here is where CLS is exciting (and it is exciting to hear Duncan Kennedy speak). Stop being a 'fusty dusty' fogey of 'a law student'; stop thinking about your 'career-as-a-lawyer'; you are a person who can engage critically, Sixties style. Take that old fogey of a teacher and trash everything he says. (There is a nasty side to CLS!) For example, take the case of *Carlill* v *Carbolic Smoke Ball Co Ltd* [1893] 1 QB 256. Don't see it as a case about 'the meaning of offer and acceptance in the law' but as a case where commercial interests in advertising are brought to bear on a woman who has been duped by false claims about a smoke ball; see it in the context of times when advertising was even less controlled than now; see how an unsympathetic analytical approach to that case is a doctrinal one liner of: 'advertisements which are 'mere puffs' are not offers that can ripen into binding contracts'.

Of course, good law teachers always pointed these sorts of facts about cases out to their students (and intelligent students always made note of them); and any barrister of decent intellect is always fully aware of this sort of factor (there are a surprising number of critical barristers about; not enough, but nevertheless a significant number). So we shouldn't be too impressed by grand CLS claims about the degree of 'false consciousness' there is about the legal profession. We ought not, either, to be swayed by claims that the CLS makes about liberalism; their claim that the liberalism inherent in the law is a false liberalism because it masks conflict and contradiction is largely unsupported and, in any case, of not much interest to pursue because the CLS thinkers appear to embrace well-known forms of liberalism: justice for all; freedom and so on (and their claim that 'modern liberalism' is 'atomistic' and 'selfish' is plainly incorrect, as any reasonable reading of Rawls, Dworkin, Nagel, Scanlon, etc, etc, will reveal).

But in the light of what has been said, reforms to my law school would be listed as follows: the formal 'two lectures followed by tutorial' pattern of teaching would cease and students would be forced to engage in discussion; law would not be taught as a set of rules, but instead as an interlocking set of open (ie anything prima facie goes) principles of the legal system and particular rules. These principles would themselves be open to continual questioning (for example, the principles of democracy). Here, incidentally, is what Dworkin refers to as being 'an internal global sceptic'. (Dworkin's work, despite the dislike CLS 'officially' has for him, has laid the intellectual groundwork for everything CLS says; but they don't seem to understand that – see Guest, *Ronald Dworkin*, 2nd edn, Chapter 6.)

There would also be studied, within the law school, with the aim of increasing the critical perspectives of the law student, subjects such as the sociology of law-making and the effects of laws, political philosophy, the history of laws (eg such as prohibition, the abolition of the caste system, the growth of constitutional independence in colonial states) and the laws of other systems (comparative law). But the depths of 'scholarship' to which the CLS aspires, in French deconstructionism and waffly pseudo-philosophers, such as Derrida, would simply be dropped; it is worse than useless as it encourages laziness. The obscurity surrounding Derrida and his followers allows support to be drawn for almost any proposition.

This is the best that can be taken from CLS; if it is just to be 'critical' then it provides no vision and no law student can be educated to be just cynical; indeed, one of the reasons that CLS manages to get a grip is (and this is a good thing) that it can feed off the natural cynicism of youth, and that, interestingly enough, was one of the causes of its rise: the (in large part, healthy) cynicism of the Sixties generation.

Part C
Justice

Chapter 12

Justice and the Legal Enforcement of Morality

12.1 Introduction

12.2 Key points

12.3 Questions and suggested solutions

12.1 Introduction

This is a large and diverse topic, which calls for a knowledge of many different theorists and theories. It is also closely linked with the jurisprudence of 'rights'. The student's response to theories of justice is bound to be partly subjective, as theories of justice are closely allied to particular political standpoints.

12.2 Key points

Rawls

His theory is of 'justice as fairness'. Justice is based on the principles which individuals in the 'original position' would choose. By his 'original position' he means a hypothetical situation where individuals would be ignorant of the likelihood of them occupying any particular social or economic position in society.

Nozick

His theory of justice rests on the tenet that the individual is inviolable. Any state besides a minimal state is unjust: for example, the Welfare State is unjust because it violates the right to property.

Dworkin

His theory of justice rests on the principle that the state should treat everyone with equal concern and respect. Redistribution can be justified but there is a host of specific rights which act as 'trumps'.

Hart-Devlin debate

Devlin argues for a conservative approach which says that English society consists of a broad consensus on moral matters. If the juryman is 'really disgusted' by, say, homosexual acts, then that makes that conduct a candidate for prohibition by the criminal law. Hart says that this kind of approach introduces bigotry in the law and that a lot of misery would be unnecessarily created by thinking that morality was merely a matter of consensus and not carefully considered conviction. The liberal approach is better, he says, because that treats as fundamental the principle that people should be in control of their own lives where what they do does not restrict the freedom of anyone else.

12.3 Questions and suggested solutions

QUESTION ONE

'Nozick's principal argument against distributionist theories of justice rests on their failure, as he sees it, to cohere with his idea of individual liberty.' (Lloyd, *An Introduction to Jurisprudence*.) Discuss. How attractive do you find Nozick's theory?

Written by the Editor

General Comment

This question calls for a critical analysis of Nozick's theory of justice. The student must be prepared to refer to other theories of justice, and to come to a firm conclusion.

Skeleton Solution

Rights – based theory – distributionist theory – need – equality – welfare state – individual rights – minimal state – taxation – subjectively unappealing.

Suggested Solution

Robert Nozick's *Anarchy, State and Utopia* stimulated much debate when it was published in the mid-1970s. Among the issues dealt with by Nozick was a rights based theory of justice, which held that any scheme of patterned distribution was unjust. In these days of the welfare state such views may seem shocking or out of step. It has, however, been pointed out that modified versions of some of what Nozick has said are not too far removed from the policies associated with 1980s 'Thatcherism'. It is proposed to examine Nozick's argument against distributionist theories before considering which theory is the most appealing.

A distributionist theory is one that advocates a patterned distribution of the benefits and burdens or 'goods' in society. Distribution is usually based on need, such need being determined on principles of equality. Distributionist theories are thus goal based: distribution is just because it achieves a certain goal (eg equality). The welfare state is clearly justified by distributive theories of justice. Money is taken from the richer members of society through taxation to benefit the needy. This is justified by the goal of equality: all individuals should have at least a minimum standard of living (it should be noted that distributionist theories do not require total equality).

Nozick utterly rejects this model of justice. For him the individual is inviolable. Man has certain rights, including the right to liberty and the right to acquire property. Such rights may only be violated with the consent of the individual. It follows from these propositions that any state beyond a minimal state is unjust. Nozick accepts that a state is necessary to protect the individual against violence and theft, and to enforce contracts. But beyond that, state intervention is unacceptable as it violates individual rights.

Thus Nozick sees distributionist theories as unjust. He views taxation, for instance, as no more than forced labour. For him the distribution of property in society is based on historical entitlement: provided property is acquired by just acquisition, legitimate transfer or rectification of past injustice, it cannot justly be taken away. According to Nozick, 'if each person's holdings are just then the total set of holdings is just'.

Although Nozick's theory is stimulating and thought-provoking it has been subjected to criticism. One might question, for example, the basis on which he arrives at his list of rights. But for many, Nozick's theory appears inherently unjust in its rejection of equality as a starting point or as a goal to be achieved. I share this view; I find distributionist theories far more appealing.

QUESTION TWO

What do you understand by Rawls' concept of the 'original position'?

Written by the Editor

General Comment

This question calls for consideration of Rawls' theory of justice. Students should note that the aspect of Rawls' theory discussed below is not the only important or interesting issue.

Skeleton Solution

Justice as fairness – original position – veil of ignorance – unanimity – social contract theory – rejection of utility – 'maximin' principle – principles of liberty and equality – criticisms – value.

Suggested Solution

The concept of 'original position' is crucial to Rawls' theory of justice. For him the ideal is 'justice as fairness' – a society organised on principles resulting from the original position. Although there are many strands to Rawls' theory, the 'original position' is one of the most central, and also one of the most criticised.

Rawls imagines a (hypothetical) situation in which a group of individuals set out to agree the principles on which society is to be organised. These individuals operate behind the 'veil of ignorance': although they are aware of the existence of different sexes, races, levels of intelligence, wealth, social status etc, they are ignorant of the characteristics they themselves possess. Thus it is not possible for an individual behind the veil of ignorance to know the probability of being at any particular economic or social level in society. Since all in the original position are equal there will be unanimous decisions as to what principles should inform society.

Rawls' theory is thus a social contract theory, although his contract is hypothetical. He attempts to justify the application of his principles on the ground that any rational person entering the original position would choose the same principles. Thus his theory goes beyond other social contract theories in that it attempts to show why the 'contract' binds those who are not a party to it. Starting with his original position Rawls believes he can deduce the principles which the individuals in that position would choose. For example, they would reject average utility as a principle upon which to organise society because of the risk of being in the lowest echelons of society. He believes that the parties in the original position would choose principles which would offer the highest possible total of basic goods such as rights, powers, health etc. They would then opt for the 'maximin' principle; in other words, principles which ensure that even the very worst situation an individual might end up in is the best of the available alternatives. Thus a person in the original position will choose the following two principles.

a) 'Each person is to have an equal right to the most extensive total system of equal basic liberties compatible with a similar system of liberty for all.'

b) 'Social and economic inequalities are to be arranged so that they are both:

   i)   to the greatest benefit of the least advantaged, consistent with the just savings principle; and

   ii) attached to offices and positions open to all under conditions of fair equality of opportunity.'

The first principle has priority over the second, as Rawls believes that no person in the original position would wish to risk his or her liberty once the veil of ignorance is lifted.

There have been many criticisms of Rawls' theory but it is proposed only to consider those relating to the concept of original position outlined above. Fisk argues that the individual cannot be abstracted from his or her material circumstances in the manner assumed by Rawls' original position, and so Rawls' theory is riddled with ideological assumptions. A more general criticism is that the original position is too artificial a device to have much meaning. It is also hard to see the justification for Rawls' assertions about which principles people in the original position will choose. Are all people risk averse? Why would people necessarily prefer liberty to equality? Perhaps Rawls' theory of justice only works for one type of character. The concept of original position is important to Rawls' theory and valid criticisms of it can only damage his theory of justice as a whole. Despite this it should be remembered that Rawls' writings are rich and stimulating and have provoked much valuable debate.

Chapter 13

What Are Rights?

13.1   Introduction

13.2   Key points

13.3   Questions and suggested solutions

13.1 Introduction

The discussion of rights can broadly be divided into two: the normative (which overlaps with Chapter 10) and the analytical. The value of the analytical approach to rights lies in the clarification of words used in legal relations so that the solution of legal problems is both easier and more certain. Since the normative jurisprudence of rights relates so closely to theories of justice, one's political standpoint will be of much greater importance here.

13.2 Key points

The normative jurisprudence of rights (see also Chapter 10)

a) The libertarian view, such as that of Nozick, is that man's rights (such as the right to property) are inviolable.

b) The liberal view espoused by Dworkin starts from the premise of equal concern and respect for individuals. This is a fundamental right and there are also other rights which are protected to preserve that fundamental right. For Dworkin, these rights are 'trumps'.

The analytical jurisprudence of rights

a) Hohfeld's scheme of jural relations is the starting point for any analysis of rights. He saw that the word 'right' can encompass the concept of right, of privilege, of power, and of immunity. He attempted to clarify legal relations in terms of jural opposites and correlatives of rights, privileges, powers and immunities.

b) The value of Hohfeld's analysis to the lawyer should be considered. If his analysis were to be really useful should law not be discussed in terms of his jural relations?

c) The 'will' theory (Hart) versus the 'interest' theory (MacCormick) is an interesting debate. For Hart, rights are legally protected choices; for MacCormick rights protect certain interests. As with the normative jurisprudence of rights, a political perspective is important to this debate.

13.3 Questions and suggested solutions

QUESTION ONE

What are rights?

University of London LLB Examination
(for External Students) Jurisprudence and Legal Theory 1998 Q12

General Comment

This is a question which should appeal to the intending lawyer. After all, lawyers are always talking about the rights and duties of the parties in a case. Surely, if the lawyer believes in the rights and duties that have been established by the law, he needs to understand these concepts enough to justify those beliefs.

Skeleton Solution

Hart's will theory – Neil MacCormick's interest theory – Bentham's utilitarianism – Dworkin's rights as trumps – conclusion.

Suggested Solution

Professors H L A Hart (H L A Hart, *Essays on Bentham* (1982)) and Neil MacCormick (Neil MacCormick, *Legal Rights and Social Democracy* (1982)) have provided an interesting debate about the nature of rights. The debate centres around Hart's will theory of rights and MacCormick's interest theory of rights.

Hart's argument is that a right is laid down in a legal rule and does not exist independently of that legal rule. Any individual has a choice whether or not to exercise his or her will over another by reference to the existing legal rule. The law can be explained in correlative terms – right and duty. Where one has a right, another person is under a corresponding duty. However, the individual can choose whether to exercise that right. Whenever the individual exercises his right, he makes a choice whether or not to enforce a rule of law.

We can use the civil law to illustrate this. If A owes B £100, B can exercise his will by waiving the debt. Where this happens, A is released from his duty to B. Duties owed in contract and trust can be waived in this manner. Criminal law is different because one cannot waive duties imposed by the criminal law. I cannot waive your duty not to murder me. Neither can I say I am exercising my will in enforcing my right that you do not murder me. This makes no sense. It is because the waiver exists in the civil law but not the criminal law that we associate rights with the civil law rather than the criminal law.

Neil MacCormick objects to correlativity. He says that correlativity obscures the fact that a duty exists to protect the interest of the right-holder. In other words, the existence of a right is a sufficient reason for the imposition of a duty. MacCormick theorises that a right is an interest, and that the holder of the right is the intended beneficiary of the duty.

Simmonds (N E Simmonds, *Central Issues in Jurisprudence, Justice, Law and Rights* (1994)) argues that MacCormick has failed to produce convincing arguments, because his rights appear to be correlative to 'oughts'. It is certainly the case that when two people are in a contractual relationship, one can waive the duty that the other person is under. I have an interest but I can decide, in exercising my will, not to enforce my strict legal right and thus waive the duty.

MacCormick's argument that people given rights are deprived of the power to contract out of those rights is easily answered by Simmonds, and I support Simmond's point. The law now stipulates the minimum hours that any person can legally be required to work. The law stipulates the minimum hours of break each employee is entitled to, and it states that employees cannot contract out of this. This law is enshrined in the Working Time Directive. It would be wrong to say that the Working Time Directive restricts the power of the employee to waive his rights. The employee always has the right which the law ensures he continues to have.

Simmonds considers the paternalistic law which requires us to wear seatbelts and argues that it would be wrong to consider that such a law places a duty on us in order to protect the interests of car and motorcycle manufacturers. MacCormick's argument is unsustainable on this score. Simmonds further considers the paternalistic law. The point must be made that the duty placed on people to wear seatbelts or helmets is not created for the benefit of the manufacturers of cars and motorcycles, who, if we must understand MacCormick, have a right which translates into their interest that we wear seatbelts or helmets in cars or on motorcycles. Plainly, this is false reasoning.

MacCormick also argues that the will theory is false because children are unable to waive any rights over the enforcement of any duty. This leads to the conclusion that children have no rights. MacCormick says that since we all know children have rights, the will theory must be false.

Hart's response is that, although babies do not exercise any rights, it is correct to say that the rights of infants are exercised for them by their parents or guardians. However, as the child grows up he increasingly begins to exercise some of these rights himself, until he reaches the age of majority when he fully exercises all of his rights without the need to sign any legal documents transferring them to him. This must mean that it is accepted that the rights always belonged to the child, but it is instructive to note that Lord Scarman in the *Gillick* (*Gillick* v *West Norfolk and Wisbech Area Health Authority* [1986] AC 112) case said that parental rights over children dwindle as the child grows older, and the child's rights grow stronger.

Jeremy Bentham believes that rights consist of those rights given by law. Bentham would draw a clear distinction between moral and legal rights. The concepts of 'right' and 'duty' are legal constructs; no one has any rights except those given by law.

Professor Dworkin (Ronald Dworkin, *Taking Rights Seriously* (1977)), on the other hand, argues that rights have a sufficiently special status to make a difference to the way social and political decisions are reached. In Dworkin's *Theory of Rights*, he states that all goals that a society pursues must be justified by reference to rights.

There are good reasons for concluding that there are no 'absolute rights'. Rights can be overridden, for example, to protect another person's right, in national emergencies and to protect the national interest as shown by the Official Secrets Act. Beyond this, there is no justification to interfere with rights such as liberty and equality. Surely, if the reasons for interfering with these rights are based on utilitarian calculation then there is a strong case that since these rights cannot be compromised, they have trumped those utilitarian considerations.

QUESTION TWO

When may rights be trumped?

University of London LLB Examination
(for External Students) Jurisprudence and Legal Theory June 1990 Q4

General Comment

A predictable question that involves analysis of a range of theorists. The work of such as Hart and Nozick are needed to supplement the more obvious Dworkin and Rawls.

Skeleton Solution

Kantian influence – Kantian ethics – liberal interpretation – liberal dilemma – Millian solution – Hart versus Devlin; what is 'harm'? – Dworkinian rights theory – utilitarianism – economic analysis of the law – differences between liberal theories – Rawls versus Nozick.

Suggested Solution

Modern jurisprudence has been much influenced by the work of Kant. His theories can be said to be the basis of much 'rights-talk', which can loosely be termed liberal jurisprudence. This is advocated by such diverse theorists as Dworkin, Hart, Nozick and Rawls. Kant believed that each person had the capacity to make his/her own decisions about what was good in life. Each individual should be allowed to form their own conception of the good, to make their own choices, plans and decisions. Society must show respect for each person's ability to make these decisions, as well as the responsibility they had for those decisions. Society should not treat persons as means to an end. It should value each person as an end in themselves; not as an instrument to achieve certain goals.

Rights can be seen as the liberal's attempt to achieve this Kantian ideal. Although there is much disagreement between liberals, all basically agree that society should provide a framework within which the individual can exercise his/her moral capacity. Rights are part of this framework because they protect the individual's plans and decisions from being overridden by other individuals and groups within society.

However, there are problems. Sometimes two legitimate rights will conflict and then a choice will have to be made. One can claim that this is an instance of rights being 'trumped'. John Stuart Mill recognised this problem within liberalism; in *On Liberty* he felt that individual rights should only be trumped when their exercise would harm or interfere with the rights of others. Beyond this there should be no trumping of people's rights, as this would reduce the quantum of utility in society. This is because there is always a danger that truth would be prevented from coming to light in the process of trumping.

Another problem, which is emphasised in the debate between Hart and Devlin, is the considerable differences as to the meaning of harm. Devlin argues that society must trump the individual's rights to prevent the decay of society's moral foundations. For him, the right to sexual freedom between two consenting male adults in private must be restricted even though no physical harm is caused to others. This is because of the harm done to the morality of society. Devlin, therefore, feels that it is legitimate for rights to be trumped on this occasion.

What about when individual rights clash with collective rights? Liberals have struggled to explain how they can advocate the importance of rights and yet at the same time accept that they are not absolute. Dworkin has claimed, in an attempted solution to this dilemma, that in order to take rights seriously one must recognise that rights have normative force. Therefore, they must be supported by judges, it being only politicians who can override rights. This seems descriptively accurate and Dworkin has been accused of placing undue emphasis upon what judges say they are doing. Even the traditionally conservative British judiciary are gradually admitting the policy element in their decisions (*Home Office* v *Dorset Yacht* [1970] AC 1004).

Utilitarianism provides a simpler answer by stating that the way to keep faith with Kant (ie treating people equally) is to accept the principle that we are all concerned to maximise our own happiness. In such a situation no one person's happiness is more important than another's. Therefore, to uphold one individual's rights against the collective interest is to treat people unequally. Utilitarians claim that rights should be trumped when to do so would maximise utility, or conversely, when the exercise of individual rights would reduce utility. Another consequentialist theory; economic analysis of the law has a similar monist (the advocation of one supreme value) approach. This theory asserts that rights should be trumped when to do so would maximise efficiency.

Consequentialist theories face severe criticism, mainly over the immoral and unjust consequences that would be justified if their views were followed. A utilitarian would countenance the activities of a sadist against an unwilling victim if the sadist derived greater happiness than the reduction in happiness of the victim. Similarly, an economic analyst would countenance the forced taking of a book that belonged to A if the taker B valued the book at £3, whereas A only valued it at £1.

At the same time as trying to reject these consequentialist theories, liberals have failed to agree on the conditions under which rights may be trumped. An example can be seen in the differences between the two liberal theorists: Rawls and Nozick. Rawls claims that rights can be trumped in order to give effect to the collective interests of society. An individual's right to his/her income can be trumped in order to redistribute it to the less well off members of society. He claims that we would agree to this if we were in the hypothetical situation he calls the 'original position'. In such a situation each individual is ignorant of his/her socio-economic position within society and his/her talents. Each realises that they could end up as one of the least well off members of society. We will agree to redistribution because of a rational fear of ending up at the bottom of the social pile. Since we would have agreed to this redistribution of wealth, the trumping of rights to income and the wealth generated by individual talent by such mechanisms as income tax is fair, according to Rawls.

Nozick (also a Kantian liberal theorist) claims to be taking rights seriously. He asserts that to redistribute wealth (eg by taxation) is theft because it trumps people's legitimate claims to what belongs to them. For him fairness is to be found in the mixing of a person's labour with an object. After such a mixing the individual has a property right in what he/she has produced. Redistribution is the worst kind of theft, since it denies that a person has rights in themselves; their talents and labour. Nozick criticises Rawl's theory as permitting individual talents and qualities to be seen as common assets available to all. Nozick states that rights can never be legitimately trumped, unless by the owner's consent.

Various theorists present different responses to the question when can rights be trumped? In so doing they also go some way to explaining why rights are trumped. The diversity of theories highlights how it is possible to have an almost infinite number of interpretations of the Kantian ideal, with the liberal's concern with rights professes to give effect.

QUESTION THREE

Assess the contribution of Wesley Hohfeld to our understanding of law.

University of London LLB Examination
(for External Students) Jurisprudence and Legal Theory June 1987 Q4

General Comment

A question calling for a critical evaluation of Hohfeld's thesis, and an evaluation of his contribution to legal or juristic thinking.

Skeleton Solution

Hohfeld's aims – his scheme of correlatives and opposites – assessment – not widely used – even though can assist in avoiding confusion – takes no account of a concept of law – no account of process of according legal character to conceptions – narrow and restrictive interpretation of rights – important though seldom acknowledged contributions.

Suggested Solution

Hohfeld has made a considerable, though hardly acknowledged, contribution to our understanding of law. In his work, *Fundamental Legal Conceptions As Applied In Judicial Reasoning*, Hohfeld stated that the aim of his theory was to clarify different kinds of legal relations and the different uses to which certain words that are employed in legal reasoning are made. He sought to expose the ambiguities and to eliminate the confusion that surrounds these words. That objective can be achieved by the concept of rights; of privilege; of power and of immunity.

For Hohfeld, these words are to be explained in terms of correlatives and opposites, as each of these concepts has both a jural opposite and a jural correlative. These contain eight fundamental conceptions and all legal problems could be stated in their terms. They thus represented a sort of lowest common denominator in terms of which legal problems could be stated. This he did by method of the following.

Jural Opposites – Right/No Right; Privilege/Duty; Power/Disability; Immunity/Liability.

Jural Correlatives – Right/Duty; Privilege/No Right; Power/Liability; Immunity/Disability.

The aim of Hohfeld was to provide a model for the correct solution of legal problems and to make that solution easier and more certain. He would advocate that the judge and the legal theorist employ the above scheme in order to ensure greater understanding of these legal concepts.

His contribution has been useful, although the difficulty is that it is not as widely used as he would have advocated. Nonetheless, as Lloyd and Freeman observe, it is the point to which all lawyers return. They perceive the value of his analysis in enabling the reduction of any legal transaction to relative simplicity and precision and in the enabling of the recognition of its universality.

Harris identifies three important advantages to his approach. Firstly that it enables real normative choices to be disentangled from verbal confusions. Secondly that if lawyers and judges were to employ his terminology that was not too far removed from that already employed, then clarity would reign. The third advantage lies in their use. Hohfeld believed that juristic problems concerning the nature of compound concepts could be dissolved.

Although he has been criticised for insisting on correlativity in situations where correlativity is hardly present, eg the criminal law, the implicit answer that Harris finds in his defence of Hohfeld is that all cases involve two parties and, as such, viewing these concepts as correlatives is in that frame quite meaningful. It does however make an explanation of rights in rem impossible. Nonetheless there are important criticisms of Hohfeld's scheme. In that he purports to analyse fundamental legal concepts, he does so without taking account of any concept of law. He fails to provide an explanation of the process by which those conceptions are given their legal character. He further assumes that there is only one concept of duty. It is said that this is because his examples are drawn from civil and private law.

As Cook observes, Hohfeld mistakenly considers all rights as sets of any number of his four elementary rights: namely, claim; privilege; power and immunity. Rights are not sets of these. Their possession entails the possession of other rights or of powers and duties. For example, the concept of ownership includes rights of possession, transfer, sale, hire and use and enjoyment. Thus, ownership creates a set of claims and powers. The concept of ownership can be seen as a set of rights; it does not denote the relationship between the owner and the tangible object.

In spite of these criticisms, viewed in a chronological frame, his contribution has been substantial. There have however, since his work, been further developments and elucidations such as the works of Hart and MacCormick on rights. They benefited from having available to them Hohfeld's analysis.

QUESTION FOUR

'A world with claim-rights is one in which all persons, as actual or potential claimants, are dignified objects of respect ... No amount of love or compassion, or obedience to higher authority, or noblesse oblige, can substitute for those values.' (Feinberg)

Assess the importance of rights in contemporary legal and political philosophy.

University of London LLB Examination
(for External Students) Jurisprudence and Legal Theory June 1991 Q4

General Comment

This is a more general question on rights which, being more difficult, will call for some thought. Since the question is potentially broad, the student must select material to be used carefully.

Skeleton Solution

Kantian ideal – Utilitarianism and economic analysis of the law's rejection of rights – Dworkin's defence – Rawls and justice – Nozick's response – Finnis and natural law rights – problem of harm – Mill's principle.

Suggested Solution

Feinberg's conception of rights envisages that their importance is in ensuring that each individual is treated in accordance with the Kantian ideal. If we take contemporary legal and political philosophy to mean Western liberalism, we can see the importance of rights as the legal expression of that political system. The Kantian ideal that underpins liberalism is that each individual should be treated as being capable of determining their own best ends; their choices should be respected equally. Most fundamentally, each person should be treated with dignity in that they should be treated as ends in themselves and not means to an end. Rights are seen as important in contemporary thinking because they are said to secure the attainment of Kantian politico-legal philosophy.

This view of the fundamental importance of rights is not without challenge or criticism. Liberals themselves disagree as to the importance of rights in achieving the Kantian ideal. Utilitarians, for example, claim that the most effective way of treating people with equal dignity and respecting their differing choices of values and aims, is to recognise their desires. Based upon a belief that all people wish to maximise their happiness (or 'utility'), they claim to accord equal respect to each person's preferences which maximise utility. Utilitarians are hostile to rights because they see them as potential obstacles to the maximisation of happiness. They privilege the happiness of some at the expense of others – thus violating the Kantian ethic.

We can understand the utilitarian hostility to rights (Bentham described them as 'nonsense upon stilts') if we examine the following hypothetical situation. If A is pregnant but would like an abortion, let us imagine that to have an abortion would increase her utility. If this is so then a right to life that prevented A having an abortion would reduce her utility – in fact it would prevent her from increasing her utility. The right has the effect of overriding her preferences. Instead, it privileges the preferences of those who are anti-abortion, instead of investigating which policy would maximise utility to the greatest extent.

Similar criticisms are made by those adherents of the economic analysis of the law movement. Like utilitarianism, this theory claims that it best gives effect to Kantian principles of equal respect and choice. The choices it respects, according to its leading exponent, Posner, are those that maximise value. Only those preferences that are backed up by the willingness and ability to pay for them can be respected. He asserts that those who value a preference most, will be willing to pay the most for it. Rights, on the other hand, may be given to those who do not value them, or at least not as much as others. These right-holders will thus be enabled to override the preferences of those who most value their preferences.

Another benefit claimed by Posner, is the avoidance of having to make comparisons between individuals as to whose preferences are to be granted. The principle of wealth maximisation provides an allegedly neutral criterion upon which a choice can be made. Judgments as to the moral worth of persons are therefore avoided, each person being treated equally in a society viewed as a market.

Rights are defended against the criticisms and claims of utilitarians and economic analysts. Against the former it is claimed that utilitarians would be unable to prevent many immoral and cruel activities. Maximising utility is not always morally sound. For example, a utilitarian sadist may derive great happiness from carrying out sadistic acts upon a victim. If the sadist's extra utility adds more to the sum total of the population's utility than the victim's disutility subtracts from it, then a utilitarian would countenance the right to perform such acts.

As far as regards the economic analysis of the law, Dworkin has criticised Posner for also being unable to prevent cruelty and exploitation. He highlights this with the example of a book belonging to A but desired by B. A values the book at £1 but B values it more highly at £3. Posner would claim that value would be maximised by A selling the book to B for £2. Both A and B would then be better off because A would have received £1 extra above the value he placed on the book, whereas B would have secured the book at £1 less than he valued it. Dworkin claims, however, that if A refused to sell the book, Posner's theory would advocate a legal rule authorising B to forcibly take the book, as this would maximise the total wealth of society.

Far from being obstacles to the Kantian ideal, those who support rights claim that it is faithful to this ideal because it protects citizen's from the circumstances described above. It is claimed that the two consequentialist theories actually violate the Kantian ethic by permitting people to be treated as means to the attainment of other people's ends, as opposed to ends in themselves.

Dworkin has emphasised the importance of rights in stressing that they may only be overriden (trumped) by arguments of principle – these typically involve the normative pull of other rights. From this strong position, he does concede that policy arguments can override rights but only in limited circumstances and judges cannot use policy arguments – that is the prerogative of the legislature. Policy arguments may often be paternalistic. Feinberg would reject overriding rights on this basis. He would claim that to override a person's choice is to privilege the legislature's choice as to the good. He clearly rejects the overriding of rights by reason of 'love', 'compassion' or 'noblesse oblige'.

Rawls agrees with the view that rights are important as a legal method of securing the Kantian ideal, but he feels that they are pointless unless there is a prior equal distribution of resources amongst citizens. He consequently advocates the overriding of rights where to do so would ameliorate the situation of the less well off in society. To secure the Kantian ideal there must be distributive justice before there can be effective rights. Rights are of secondary importance to Rawls, the primary value being justice.

Nozick rejects Rawls' view of rights. Instead, he sees them as primary. They secure a sphere of freedom around each individual, in which persons, property and values are free from the interference of other citizens and government. He describes Rawls' re-distribution of wealth as theft, since it overrides individuals' property rights. More fundamentally, it fails to treat the individual with Kantian dignity because their choices (as manifested by their rights) are sacrificed to the collective interests of society.

In rejecting any resort to higher values as overriding rights, Feinberg underlines the importance of rights over natural law doctrines of fundamental values. Rights are expressions of individual choice as to conceptions of the good in life. These choices cannot be dictated to people by reference to a set of fundamental values. To do so would once again violate the Kantian basis of liberalism. Finnis has attempted to formulate a natural law concept of rights. He envisages that people should be free to make choices, but that these choices will be limited by the aim of choosing the best methods to attain the seven 'basic goods' of life. These are fundamental values, without which human flourishing would be impossible.

In his concern for human flourishing, Finnis reflects the Kantian belief that free individuals are the best people to decide which ways of life will lead to their personal fulfilment. The inherent problem, which Finnis tries to resolve, is that people may exercise their rights, and the freedom that these secure, in order to make choices that are harmful to themselves, or others. We saw this possibility with the utilitarian and economic analysis theories. Given the avowed importance of rights to liberalism, how can restrictions on those rights, when they cause harm, be justified?

Mill's thesis that citizens should have the right to as much freedom as possible, as long as the exercise of their rights does not harm others, provided liberalism with a principled response to this problem. Rights, although important, had limits. Even though Feinberg appears to reject any limits on rights, most liberals agree that the unlimited exercise of rights would destroy the rights and freedom of other members of society.

Essentially, Feinberg is correct in seeing the importance of rights within contemporary politico-legal philosophy as being a mechanism for allowing people to be self-determining agents. Nevertheless, despite this importance, there is much disagreement as to just how important rights are. Some claim they are a hindrance, others that they are not as important as other mechanisms (eg justice). It has also been shown that an over-emphasis of the importance of rights can lead to a situation in which some are prevented from exercising their own rights. Whilst seeing rights as important elements of liberal thought, we must recognise their limitations and the existence of other essential concepts.

Part D
Judicial Reasoning

Chapter 14

Legal Personality

14.1   Introduction

14.2   Key points

14.3   Questions and suggested solutions

14.1 Introduction

The concept of legal personality has been the subject of some jurisprudential debate. The student might wish to consider why certain bodies are treated as having such 'personality' whilst others are not, and also why (if at all) we need such a concept. This is a subject where it is necessary to consider case law and practical situations.

14.2 Key points

The different types of legal personality

a) Human beings – this could be a more complex notion than at first appears. What, for example, is the legal status of a foetus?

b) Corporations sole, such as the Crown.

c) Corporations aggregate; these are treated as persons in law unless the contrary is stated.

The theories of legal personality

a) The 'fiction theory' – the treatment of legal persons as persons is merely a fiction.

b) Hohfeld's theory – companies must be explained by looking at the capacities, rights, powers and liabilities of the individuals involved.

c) The Realist theory – 'artificial' persons have a real personality with a real mind, will and power of action.

d) The 'purpose' theory – the law protects certain purposes in addition to human beings.

Evaluation of theories of legal personality

a) The 'fiction theory' fails to explain why the concept of legal personality is used at all.

b) The Realist theory has, according to Hart, illogical boundaries.

c) The 'purpose' theory fails to explain why the purposes protected by law need to be called, and treated as, persons.

d) Theorists such as Paton and Hart think that the above theories deal with the wrong issues: to consider the nature of legal personality is unhelpful.

14.3 Questions and suggested solutions

QUESTION ONE

'... we constantly need in modern law the conception of an artificial person ...' (Sir Frederick Pollock) Examine critically the attempts made by English legal theory to provide for this need.

University of London LLB Examination
(for External Students) Jurisprudence and Legal Theory June 1983 Q8

General Comment

This question requires a relatively straightforward analysis of the theories of legal personality. The only difficulty lies in deciding which are the more important theories, and thus how much detail to ascribe to each.

Skeleton Solution

Fiction theory – artificial persons treated as persons – no explanation for idea of 'personality' – Realist theory – artificial person as a real personality – illogical boundaries – corporate veil – purpose theory – attempts are unsuccessful – is the wrong question being considered?

Suggested Solution

Legal theory constantly wrestles with the problem of the nature of an artificial person. This strange animal appears in the notion of 'legal personality'; that a body or group or office is in the eyes of the law a 'person', and is treated in the same way as a natural person – a human being – is treated. It might be thought that this notion requires little explanation: an artificial person is an entity which the law (a legal system) considers 'a person' (ie clothed with some of the rights and duties of a person). This simple view has not been enough for legal theorists, and we must consider those theories giving more complex explanations which appear in the English writings on the subject. (Some views, such as those of Ihering and Kelsen, find no support over here, and are thus not treated). Our criticism will concentrate on the implications of the theories, and whether the English law of 'artificial persons' can be said to be based on them.

First, we will look at the 'fiction theory', supported in England by Coke, Blackstone and especially Salmond. Juristic or artificial persons are only treated as if they are persons, under this view. They are fictitious, not known as persons apart from the law. The law gives them proprietary rights, grants them legal powers and so on, but they have no personality and no will (except to the extent a will is implied by the law). This is an obviously flexible viewpoint, since it can account for any apparent inconsistency in legal treatment by simply saying that they are only treated as persons 'to that extent'. The doctrine of ultra vires, under which a company cannot do anything not authorised by its memorandum of association, might be thought to support the fiction theory, for example (the law only gives personality to the limit of the memo), and so might the doctrine that a company is separate from its members, epitomised in the leading case of *Salomon* v *Salomon* [1897] AC 22 (the law treats the company as a separate unit, even though in fact it is not, especially in the one-man company cases like *Salomon*). Further support for the theory could be claimed from the criminal law, which originally accepted that a company could not commit a criminal offence, which depends on mental intention. The fiction view explains this on the basis of the 'will' of the 'person' only being that given by law, and therefore presumably limited to lawful intention. Recent developments show a more pragmatic and sensible approach, with companies subject to more criminal liability (and also subject to liability for the torts of their servants). Also, the cases where the law allows the veil to be turned aside can be explained as limitations on the grant of the fictitious personality.

Acceptable explanations, then, for many aspects of company law (although many of them can be explained acceptably by other theories, see below). However, no explanation is given for why the law uses the idea of 'personality': is there an essential similarity to real persons or not?

Some other theories are similar to and bound up with the fiction theory, notably the concession theory (that legal personality flows from the state) and the symbolist theory of Ihering.

The second main theory is termed 'Realist' and is expanded in English theory by Maitland, Pollock and Dicey. (Closely related is the 'organism' theory, the name of which gives an accurate guide to the contents.) This view sees an 'artificial person' as a real personality, having a real mind, will and power of action.

If independent power of action was the only requirement of our definition of 'person' and 'personality', perhaps an artificial person would qualify (but has a company really got a power of action independent of its members and officers?); surely though there is something more. To say a corporation is a real person implies an individuality, and that implies some consciousness, experience, inner unity. Some groups may seem to have such an unity and consciousness – one could talk of such a feeling over the British reaction to the Falklands crisis, for instance – but do all legal personalities fit? Surely a corporation sole (consisting of successive holders of one office) hasn't a 'consciousness', nor a multi-national company, nor even a small company? Perhaps a university might be thought to fit?

In any case, even if the legal personalities could be counted as real persons, a further problem arises. If a two man company is a person in reality, why not a two man partnership? If a one man company, why not a one man business? In everyday life, ordinary people treat them as if they did have real personality, though in law they did not. The 'Realist theory' fails to explain why the legal definition of personality does not match the extended Realist definition.

Returning to some of the aspects of English law already considered, Realist theory can account for ultra vires (the real personality constituted by the company as set up by its documents), albeit rather weakly (isn't it a weakness to have to refer to the legal documents to establish the limits of reality?); but can't successfully accommodate the tearing aside of the corporate veil. If the company is a real entity distinct from its members, surely it should always be viewed as such and not sometimes viewed as a collection of its members? Finally, Realism can account for those instances where criminal law applies to a company: can it account for those when it doesn't (if a Board meeting orders an 'execution', the company isn't guilty of murder: why not?).

The third major opinion is the purpose theory developed in England by Barker. Only human beings are persons, but the law protects certain purposes other than those human beings. The creation of artificial persons just gives effect to that purpose (for example, a charitable corporation is created to give effect to various devices by which the law aids the charity). So company property is held not by a person, but for a purpose; the company is 'subjectless property'.

This view has a fundamental flaw. It does not answer the question. It is obviously true that companies and other artificial legal persons are given their status for a purpose (or various purposes). The question remains: why call them 'persons'? What aspect of these entities makes them so akin to real people that the law uses the same name and, to a great extent, applies the same rules?

A purpose view can explain ultra vires (a company is limited to its express purposes, as mentioned in the memo), and even the tearing aside of the veil (the countering weight of other legal purposes), but cannot explain the concept of an artificial person.

The various attempts of English legal theory to provide an adequate concept of artificial persons do not succeed. Paton, in *Jurisprudence*, suggests that the reason for the failure is that the wrong question is being considered. Asking what is the essence of, the connecting factor between, the various different types of legal 'persons', natural and artificial, is the wrong approach, since there is no essential connecting factor except the similarity in treatment meted out by the law.

Perhaps, instead, legal theorists should ask why artificial personality is given by the law, and why and when it should be given.

QUESTION TWO

'As to what the nature of corporate personality may be in itself, no positive rule at all is laid down.' (Sir Frederick Pollock) Discuss how far you believe this still to be true.

University of London LLB Examination
(for External Students) Jurisprudence and Legal Theory June 1984 Q10

General Comment

This question is both interesting and difficult. It leaves scope for discussion of the Hartian view that theories of legal personality have floundered because theorists have used the wrong approach.

Skeleton Solution

Realist theory – corporate person has mind, will and independent power of action – consciousness? – 'fiction theory' – how can companies commit crimes? – 'purpose theory' – why 'persons'? – Hart – asking the wrong question – no such rule possible.

Suggested Solution

There have been many attempts to lay down a positive rule to explain the nature of corporate personality. It is my view that none have been totally successful, each attempted explanation illuminating some characteristics of such personality while obscuring or distorting others. I will set out and discuss some of the main theories which have been developed to illustrate my point. I will then consider the application by Professor Hart in his inaugural lecture *Definition and Theory in Jurisprudence* of modern linguistic theory. Hart concludes, in effect, that the search for a positive rule has been misconceived and misleading; and he thinks that a new approach is required.

The first theory we shall look at is the 'Realist' theory, expounded by Gierke, Maitland and others. Under this theory, a corporate person is a real person, with a mind, will and independent power of action. Clearly there is an extent to which a company has a power of action independent of its members, at least when it is a big company and the members are not in control of its management. But surely something further is required to constitute a 'real person' – consciousness, experience, inner unity. Has a corporate personality (even a small company or a traditional organisation such as Marks & Spencer) these characteristics? Even if it has got those characteristics, the Realist view does not explain why a two man company has them but not a two man partnership, a one man company and not a one man business. The specific legal definition of a corporate personality is not sufficiently explained.

A second major attempt to lay down a rule to explain the nature of corporate personality is the 'fiction theory', evolved by Savigny and Salmond. This theory denies that corporate persons are real 'persons' at all: their 'personality' is a fiction, they are not persons at all apart from the legal treatment. The law gives them rights and duties. This is a flexible 'rule'; any apparent inconsistency in treatment can be explained as the law treating the organisations as persons only to a given extent. Support for this view can be taken from *Salomon* v *Salomon* [1897] AC 22: the law treats a one man company as a person separate from its owner, even though they are clearly identical. The ultra vires rule is explained by the fact that the law allows 'personality' only to a defined extent, in this case the extent set out in the memorandum.

The problem for the fiction theory is that no explanation is given of why the law imputes a corporate personality: why is the idea of 'personality' used. And if the idea is a fiction, how is it that companies are now held able to intend to commit crimes and torts? There is at least one aspect, then, of the phenomenon that the 'fiction' theories have failed properly to capture.

A third major theory is the 'purpose theory', expounded by Barker. Companies are not persons, but the law protects certain purposes other than human beings. A company's property is held not by a person but for a purpose; similarly the right to bring a court action is given to a corporation for a purpose (the purpose differing, presumably, between the different types of corporation). Again, this view leaves the fundamental question unanswered: why are they called 'persons'? Is there a necessary similarity between corporate and individual personality?

Many other answers have been put forward to the search for a rule to explain the nature of corporate personality. The 'organism' theory, similar to the Realist viewpoints, sees a company as a living organism; the symbolist or bracket theory, allied to the fictional 'school' of thought, is a perhaps self-explanatory view. There are others.

Our conclusion at this point must be that, as in Pollock's time, no positive rule is laid down as to the nature of such personality. Professor Hart has argued persuasively in *Definition and Theory in Jurisprudence* for a viewpoint which can be considered as amounting to a claim that the search for such a 'positive rule' is misguided.

In Hart's view, attempts to understand and explain the concept of corporate personality have floundered because the wrong question is being asked. To put it in perhaps an over-simplistic fashion, the question 'what is corporate personality' can never be answered because, in common with other concepts to be found in different areas of law and different legal systems, there is no physical referent to which the concept relates. The usual form of definition 'per genus et differentiam' is therefore not suitable and a different mode of explanation is required.

This role of explanation involves looking at and explaining in context a typical sentence using the concept. To explain the concept of a 'legal right', for example, one must look at a sentence in the form 'X has a legal right as against B' and explain what the sentence means – which explanation will include the complex details of the legal system, a law passed by one of its law-making organs, the possibility of sanctions if the legal right is not properly fulfilled. A similar explanation of sentences in the form 'Smith and Co Ltd owes wife £10' must be used to explicate the concept of legal personality.

Let us revert to the concluding sentence of the third last paragraph. Is Hart saying that the search for a positive rule is misguided, or is his just an extension (in a rather Hohfeldian direction) of the fiction theory? Hart himself is clear that he is rejecting the theories (even that of Hohfeld, which sees corporate personality as a complex myriad of rights, duties and so on, which seems at first sight to be similar to Hart's own position). We must, I think, agree with him that his answer (in rejecting the theories and the very idea of there being an answer to the question 'what is corporate personality') is a denial of the claim that there is any positive rule to be found as to its nature.

In short, then, not only is Pollock right to say no positive rule is laid down: there is strong support for the view that no such rule is possible.

Chapter 15

The Judicial Process

A JUDICIAL DISCRETION

15.1   Introduction

15.2   Key points

15.3   Questions and suggested solutions

B LEGAL REASONING

15.4   Introduction

15.5   Key points

15.6   Questions and suggested solutions

C PRECEDENT

15.7   Introduction

15.8   Key points

15.9   Question and suggested solution

D STATUTORY INTERPRETATION

15.10 Introduction

15.11 Key points

15.12 Question and suggested solution

A JUDICIAL DISCRETION

15.1 Introduction

Since the publication of Dworkin's *Law's Empire* this has become a hotly debated topic. Students should not only consider judicial discretion from both a descriptive and a prescriptive viewpoint but consider, too, Dworkin's invocation that we interpret – that is, make best sense of what judges and lawyers do. It is useful to revise this topic in conjunction with Hart's theories. Furthermore a consideration of the Realist approach may provide an interesting point of comparison.

15.2 Key points

a) Dworkin – *Taking Rights Seriously* and more importantly, *Law's Empire*. This is both a descriptive and prescriptive account, which sees law as a 'seamless web'.

b) Criticisms of Dworkin – Hart, internal scepticism etc.

c) Alternative views – what do pragmatists or Realists have to say?

15.3 Questions and suggested solutions

QUESTION ONE

'The principle of integrity in adjudication ... explains why judges must conceive the body of law they administer as a whole rather than as a set of discrete decisions that they are free to make or amend one by one.' (Dworkin)

What are the consequences of this conception of law for the lawyer?

University of London LLB Examination
(for External Students) Jurisprudence and Legal Theory June 1998 Q7

General Comment

This question can only be properly tackled if you have read Dworkin's *Law's Empire*. Candidates are strongly advised to read this book as part of their studies.

Skeleton Solution

The idea of integrity – the single voice of the law – the ideas of fit and substance – the question of emotional damage – conclusion.

Suggested Solution

Dworkin's (Ronald Dworkin, *Law's Empire* (2nd edn, 1991)) idea that legal argument must be justified by an appeal to integrity holds a method of adjudication for judges which looks bold and daring.

The programme of law as integrity holds a vision for judges, which states that as far as possible they should identify legal rights and duties on the assumption that they were all created by the community as a single entity, and that they express the community's conception of justice and fairness.

According to law as integrity, propositions of law are true if they figure in or follow from the principles of justice, fairness and procedural due process, which provide the best constructive interpretation of the community's legal practice. Law as integrity states that the law must speak with one voice, so judges must assume that the law is structured on coherent principles about justice, fairness and procedural due process, and that in all fresh cases which come before them they must enforce these so as to make each person's situation fair and just by the same standards – that is to say, treat everyone equally.

Because law as integrity sees the law as a coherent phenomenon, rather than a set of discrete decisions, judges are required to justify their decisions to the entirety of the law, which is considered to have an integral life of its own. There must be an essentially interpretive study of legal doctrine. Positivism does not require judges to justify their decisions to the entirety of the law. In this sense, positivism does not consider the law as having an integral life of its own. Positivism will present the law as comprising of a set of discrete decisions, which judges have the discretion to make or amend.

Taking the law as a coherent whole, law as integrity requires that judges go through the whole law to consider an interpretation: this throws into focus the question of whether legal practice is seen in a better light if we assume that the community accepts the principle that people deserve to be treated equally. The interpretation law as integrity holds for the judge is one which both fits and justifies what has gone on before as far as possible. In law, as in literature, the interplay between fit and justification is complex. Just as the interpretation within a chain novel is, for each interpreter, a delicate balance of different types of the literary and the artistic, so in law it is a delicate balance of political convictions of different sorts. In law, as in literature, these must be sufficiently related, and yet disjoint to allow an overall judgment that trades off an interpretation's success on one type of standard against its failure on another.

If, for example, it is decided in the case *McLoughlin* v *O'Brian* [1983] AC 410 that Mrs McLoughlin deserves compensation for her injury, then the question that we need to analyse is whether legal practice is seen in a better light if the community accepts the principle that people in Mrs McLoughlin's position deserve compensation. Positivism as a theory insists that in difficult cases, post-political decisions yield no rights tenable in court (this is only true for simple cases). To the positivist in the *McLoughlin* case, the judge must exercise discretion and make law which is then applied retrospectively to the parties in the case.

We must note that, if the judge is guided by law as integrity, which does not limit what convention finds in past decisions but directs him also to regard as law what morality would suggest to be the best justification for past decisions, then such a judge deciding *McLoughlin* employs his own moral convictions. If he is satisfied that the law as he understands it favours Mrs McLoughlin, he will feel justified in thus deciding whatever the present legislature thinks, whether or not popular morality concurs.

Law as integrity provides a consistency in principle which requires that various standards governing the state's use of coercion against the citizen be consistent in order to have a single vision of justice. If a judge deciding the *McLoughlin* case is tempted to decide against Mrs McLoughlin, he would first ask himself whether any principled distinction can be drawn between her case and other mothers who suffer emotional damage at the scene of an accident. Positivism is different from law as integrity precisely because it rejects consistency in principle as a source of legal rights.

Consistency in principle supposes that people have legal rights which follow from legislation and precedents which enforce coercion. Mindful of this, law as integrity supposes that people are entitled to a coherent and principled extension of past decisions, even when judges disagree about what that means. Positivism denies this, since it denies consistency in principle as a judicial virtue for disssecting ambiguous statutes and inexact precedents to try to achieve this. The methodology of Dworkin's model judge, Hercules, emphasises this point.

Law as integrity requires judges to treat the techniques that they use in interpreting statutes and measuring precedents not simply as tools handed down by the legal system, but as principles they assume can be justified in political theory, and when that is in doubt they construct a theory of the system to better them.

The consequences of this conception of law for lawyers have hopefully been made clear in the preceding paragraphs. More importantly, this theory invites lawyers to search for an answer in legal materials, using innovation and lots of imagination. In doing this, lawyers should not be afraid to draw on their own moral convictions to determine the best way to interpret legal data. By drawing on their moral convictions, they are able to interpret legal data in order to bring consistency into the law and portray the community's legal practice in its best light.

QUESTION TWO

'... the skeptical challenge, sensed as the challenge of external skepticism, has a powerful hold on lawyers. They say, of any thesis about the best account of legal practice in some department of the law, "That's your opinion," which is true but to no point. Or they ask, "How do you know?" or "Where does that claim come from?" demanding not a case they can accept or oppose but a thundering knock-down metaphysical demonstration no one can resist who has the wit to understand. And when they see that no argument of that power is in prospect, they grumble that jurisprudence is subjective only. Then, finally, they return to their knitting – making, accepting, resisting, rejecting arguments in the normal way, consulting, revising, deploying convictions pertinent to deciding which of competing accounts of legal practice provides the best justification of that practice. My advice is straightforward: this preliminary dance of skepticism is silly and wasteful; it neither adds to nor subtracts from the business at hand. The only skepticism worth anything is skepticism of the internal kind, and this must be earned by arguments of the same contested character as the arguments it opposes, not claimed in advance by some pretense at hard-hitting empirical metaphysics.' (Ronald Dworkin, *Law's Empire*.)

Discuss.

University of London LLB Examination
(for External Students) Jurisprudence and Legal Theory June 1993 Q6

General Comment

Candidates always have difficulty with questions generally on what has become known as 'Dworkin's one right answer thesis'. It is not a question to make a big meal of; nor is it a question to dismiss lightly. Rather, it requires very careful preparation. Don't be frightened by the fact that the question of truth and objectivity is one of the most difficult questions of any discipline – not just philosophy! If you show an examiner that you are dismissive you will get few marks. You must show that you've thought carefully about the matter. It is a topic that displays sloppy logic very easily. For example: 'There is no right answer because people disagree' is just a foolish comment. True, there may be no right answers, but not for that reason, because people disagree all the time about what the right answer is (note: courtrooms!). Or, 'There is no right answer because morality is subjective'. Here by 'subjective' it is usually meant that 'no right answer is possible', so the sentence is as tautological as: 'There is no right answer because morality doesn't have one right answer'. If, on the other hand, by 'subjective' is meant 'people's beliefs differ' then we have the same mistake as before. The moral: tread very carefully!

The way to answer this sort of question is to discuss obvious distinctions such as these just pointed out, after having discussed what the question means. Use Dworkin's arguments, and that means referring to his distinctions between internal and external scepticism, and taste and judgment. Refer to the construction of the best theory underlying legal practice by Hercules, the superhuman judge. Also, difficult perhaps as the idea is, try to grasp his criticism of the idea of 'demonstrability' (see Guest, *Ronald Dworkin*, Chapter 6) and explain that. Best of all, though, refer to one or two of the cases that have struck you as either confirming or contradicting what he says. Referring to what goes on in court is always useful in jurisprudence – try to bring the subject alive. After all, it must be an important question whether lawyers and judges in court are disputing about a correct decision or whether they are just 'trading tastes'.

Skeleton Solution

What question means; the arguments for subjectivity; the futility of the simple arguments for subjectivity; Dworkin and the consequences for his theory if morality were subjective; morality's being subject to a 'sieve' of rationality; the idea of external and internal scepticism; the difference between 'taste' and 'judgment' – the demonstrability thesis.

Suggested Solution

The question refers to the facts, which seem undeniable, that people who suppose that there is no objectivity to questions involving controversial issues of law and morality, will, in their ordinary lives refer constantly to the 'right' way of doing things, to producing arguments that are 'better' than others and so forth. This seems particularly true of legal argument; after all, what is the business of legal argument – working out what judges should do in relation to putting people in prison, or taking money by way of fine of compensation from them – if it is not about rival accounts of what should be done? If people really thought there was no 'right' or 'wrong' to the matter why would they bother to supply arguments? Why wouldn't they just say: 'this is my opinion' and 'your opinion is as good as mine'?

There are some arguments for this approach; some people would say that is in fact all that people can do, that is, give their opinion. Further, if we accepted, like Fuller and Dworkin, that moral reasoning were an integral part of legal reasoning, we would have to accept that moral reasoning was objective, and that is one idea that many people just cannot accept. Even further, what sense can be given to an argument's being right if there is no way at all of establishing, ie proving, it to be right?

But these three arguments for the subjectivity of legal reasoning, which are very common, cannot be sufficient in themselves. Take the first one; does the mere fact that something is a person's 'opinion' make it thereby 'subjective'? The answer is a crashing 'no' because even scientists, who clearly accept that there is an objectivity to many, if not all, statements of science, use the phrase 'in my opinion' with great frequency. Further, in courtrooms, opinions are frequently expressed about the truth of objective matters; the giving of expert evidence is an obvious example, but (although barristers are not permitted to give evidence of 'their opinion') virtually all arguments on questions of law are without doubt the result of the 'opinions' of barristers, solicitors, government departments and pupils. Indeed, the usual phrase is: 'let's seek the opinion of a barrister'. Maybe one thing that is being claimed here is that when someone gives an opinion, he is not saying he is right, just that he wants to convince the other so that the other will accept the opinion.

But it cannot be true that if you say that X is your 'opinion', you mean that there is no right or wrong of the matter. Tell that to the flat-earthers: they believe that their opinion that the world is flat is right and we believe that their opinion is wrong. Any barrister, too, will claim that his opinion is the right one (otherwise, we might wonder why he was advancing it: no-one has an interest in a wrong opinion). Further, it cannot be an answer to say that something is put forward as an opinion in order only to convince; what is it that 'convinces'? Is it conceivably possible that it is the objective truth for the opinion that has to convince?

The second argument suggested above for the subjectivity of legal reasoning arises from the supposed subjectivity of moral reasoning; if Dworkin is right that morality is part of the law, then, if morality is subjective, so is legal reasoning. Is morality subjective? In some senses it is clearly not; although equally clearly, matters of morality cannot be proved in any way. First, people argue about morality (eg about the rightness and wrongness of abortion), as in law, as if they believed there were right answers ('abortion is a right'; 'abortion is murder'; etc). Second, people assume that arguments about morality should be subject to rational enquiry. They assume, for example, that moral judgments that are illogical ('pacifism is wrong because people like Bertrand Russell are pacifists'); based on false premises ('homosexuals have weak wrists'); assertive ('abortion is just wrong'); or just amount to parroting ('adultery is wrong because my father said it was') are all ruled out as sensible, intelligible statements of moral positions. We might accept that abortion, homosexuality, adultery, pacifism etc are wrong; but we certainly do not do so for these reasons.

All this shows that there is a difference between assertions of 'taste' and 'judgment'. 'Taste' refers to our subjective states such as when we say that we like vanilla ice-cream; there is no right or wrong of it. Judgment, on the other hand, is a matter of right and wrong; it is just that the arguments are controversial and, in a nutshell, very difficult! Dworkin puts the point in another way. He distinguishes between external skepticism, whereby one stands outside some intellectual scheme (eg legal argument) and says that there can be no truth there because there is nothing in the external world, by virtue of which it could be true; and internal skepticism, where one says, there *could* be truth, but the arguments are just not convincing! Dworkin says the internal sceptic doesn't say anything contrary to there being right answers; only the external sceptic does that and, he says, this is exemplified by the passage in the question, there are few, if any, of them. The CLS movement, despite what they say, are not external sceptics, but (dubious) 'global internal sceptics'; they claim there is no truth for legal reasoning on the grounds that the law is too conflicting and contradictory. 'Being non-conflicting and non-contradictory' is therefore the CLS criterion for truth in law; and hence their argument of saying that there is no truth in law does not rest upon any external premise such as, in the external world there is nothing by virtue of which 'law is true'!

The final argument is straightforward: there can be no truth unless it can be demonstrated. Look, we can cut the argument very short on this one. The statement 'there can be no truth unless it can be demonstrated' cannot itself be demonstrated and yet it is put forward as true. Enough said? Well, if we are being urged to adopt this view of truth for law, which is possible, but not the way proponents of the demonstrability thesis put it, why should we accept it? The usual answer is that it makes for certainty, objectivity and clarity. Well, we've heard those arguments before. They are not arguments about law's truth, but the arguments for legal positivism, which moves us to an entirely different battlefield.

QUESTION THREE

'Since no real judge can be Hercules, Dworkin's picture of judicial integrity is a myth and has no use for real judges.'

Discuss.

University of London LLB Examination (for External Students) Jurisprudence and Legal Theory June 1995 Q9(a)

General Comment

A relatively easy question which relies on an evaluation of Dworkin's creation. This thought-provoking quote requires a strong defence of the purpose behind the concept of 'Hercules' with an examination of the criticism levelled at Dworkin for creating him in the first place.

Skeleton Solution

What is Hercules about? – Hercules and 'hard cases' – the real value of Hercules – conclusion.

Suggested Solution

To suggest that Dworkin's creation of Hercules in his article 'Hard Cases' is a 'myth' is to misunderstand the very nature of his fascinating and highly practical theory. The quote is in danger of being interpreted with an underestimation of Dworkin's subtlety and intellectual power as our most important contemporary in legal philosophy.

There is a tendency to dismiss Hercules by suggesting that no such judge ever existed. However, this view is too glib. Hercules is a model against which, like any other ideal, legal arguments are to be judged. A good illustration of this can be found with the idea of the ideal market. The commentator would go away from the main point if he were to argue that the ideal market does not exist, because saying such a thing is to recognise the idea of the ideal in any case. The concept of an ideal market illustrates how, in the real world, imperfections exist because of monopolies or other restrictive practices which 'distort' the real market.

Dworkin posits the ideal judge because his theory is about law as an argumentative attitude. He provides a scheme of argument which is sufficiently abstract to draw controversy. However, he does not provide a set of premises from which conclusions may be drawn by the use of syllogisms because Hercules is not that sort of theory. Hercules is intended to point the way to correct legal argument. It is not a method to point towards a right answer, but to raise the question of whether there could be such a right answer. Thus, it is about objectivity and not a criticism of the ideal module of Hercules.

Dworkin establishes his idea by saying:

> 'If a judge accepts the settled practice of his legal system – if he accepts, that is, the authority provided by its distinct constitutive and regulative rules – then he must according to the doctrine of political responsibility, accept some general political theory that justifies these practices.'

The judge has convictions about his role and his duties which are defined by his judicial oath and by other sources. It would certainly be surprising if he did not. Thus, the judge has an idea about legislative purpose and the principles enshrined in common law.

Hercules has a use for real judges because, to make sense of his position, he must be able to make general statements about what judging entails. It is not enough to declare that he accepts a set of rules without the need to explain or justify why he accepts them. For real judges, the magnitude of their coercive powers indicates a requirement for some form of justification when such powers are used. It is, therefore, eminently reasonable to suggest that there is a rationale behind the business of judging.

Dworkin says that we can assume that Hercules accepts most of the settled rules of his jurisdiction. Such rules lay down the familiar characteristics of the law. An example is given of the constitutive and regulative rules that grant the legislature powers to legislate, and give judge the powers to adjudicate and to follow previous decisions in addition to settled areas of law such as contract.

Hercules has, however, a real and not merely mythical value because he goes further. He can produce theories underlying all the above rules. 'Democracy' underlies, albeit in different forms, jurisdictions in both the United States and the United Kingdom. In such examples there is the basic justification for judicial coercion which exists in accordance with the requirements created by the legislature, democratically elected.

However, from these beginnings, a justification for common law precedent is based upon fairness where citizens are treated in a consistent fashion. The justification for particular statutory or common law applications comes within more elaborately worked out theories such as a theory of responsibility in criminal law, and so on. From each theory, there are sub-theories. A good example is the defence of duress in criminal law. One theory suggests that duress is a justification for action (ie for self-preservation), whilst another suggests duress is an excuse which absolves the defendant from blame, and is a recognition of human weakness in dire circumstances. An extension of such theories questions what constitutes 'dire' circumstances, such as whether duress can be a defence for murder in the first degree. A further theory then examines the question of a moral difference between degrees of murder and how far the defence can be extended.

Whilst such theories are discussed in law reports and by academics, one's own theories and arguments can also be perfected. Dworkin uses Hercules to illustrate the general form, or scheme, of the types of arguments which are used. Hercules can be thought of as producing all these theories for all areas of law but he will have to justify the particular settled rules with such substantive theories as he has devised.

There is, too, the need to do more. A judge may draw a conclusion about the 'clear' law in a way which is different from merely 'reading off' the law. Such a judge might conclude that he would exceed his judicial powers were he to depart from clear law and extend, for instance, the defence of duress. Lord Kilbrandon, in *Lynch* v *DPP for Northern Ireland* [1975] AC 653, expressed such a warning by suggesting that such a decision to so extend the law would step 'outside the proper functions' of the court. It is submitted, therefore, that whilst the purpose of Hercules, as a judge of integrity, is an ideal, it has a very real value for the responsibilities exercised by real judges.

QUESTION FOUR

'Judges neither should be nor are deputy legislators, and the familiar assumption, that when they go beyond political decisions already made by someone elsse they are legislating is misleading. It misses the importance of a fundamental distinction ... between arguments of principle on the one hand and arguments of policy on the other.' (Dworkin) Discuss critically Dworkin's theory of adjudication.

Written by the Editor

General Comment

Analysis of the judicial role is required. Dworkin is of course central to the debate. Reference to actual decisions of the courts must be part of your answer.

Skeleton Solution

Taking Rights Seriously – *Law's Empire* – principle and policy distinction – theory of adjudication – rejection of Hart's free discretion – affirmation of principle decisions – nature of principles – one Right Answer Thesis – interpretation – constraint and freedom – rejection of law as pragmatism (policy arguments) – criticisms of theory.

Suggested Solution

In *A Matter of Principle* Dworkin makes a distinction between arguments of principle and those of policy. He argues that judges should only adjudicate on cases that concern principles, whereas politicians should, and indeed, are engaged in questions of the collective interests. These he terms issues of 'policy'. In *Law's Empire* Dworkin places within a wider conception of the nature of law and adjudication. Central to Dworkin's thesis is that what judges say they are doing must be taken seriously. He notes how judges deny that they are legislating, on the contrary they talk as if they are making decisions according to what the law requires. Dworkin sees law as a seamless web and strongly rejects Hart's view that there are penumbral areas within which a judge exercises 'free discretion'.

Dworkin claims that a judge is always free and yet constrained when he/she adjudicates. Another claim is that judges can make decisions that are political in content and implication without at the same time law-making. This theory seems most relevant when seen as an attempted explanation of American Supreme Court practice – his wider message is that judges (but more especially Supreme Court judges) can be political without merely expressing subjective judgements.

How does Dworkin support these claims? If we begin with the distinction between policy and principle, we see how in *Law's Empire* Dworkin offers a view of law called 'Law as Integrity'. According to this view, judges should make decisions with integrity. This integrity is displayed by his ideal type of judge (called Hercules) who adjudicates by following principles which run through the political and legal culture. Such principles include: 'due process' and 'equality of resources'. These principles can be political but they may conflict with policy goals. In such instances, a judge must give effect to politico-legal principles.

Earlier in *Taking Rights Seriously* Dworkin explains the nature of principles. He feels that unlike rules, they can be applied or not applied without affecting their existence. A principle is not all or nothing in its application, instead it has weight. A principle does not depend for its existence upon judicial pronouncement; a judge may never have articulated a particular principle but it is not right to say that it does not exist within a legal system. To illustrate the nature of principles, Dworkin uses the case of *Riggs* v *Palmer* 115 NY 506 (1889) where the judges 'found' and applied an equitable principle that one should not benefit from one's own wrong doings.

When a judge adjudicates he ideally should recognise these principles because they make sense of the enterprise of adjudication he/she is involved in. A judge is forced to recognise these principles because of this reason. As a result a judge cannot simply apply his/her subjective prejudices (as someone like Griffith in *Politics of the Judiciary* would claim) to a case before him/her because she/he is constrained by principles of impartiality and fairness which permeate his/her judicial activity.

In addition, where Hart would claim there is no law covering a particular situation – a gap – Dworkin claims that there lie principles. Sometimes these principles conflict but there can be a right answer. The 'one right answer thesis' is the most controversial aspect of Dworkin's theory of adjudication. His claim is not as absurd as it initially sounds. Like Hercules, a judge, when adjudicating must choose the appropriate principles. He/she is restrained from simply making new law but instead looks within the legal system to see what decision would best give effect to the principles which that particular legal and political system claims to embody. His/her choice or decision is therefore a principled one; not one of policy. What makes it right? The answer is somewhat complex but essentially a judge's adjudication is said to be right when he/she has made an interpretation of what the best adjudication would be.

Dworkin claims that adjudication is an interpretive exercise, it is like writing a chain novel. The next writer is simultaneously free to carry on the story in an infinite number of ways but at the same time is constrained by the enterprise he/she is engaged in and the preceding text. According to Dworkin, the chain novelist faces two threshold requirements; to find the best textual fit (what particular manner of continuation best fits in with the preceding text?) and secondly, the best justification (what particular continuation best carries out the claims made by the chain novel and the novelists?).

When these two requirements are transferred into the realm of legal adjudication we can see that institutional fit and justification permit a judge to be engaged in political decisions, but at the same time be constrained by principle so that he/she does not legislate. If, as Dworkin claims, the law professes to use coercion because of past political decisions, then a judge's adjudication must justify such use. Dworkin personifies the state as acting coherently according to principle. A judge's function is to try to trace the thread of the state's principled coherence – its 'integrity'. In order to fulfil this function, he/she must engage his/her own interpretative skills and providing this is done genuinely the adjudication that results is said by Dworkin to be the correct one.

A number of criticisms can be made of Dworkin's theory. Firstly, virtually any policy decision can be dressed up as a decision based upon principle, as long as judges talk the language of 'institutional fit' and 'justification'. A second objection was most clearly made by the American Realists; one should avoid excessive interest in what judges say they are doing and pay more attention to what they are actually doing. Thirdly, the law must perform mundane, everyday functions but Dworkin's method of adjudication is so incredibly complex that no judge could attempt it in practice without sacrificing this mundane function. If a judge did aspire to Dworkin's Herculean ideal there would be of a great cost in legal certainty. Fourthly, what if a judge is under a state of false consciousness and therefore believes that he/she is institutionally constrained, but in reality he/she is expressing his/her own subjective/political bias in his/her adjudications? Here a judge may justifiably be accused of not merely applying, but making the law instead.

Finally, it may be claimed that Dworkin's theory is very culture specific; concerned with defending the liberalism of the Supreme Court. This liberalism can be seen in the landmark cases of *Roe* v *Wade* 410 US 113 (1973) and *Brown* v *Board of Education* 347 US 483 (1954). Dworkin claims that we can trust the judiciary, even when their decisions seem highly charged politically. However, in claiming that political decisions are part of the legitimate judicial adjudication, Dworkin's theory can defend the modern day conservatism of the Supreme Court. It may be said that contemporary Supreme Court decisions are examples of the judicial politico-legal interpretation that Dworkin puts forward as the ideal.

B LEGAL REASONING

15.4 Introduction

Questions often concern logic – is legal reasoning logical? It is thus necessary to consider what 'logical' means. Some useful cases for illustrating points about legal reasoning are *Donoghue* v *Stevenson* [1932] AC 562; *R* v *Allen* (1872) LR 1 CCR 367; and *Fisher* v *Bell* [1961] 1 QB 394.

15.5 Key points

Deductive reasoning

A logical necessary conclusion is drawn from major and minor premises. What is the meaning of logical?

Inductive reasoning

Propositions are arrived at after collection and sorting of data.

15.6 Questions and suggested solutions

QUESTION ONE

'There are good reasons for supposing that judges ought to consider and evaluate the consequences of various alternative rulings open to them ...' (MacCormick)

What are these reasons?

University of London LLB Examination
(for External Students) Jurisprudence and Legal Theory June 1999 Q12

General Comment

This question may seem difficult because it can easily be misunderstood. Since the quotation is taken from Neil MacCormick, one will do well if his book *Legal Reasoning and Legal Theory* is familiar to you. However, an understanding of the requirement of the question should be enough to fetch you good marks.

Skeleton Solution

The purpose of legal reasoning: MacCormick – policy/principle dichotomy – *Alcock* v *Chief Constable of South Yorkshire* – *Donoghue* v *Stevenson* – conclusion.

Suggested Solution

Professor Neil MacCormick (Neil MacCormick, *Legal Reasoning and Legal Theory* (1978)) argues that it is part of legal reasoning to eliminate logical conflicts between rules. To him, this leads to coherence in the law. He argues that the concept of coherence involves offering a rational purpose to the law, rather than regarding it as something existing on its own.

For example, in formulating the 'neighbour principle' (which said that a duty is owed to persons whom one can reasonable foresee would be likely to be injured by one's careless acts or omissions) Lord Atkin said, 'In English law there must be, and is, some general conception of relations giving rise to a duty of care of which the particular cases found in the books are but instances'.

According to MacCormick, so long as a proposed ruling is consistent and coherent with the rest of the system, it is legally permitted: that it is authorised by a principle or by analogy, and is therefore legally justified, has better consequences than any other similarly authorised ruling. It is because of this view that he rejects Dworkin's theory of principles (Ronald Dworkin, *Taking Rights Seriously* (1977)) as propositions that describe legal rights. He is of the view that rules are superior to principles. To him, rules owe their status as rules to their pedigree, and principles have their status offered to them by those who use them as a rationalisation of rules.

MacCormick would explain that a case such as *Donoghue* v *Stevenson* [1932] AC 562 is one involving the problem of relevancy, where it was disputed in case law whether or not there was a rule of law imposing a duty of care on manufacturers relative to the consumer. We know that the majority of the House of Lords thought that there was such a rule, while the minority thought there was not. We should remind ourselves that in this case Lord Buckmaster said that Mrs Donoghue could only recover if her claim was based on an existing law, as she was not the immediate purchaser. Lord Atkin's 'neighbour principle' extended the liability of the manufacturers to the ultimate consumer.

We can see the point MacCormick is making with the quotation in this question if we consider the different standpoints of both Lord Buckmaster and Lord Atkin in *Donoghue* v *Stevenson*. Lord Buckmaster preferred to think that, in giving a decision in court, a judge must be open to evaluate the consequences of alternative rulings open to him. The judge may want to consider the utilitarian purpose of the existing law. Let us assume that the purpose of the existing law is to encourage inward investment in a rundown economic zone. The government would not want to frighten such investors away with punitive taxes and other restrictive laws, and investors would be concerned about the law making them potentially liable to millions of claimants in negligence. Investors would be scared off.

Since the government believes capital must be wooed, pampered and cossetted, it would be policy that the flood gates are not opened by judicial decisions. Judges are aware of the position they occupy as vital cogs in the wheel of investment attraction, and must thus be aware of the consequences of the alternative rulings open to them.

It is arguable that a judge might decide to rule on policy ground because that to him is the only way to achieve an increase in the welfare of the community. We see an example of this point in the case of *Alcock* v *Chief Constable of South Yorkshire* [1992] 1 AC 310 regarding the Hillsborough football disaster, where the court decided the case on policy grounds.

However, we are warned of the danger of deciding a case on policy grounds by Professor Dworkin, who states that the judge must assume that the law he is called upon to interpret is structured on a coherent principle of justice, fairness and procedural due process, and that in all the fresh cases that come before him he must make each person's situation as fair and just by the same standards. It is only by this method that the law will treat people equally.

Dworkin's point is that judges, although they must give thought to the consequences of their rulings, must be alive to the fact that they can only decide a case by constructing a theory of the system and giving weight to competing sets of principles. Giving a ruling on the basis of principles and not policy means that the judge gives consideration to the rights of the parties before him. Policy-based arguments concern the community's goals, not the individual's rights: this leads to inequality.

MacCormick would urge judges to consider both policy and principle during adjudication. He has no problem in advising that the community's goal is important; judges must pay as much attention to this as they pay to the individual's rights. However, it is instructive to find in Dworkin a neat idea which states that arguments for community's goals have the consequence of stifling the individual's rights. It is for this reason that the individual's rights must always trump community-based ones. It is with this point in mind that we recall the late Lord Denning, who always put adaptability first. His view that the legal authorities should be interpreted so as not to impede justice is found in the expression 'justice according to the law', which to him meant that the law should not prevent the application of justice.

Other judges declare that they dispense 'justice according to the law'. However, they are more orthodox and limit their choices to rulings found in the existing law, which may well have been made for policy reasons. They would reject arguments on principled grounds. To them, society's needs are greater, but we ask whether it is such a bad thing to ask judges to rule on alternatives which yield justice and equality for all.

QUESTION TWO

Why are judges bound by legal precedents?

University of London LLB Examination
(for External Students) Jurisprudence and Legal Theory June 1995 Q11

General Comment

This is a very wide-ranging question. The student should take great care with it. Detailed books on the subject have already been written, so the main solution is to select points which attract comments when judges do not feel bound by legal precedent. Explain why judges apply precedents, and how they interpret the ratio decidendi of a particular case.

Skeleton Solution

Introduction – what is precedent? – the doctrine of stare decisis – ratio decidendi – conclusion.

Suggested Solution

The judge has two tasks:

a) to resolve the dispute before him;

b) to reach his decision by reference to some impartial rule of law.

A main aspect of formal justice is that all cases should be treated alike where there is a repetition of earlier practices which follow earlier patterns. Most legal systems have developed a system of precedent, including the use of past decisions as a guide to present decisions.

In England, precedents of an appropriate authority not only guide decisions in later cases but they bind the judges in those later cases. The doctrine of stare decisis has developed whereby a judge in an inferior court may obey the decision of a higher court on the same point. The main argument for stare decisis is certainty, which is valued in our legal system because it allows people to arrange their affairs in accordance with the law, by not breaking it, or by taking advantage of it. If judges depart from previous decisions at will such arrangements are upset. Also, individual earlier cases would become, in effect, retrospective laws which change the old law and apply a new law in the present case to be decided.

Cardozo J, in *Great Northern Railway Co* v *Sunburst Oil* (1932) (unreported) suggests that in order to avoid this problem, the court could adopt prospective overruling. The present case would then be treated in accordance with the old law, whilst a new law would be announced for future cases. Although retrospective argument is avoided, could it be so arranged (by applying the new law to future arrangements only) to avoid affecting settled arrangements? It would seem to be unfair to the losing litigant because he would have persuaded the judge to accept his legal submission, but would still lose the case. It is submitted that the question posed is whether certainty and the development of the law go together.

The doctrine of stare decisis has been criticised for its rigidity and inflexibility. In practice, however, judges do have a wide measure of flexibility and movement where devices can be used to avoid a particular precedent. The authority of a particular law report is weighed up, with more weight becoming attached to those reports thought to be of a higher quality than others. The judge then decides which parts of an earlier case will actually bind him. He will distinguish the 'ratio decidendi' of the earlier case from the 'obiter dicta' which will not bind him, hence the measure of flexibility.

A traditional definition of the ratio decidendi is that it is the rule of law enunciated by the judge to the extent that it is necessary for the decision of the case. Therefore, the question is what part of the judgment is relevant: see *Donoghue* v *Stevenson* [1932] AC 562 per Lord Atkin who developed the neighbour principle, as compared with the narrower principle concerning manufacturers' liability first pleaded in the lower court.

Some judges are said to decide the case before them rather than stating the law. Certainly the House of Lords, which no longer binds itself with earlier decisions, attempts the latter course, although often a policy of law rather than the law itself can emerge. Wallbaugh puts forward a reversal test against this traditional view. He suggests that if the reverse of the proposition leads to a different decision in the case, that is the ratio decidendi. Such a distinction, highlighted in *Donoghue* v *Stevenson*

[1932] AC 562, suggests, however, that Wallbaugh's reversal test will tell us what is not the ratio whilst failing to assist us with what it is.

Lord Devlin's approach says that the ratio is the reason for the decision which the judge wishes to be the source of precedent. Therefore, would it be incorrect to say that a case is a precedent, and, as such is binding in a way the judge never intended?

Goodhart sees the ratio as the decision based on the facts which are treated as 'material' by the judge, putting less emphasis on the judge's statements of law. He sees the judge as viewing certain facts, explicit and implicitly, as 'material' where his decision on those facts becomes binding as the ratio.

Stone, however, maintains that there is not a unique ratio of a case, but a choice of rationes available to later judges to make a choice from. The two possible rationes are the descriptive and the prescriptive, whereby a descriptive ratio is ascertainable from the decision once given, but the prescriptive ratio is how a subsequent court treats the earlier decision: see *Evans v Triplex Safety Glass Co Ltd* [1936] 1 All ER 283 where a windscreen smashed causing injury. The court, bound by *Donoghue v Stevenson*, held that the ratio of the earlier case was that a duty of care arose only when there was no possibility of interference with the product between the time it left the manufacturer and the time the loss was caused. In the later case, the court held that there was such a possibility and the plaintiff did not recover.

Dias goes further by saying that the ratio should be viewed in a continuing time framework, as the interpretation of the case given by later judges.

Whilst such views give an understanding of the central feature of why judges are bound by legal precedents, it is nevertheless important to identify how cases are treated in later cases to discover for what they are taken as authority. Montrose argues that the ratio is essentially one of a terminological nature, reasserting the common law tradition by suggesting:

a) the rule of law is to be found in the actual opinion of the judge which forms the basis of his decision;

b) there is the rule of law for which the case is binding authority;

c) any reason which ultimately brings about the decision – which essentially relates to the reasons for the ratio.

It is submitted that Montrose takes the argument little further.

It is worth noting de Smith's view from *Nissan v Attorney-General* [1970] AC 179 where it is possible that the case will have no ascertainable ratio at all. However, today the doctrine of stare decisis appears fixed and settled – in practice it is a flexible weapon in the hands of a judge. What occurs is the establishment of a core area of fixed law surrounded by a fringe area where the judges distinguish, approve or follow cases whilst steadily developing the law.

QUESTION THREE

What, in your view, does interpretation of the law involve? Does it bear any analogy with intepretation in other fields, such as the interpretation of literature, or art?

University of London LLB Examination
(for External Students) Jurisprudence and Legal Theory June 1993 Q8

General Comment

This is a difficult question although, for a person who has interests in fields other than law, such as literature or music, it is possible to write very interesting answers. It requires a close look at Dworkin's theory of interpretation and then some views of your own; it is best to contrast the idea of interpretation with that of description (note Hart's descriptive sociology of law) and 'normativity', with a look at some cases. Then it is important to explore the analogy; don't be dismissive because legal argument shares many features with interpretation in the arts (both discourses, for example, make extensive use of the idea of interpretation). Explore the strengths and the weaknesses of the analogy. The best way to do this is to pick on (if you have one) your own speciality, whether it be music, literature, poetry or painting. Remember, too, in this kind of question, to come to some kind of answer: do you think that there is a reasonable analogy to draw?

Skeleton Solution

The meaning of interpretation as opposed to describing and saying how things ought to be – Dworkin's theory of interpretation and how it is supposed to apply to law – an analogy with interpretation in music.

Suggested Solution

The idea of interpretation is one that occurs frequently in the law; the barrister, solicitor, judge and law student have to 'offer an interpretation' of some legal point. What does it actually mean? We could take the famous case of Hart's statute prohibiting 'vehicles' in the park; we could, for example, be asked by a client to say whether his having taken a skateboard through the park was in breach of this statute. We start with a baseline, that of agreement with the provision 'Vehicles are prohibited from the [such and such] park'; after that, however, we have only interpretations as to whether 'vehicle' includes skateboards. There is no 'read off' sense in which we can find the answer to this difficult question, yet barristers spend all the time trying to make their living out of making this sort of interpretation. Put in another way, there is no descriptive sense in which we can simply describe what the law says. Further, it does not seem to be correct that, say as barristers, we can merely exhort a judge with the normative statement: skateboards either ought or ought not to be covered by the word 'vehicle'. What is it, then, that we do?

Ronald Dworkin claims that interpretation is central to legal argument and that we cannot have a proper account of law until we have a proper account of legal interpretation. He says that interpretation means 'making the best sense' of some activity (like legal practice) in the following way: we try to construct the most coherent account of the practice in terms of what is of moral importance. He imagines a society in which one of the rules is that people doff their hats to their superiors; if they do this unthinkingly, he says that the rules function in that society in a pre-interpretive way. It is only when people start to question the point of such rules that the society (perhaps only by its officials) has entered the interpretive phase. People might ask why they do this and come up with some interpretation such as that hat doffing is a mark of deference to people whom they perceive to be superior; others might come up with the idea that hat doffing is a mark of respect to all members of the society. In fact, there may be arguments about which interpretation is the 'better' one; some will argue that members of the society are better than others and that deference is therefore in order while others will argue that deference between people is wrong and that all people deserve respect equally. If a decision is made on the correct interpretation, say, in some test case where a member of the society refused to doff his cap to a dinner lady because she 'was inferior', and the result is that the action was wrong because hat doffing was a required mark of respect, Dworkin says that the society has entered a 'post-interpretive' phase, in which 'interpretation folds in on itself' to change the practice.

How could we apply this method to the famous vehicle case? Well, what is the 'best sense' we can make of 'Vehicles are prohibited from the park'? It seems that the most natural thing we would want to do is look to a thing we call 'the intention of Parliament'; we might then go to some principle of construction of statutes that requires ambiguous penal statutes to be resolved in favour of a criminal defendant. This seems natural, but why? Dworkin's explanation is that we understand the language of the statute in the context of the theory of democracy (parliamentary supremacy; hence the attention paid to 'the intention of Parliament') underlying it. He says that barristers do this sort of thing all the time. We assume that we have to construct an understanding of the words of the statute that makes best sense of the words that the major institution of our democratic legal system has produced; making best sense means, for him, best moral sense, by which he refers to the way in which we suppose that all decisions relating to taking away freedoms from people, whether money for compensation or fines, or imprisonment, should be in accordance with morality.

Does this form of interpretation bear any analogy with interpretation in art? What would be the analogy with 'Vehicles are prohibited in the park'? The first thing to note is that no-one (except the rare Marxist) disagrees that this phrase states the law; rather, the difficulty lies in working out whether it excludes skateboards. Are there equivalent consensuses on what counts as, say, part of a novel? The answer must surely be yes; we all accept that Shylock is the name of the Jew in Shakespeare's *The Merchant of Venice*; no-one disputes that. However, people could dispute that *The Merchant of Venice* is a play, as opposed to an anti-Jewish tract. But that is not enough to ruin the analogy, because, as pointed out with the Marxist above, it is always going to be possible to dispute. After all, even clear statutes enacted by Crown-in-Parliament which purport to bind Parliament's successors, can be laid open to the same charge. What is the analogy with the vehicles through the park legislation and *The Merchant of Venice*? We can easily imagine two rival interpretations (and such interpretations are common and widely argued over). Some will argue that Shylock is mean, self-defensive and whingeing, citing various of his actions and drawing evidence from his use of language; others will argue that he has a soul and is sensitive to human suffering and joy, drawing similarly from the work.

Who is to say who is right? Perhaps the analogy breaks down here; after all, we have a judge to decide in the field of law. But it is only an analogy, after all. One of the things people feel about interpretation in the field of literature is that is subjective in a way that interpretation is not in law. But it is difficult to give a rational explanation of that feeling; literary critics as much wrestle with the problems of rival interpretations as do judges and barristers; certainly, literary critics do not sit back and say 'Well, it is just a matter of taste, either you like it or not'. To conclude, then, it seems as though there is a great deal to the analogy between legal argument and literary criticism.

QUESTION FOUR

To what extent does Dworkin's image of legal development as similar to constructing a chain novel illuminate important features of the legal process?

University of London LLB Examination
(for External Students) Jurisprudence and Legal Theory June 1996 Q8

General Comment

To gain good marks for this question the candidate must exhibit a good grasp of Dworkin's idea of interpretation. This is not a question to be treated casually. Do not attempt it if you do not understand Dworkin's idea of constructive interpretation.

Skeleton Solution

Dworkin's idea of interpretation – law as integrity – the chain novel analogy – Hercules methodology.

Suggested Solution

Dworkin's idea of interpretation is about legal reasoning in the judicial process. There are three stages of interpretation in the legal process:

a) the pre-interpretive stage;

b) the interpretive stage; and

c) the post interpretive stage.

At the pre-interpretive stage, the judge considers the pre-interpretive legal data. This means the judge is bound to consider the actual legal materials at his or her disposal. Some interpretation is required even at this stage to find what legal materials to consider. This is about considering the relevant existing law.

At the interpretive stage, the judge constructively interprets the legal material. He or she makes the best possible sense of the legal material. This is Dworkin's best light thesis. The interpreter of the legal materials (the judge) questions and examines the issues in the light of his or her constructive interpretation of the law. To Dworkin, this constructive interpretation leads to the morally best interpretation of the law.

At the post interpretive stage, changes, if any, are announced, and the existing law is overruled if necessary.

Let us assume that someone is required to interpret a particular communal practice. It will help to assume that the community we are concerned with is a distinct person with opinions and convictions of its own, a group consciousness of some sort, and that assumption means that the interpreter must judge and dispute the opinions of a person, and not simply discover and report. He or she must distinguish between the opinion the group has about what is needed, which he can find out by reflecting on its distinct motives and purposes, and what the interpreter thinks the practice really requires.

The idea of interpretation is linked to Dworkin's idea of law as integrity. For interpretation to be successfully carried out the judge must accept law as integrity. Integrity says law must speak with one voice. Judges must assume that the law is structured on coherent principles about justice, fairness and procedural due process, and that in all fresh cases that come before them they must enforce these so as to make each person's situation fair and just by the same standard (Dworkin, *Law's Empire* (1986), p243). Law as integrity rejects the positivist 'law is law' as well as the cynicism of the Realist school.

To Dworkin, the dividing force of judicial practice is integrity, which is a public virtue comparable with justice and fairness. It demands that the judge justify his or her decisions by making them conform to the entirety of the law which has a life of its own.

It is against this background that Dworkin's image of legal development is compared to the construction of a chain novel. Dworkin says that judges, like novelists, undertake constructive interpretation when they undertake legal reasoning in judicial practice. The aim of constructive interpretation is to discover the intention of an author, not because the aim is to discover the purposes of the former author, but to impose purpose over the test or data being interpreted (Dworkin, ibid, p228). To Dworkin, since all constructive interpretation shares this feature, which is normative, it explains why judicial interpretation can be compared with the constructive interpretation of a novel by a novelist. Judges are authors as well as critics, and a judge adds to what he or she interprets; future judges are confronted with what the previous judge has done.

The comparison between literature and law leads to Dworkin's idea of chain novel. In this enterprise a group of novelists are expected to write a novel seriatim. Each novelist in this chain is supposed to interpret the chapter given to him or her in order to write a new chapter, which is passed on to the next novelist. This goes on down the chain. The job of each novelist is to write his or her chapter so as to make the novel under construction the best it can be, and Dworkin says the complexity of this enterprise is similar to the complexity of legal reasoning in deciding cases under law as integrity.

Each novelist's aim is to make a single novel with the material supplied, and the single novel will have to encompass what he or she adds to it, and within limits, what future authors would want or be able to add. He or she must endeavour to make the novel the best novel constructed by a single author rather than make it seem the work of different authors. The novelist has to make a judgment or a series of judgments as he or she writes and rewrites. He or she has to decide on a working theory about the novel's characters, plot, theme and aim in order to come to a certain decision about what would constitute continuing a chain novel and starting a new one.

If the novelist is a good critic, his or her views will be various and complex because the value of a good novel cannot be encapsulated from a single view point. There are two dimensions which the novelist considers to structure any interpretation he or she adopts. The first is the dimension of fit. The chain novelist cannot make any constructive interpretation unless he or she believes the material given him or her was not written by a single author. Any interpretation which he or she adopts must flow from the text supplied. The second dimension says that the novelist is required to judge which of the available interpretations makes the work in progress best, all things considered. The novelist might find that he or she has written a rather different interpretation, or may find it impossible to sustain the existing theme. In this case, the novelist will reconsider other interpretations which he or she at first rejected, and at all times return to the text to reconsider the interpretation that construes its best meaning.

Someone may accuse the novelist of rewriting the 'real' novel to produce a different one that he or she likes; that the 'real' novel can be discovered in some other way than by the novelist's method. Such a person can be said to have misunderstood not only the chain novel enterprise but the nature of literary criticism.

To Dworkin, judicial reasoning is exactly the same as the chain novel process; that cases which come before judges must be treated like the chain novel analogy. The judge, like the novelist, must undertake constructive interpretation of the legal data and follow the two dimensions, like the novelist. First is the dimension of fit. The judge similarly cannot make any constructive interpretation unless he or she believes the legal data before him or her does not come from a single author. Here the judge will think that the legal materials come from the legal system generally. The different judges in the legal system represent the different authors. Any interpretation the judge adopts must flow from the text supplied. This accords with Dworkin's idea of interpretation.

The stage where the judge begins with the text is the pre-interpretive stage. At the interpretive stage, the judge considers possible inter-pretations to adopt.

It is here that the second dimension which the novelist follows applies to the judge. The judge is required by the second dimension to decide which of the available interpretations makes the decision the best one. When the novelist has produced the finished work, the novel gets handed to his or her successor down the chain. This represents the post interpretive stage in Dworkin's theory. When the judge has made a decision it is handed down the chain to other judges to consider as precedent.

A judge deciding a common law case like *McLoughlin* v *O'Brian* [1983] 1 AC 410 must think of himself or herself as an author in the chain of common law. The judge is faced with existing precedents which deal with problems analogous to the case under consideration. The judge must think of the precedents as part of the long story which he or she must interpret, and then continue using his or her own judgment to make the unfolding story as good as can be. Like the novelist, the judge during legal reasoning constructs the precedents in the best possible light, and best here means morally best.

The judge's decision, which is his or her post interpretive conclusion, represents an interpretation that fits and justifies the practice that has gone on before, as far as possible. Just like the interpretation in a chain novel for which each interpreter considers the enterprise as a delicate balance between different types of literary and artistic attitudes, so with law, judges consider the practice as a delicate balance between different political convictions.

As an example of how a judge acts like the chain novelist in judicial practice, Dworkin offers Hercules, a superhuman, patient and intelligent judge who accepts law as integrity and who, like a chain novelist, has to decide a hard case like *McLoughlin* v *O'Brian* [1983] 1 AC 410. Like the chain novelist, Hercules will first construct a moral theory of the system, draw up a list of different interpretations from the precedents, and go through the list until he comes to a decision as to which interpretation best fits the settled law and provides the best justification of it. This means that the judge's constructive interpretation of the existing precedents best fits the law and provides the morally best interpretation of them.

Dworkin's chain novel idea certainly throws light on judicial practice in the common law, especially in hard cases. The chain novel analogy mirrors judicial interpretation of the legal data, illuminating the process in a way which even the non-lawyer will find helpful.

C PRECEDENT

15.7 Introduction

In England, precedent is of much importance. Past precedents not only guide later decisions, but if appropriate within the hierarchy of courts, bind judges in later cases.

This is the theory of stare decisis. In considering this doctrine the student might like to ask whether stare decisis is absolute and inflexible, or whether its rigidity is more apparent than real. As with the whole of this chapter, it is important to know some case law.

15.8 Key points

The English system of stare decisis

a) Decisions of superior courts bind lower courts in later cases.

b) The advantages of this system are certainty and uniformity.

Comparison with civil law countries

a) Past decisions do not bind but are merely persuasive.

b) This system has more flexibility, although it sacrifices a degree of certainty and uniformity.

15.9 Question and suggested solution

'Nevertheless, the basic flexibility of the system is preserved, not so much by the formal limitations on the rule of stare decisis but by the relative freedom with which the courts may and often do determine the scope and limits of past precedents ...' (Lloyd, *An Introduction to Jurisprudence*.)

Discuss.

Written by the Editor

General Comment

Quite a straightforward general question on precedent. It involves both the basic rule and the exceptions to it. Knowledge of illustrative cases is important.

Skeleton Solution

Precedent – stare decisis – civil law countries – lack of flexibility? – ratio decidendi – obiter dicta – traditional view – *Donoghue* v *Stevenson* – Goodhart – Stone – no definition.

Suggested Solution

In England precedents have great importance. According to the rule of stare decisis, the decisions of superior courts bind lower courts in later cases. There is thus a hierarchy of courts – for example the House of Lords is superior to the Court of Appeal. This contrasts with the place of precedent in civil law countries where past decisions are merely persuasive, not binding. The rule of stare decisis provides for much uniformity and certainty of decisions. It is, however, open to the criticism of extreme inflexibility, with the attendant risk of injustice in some cases. It will be shown that stare decisis does actually give judges a wide measure of flexibility, and that one of the major reasons lies in the definition of ratio decidendi.

As Lloyd points out, one of the functions of the judge is determining the 'scope and limits of past precedents' and thus which parts of an earlier case are binding on him. The binding part of a case is known as the ratio decidendi, as distinguished from the obiter dicta. The reason why this technique provides flexibility is that the definition of a ratio decidendi is uncertain; it is thus up to the judge to decide its exact scope.

The traditional view of ratio is that it is that rule of law enunciated by the judge to the extent that it is necessary to decide the case. But an examination of a well-known case shows the unhelpfulness of this definition: in *Donoghue* v *Stevenson* [1932] AC 562 was the relevant and necessary part Lord Atkin's 'neighbour principle' or merely a narrow principle of manufacturer's liability?

An alternative definition is that put forward by Professor Goodhart for whom a ratio is the decision based on the facts treated as material by the judge. There are difficulties with this – it may be difficult to tell which facts the judge took into account. Professor Stone takes a rather different view. For him there are two possible rationes – the prescriptive and the descriptive. The latter is ascertainable from the given decision but the former is how the courts treat the earlier decision in subsequent cases.

It should be pointed out, however, that none of these approaches tells us how a judge may decide the ratio of a case. All he can do is take as the ratio the principles that seem to him appropriate. It is this which gives flexibility. For example, judges in cases subsequent to *Donoghue* v *Stevenson* look the wider principle as being the ratio. Had they confined themselves to the narrower principle of manufacturer's liability, the law of negligence might have developed quite differently. It is therefore clear that I agree with what Lloyd says in the quotation.

D STATUTORY INTERPRETATION

15.10 Introduction

Once again it is useful to demonstrate points made about the three 'rules' of statutory construction by means of case law. The ever growing flow of statutory law, combined with the inherent ambiguity of many words and phrases, means that statutory interpretation is becoming increasingly important. Despite this, it is fair to say that this has not been the most popular examination topic in recent years.

15.11 Key points

The canons of construction

a) The statute must be read as a whole.

b) Ejusdem generis.

c) Narrow construction of penal provisions.

d) Interpretation Act 1978.

Presumptions

a) Against alteration of law.

b) Against imposition of no-fault liability.

c) Against ousting the jurisdiction of the courts.

d) Against depriving a person of a vested right.

The three 'rules' of statutory construction

a) Mischief rule.

b) Literal rule.

c) Golden rule.

Later developments

a) The modern purposive rule.

b) *Pepper* v *Hart* [1993] 1 All ER 42.

15.12 Question and suggested solution

Which of the three rules of statutory construction do you consider to be the most accurate description of the way in which judges interpret statutes?

Written by the Editor

General Comment

A fairly straightforward question concerning the three rules of statutory construction. The answer should be backed up by case law.

Skeleton Solution

Mischief rule – *Heydon's Case* – purposive – *Mandla* v *Dowell Lee* – literal rule – RRB v *London Borough of Ealing* – golden rule – *R* v *Allen* – inconsistent approach – rules conflict – Rupert Cross – *Pepper* v *Hart* – modern purposive rule.

Suggested Solution

The three rules of statutory interpretation which are most commonly suggested are the literal, the golden and the mischief rule. Although support can be found in the cases for all three rules, they are somewhat contradictory. It is thus proposed to consider which, if any, rule most accurately reflects the way in which judges interpret statutes.

The mischief rule was probably at the height of its popularity in the sixteenth century. In *Heydon's Case* (1584) 3 Co Rep 74, the classic statement of the rule was laid down: there are four things to be considered when interpreting statutes: the common law before the Act; the mischief that the common law did not provide for; the remedy appointed for that mischief; and the true reason of the remedy. Thus interpretation is purposive. There is still some support for this rule today. For example, in *Mandla* v *Dowell Lee* [1983] 2 AC 548 the House of Lords considered the purpose of the Race Relations Act 1975 before applying it to the facts of the case.

The mischief rule is not, however, the only approach used in recent years. In *RRB* v *London Borough of Ealing* [1978] 1 All ER 497 for example, the literal approach to the Race Relations Act was taken. According to this approach the literal meaning of words must be taken – the intention of parliament is taken to be contained in those literal words. Clearly this approach stems from constitutional principles of the separation of power. One might query, however, whether there is usually only one 'literal' interpretation of words and phrases – words are often unclear or ambiguous.

The strictness of the literal rule has often been mitigated by the 'golden rule'. Where a literal interpretation results in a meaning which parliament could not possibly have intended, a secondary meaning can be taken. An example is *R* v *Allen* (1872) LR 1 CCR 367 where the literal definition of bigamy in the Offences Against the Person Act 1961 was not applied since that would have led to the absurd conclusion that bigamy could never be committed.

From an examination of case law it becomes apparent that there is no one consistent approach to statutory interpretation. All three rules are sometimes applied although in many ways they conflict. For example, both the mischief and the golden rule are to some extent purposive, whilst the literal rule masks the statutory purpose. Professor Cross has put forward a pleasing formulation of what judges do. He suggests that the mischief and literal rules are mixed, and the element of context added. Thus judges look at the ordinary English meaning of words in the general context of the statute. That ordinary meaning may be displaced of the result would be absurd. Perhaps this is a better description of how judges interpret statutes than a strict adherence to one or other of the three rules. Additionally, in recent years there have been signs of judicial activism by reason of the use of a purposive approach to interpretation and the ability to refer to Hansard in light of the decision of the House of Lords in *Pepper* v *Hart* [1993] 1 All ER 42.

Unannotated Cracknell's Statutes for use in Examinations

New Editions of Cracknell's Statutes

£11.95 due 2002

Cracknell's Statutes provide a comprehensive series of essential statutory provisions for each subject. Amendments are consolidated, avoiding the need to cross-refer to amending legislation. Unannotated, they are suitable for use in examinations, and provide the precise wording of vital Acts of Parliament for the diligent student.

Commercial Law
ISBN: 1 85836 472 8

European Community Legislation
ISBN: 1 85836 470 1

Conflict of Laws
ISBN: 1 85836 473 6

Family Law
ISBN: 1 85836 471 X

Criminal Law
ISBN: 1 85836 474 4

Public International Law
ISBN: 1 85836 476 0

Employment Law
ISBN: 1 85836 475 2

For further information on contents or to place an order, please contact:

Mail Order
Old Bailey Press
at Holborn College
Woolwich Road
Charlton
London
SE7 8LN

Telephone No: 020 7381 7407
Fax No: 020 7386 0952
Website: www.oldbaileypress.co.uk

Suggested Solutions to Past Examination Questions 2000–2001

The Suggested Solutions series provides examples of full answers to the questions regularly set by examiners. Each suggested solution has been broken down into three stages: general comment, skeleton solution and suggested solution. The examination questions included within the text are taken from past examination papers set by the London University. The full opinion answers will undoubtedly assist you with your research and further your understanding and appreciation of the subject in question.

Only £6.95 Due December 2002

Constitutional Law
ISBN: 1 85836 478 7

Jurisprudence and Legal Theory
ISBN: 1 85836 484 1

Criminal Law
ISBN: 1 85836 479 5

Land Law
ISBN: 1 85836 481 7

English Legal System
ISBN: 1 85836 482 5

Law of Tort
ISBN: 1 85836 483 3

Elements of the Law of Contract
ISBN: 1 85836 480 9

For further information on contents or to place an order, please contact:

Mail Order
Old Bailey Press
at Holborn College
Woolwich Road
Charlton
London
SE7 8LN

Telephone No: 020 7381 7407
Fax No: 020 7386 0952
Website: www.oldbaileypress.co.uk

Old Bailey Press

The Old Bailey Press integrated student law library is tailor-made to help you at every stage of your studies from the preliminaries of each subject through to the final examination. The series of Textbooks, Revision WorkBooks, 150 Leading Cases and Cracknell's Statutes are interrelated to provide you with a comprehensive set of study materials.

You can buy Old Bailey Press books from your University Bookshop, your local Bookshop, direct using this form, or you can order a free catalogue of our titles from the address shown overleaf.

The following subjects each have a Textbook, 150 Leading Cases/Casebook, Revision WorkBook and Cracknell's Statutes unless otherwise stated.

Administrative Law
Commercial Law
Company Law
Conflict of Laws
Constitutional Law
Conveyancing (Textbook and 150 Leading Cases)
Criminal Law
Criminology (Textbook and Sourcebook)
Employment Law (Textbook and Cracknell's Statutes)
English and European Legal Systems
Equity and Trusts
Evidence
Family Law
Jurisprudence: The Philosophy of Law (Textbook, Sourcebook and
    Revision WorkBook)
Land: The Law of Real Property
Law of International Trade
Law of the European Union
Legal Skills and System
    (Textbook)
Obligations: Contract Law
Obligations: The Law of Tort
Public International Law
Revenue Law (Textbook,
    Revision WorkBook and
    Cracknell's Statutes)
Succession

Mail order prices:	
Textbook	£14.95
150 Leading Cases	£11.95
Revision WorkBook	£9.95
Cracknell's Statutes	£11.95
Suggested Solutions 1998–1999	£6.95
Suggested Solutions 1999–2000	£6.95
Suggested Solutions 2000–2001	£6.95
Law Update 2002	£9.95
Law Update 2003	£10.95

Please note details and prices are subject to alteration.

To complete your order, please fill in the form below:

Module	Books required	Quantity	Price	Cost
		Postage		
		TOTAL		

For Europe, add 15% postage and packing (£20 maximum).
For the rest of the world, add 40% for airmail.

ORDERING

By telephone to Mail Order at 020 7381 7407, with your credit card to hand.

By fax to 020 7386 0952 (giving your credit card details).

Website: www.oldbaileypress.co.uk

By post to: Mail Order, Old Bailey Press at Holborn College, Woolwich Road, Charlton, London, SE7 8LN.

When ordering by post, please enclose full payment by cheque or banker's draft, or complete the credit card details below. You may also order a free catalogue of our complete range of titles from this address.

We aim to despatch your books within 3 working days of receiving your order.

Name

Address

Postcode   Telephone

Total value of order, including postage: £

I enclose a cheque/banker's draft for the above sum, or

charge my   ☐ Access/Mastercard   ☐ Visa   ☐ American Express
Card number

☐☐☐☐ ☐☐☐☐ ☐☐☐☐ ☐☐☐☐

Expiry date   ☐☐☐☐

Signature: ....Date: ....